DOWN THE RHODES
THE FENDER RHODES STORY

DOWN THE RHODES
THE FENDER RHODES STORY

Based on a film documenting the Fender Rhodes Electric Piano

Gerald McCauley and Benjamin Bove

Edited by A. Scott Galloway

Hal Leonard Books
An Imprint of Hal Leonard Corporation

Published in 2013 by Hal Leonard Books
An Imprint of Hal Leonard Corporation
7777 West Bluemound Road
Milwaukee, WI 53213

Trade Book Division Editorials Offices
33 Plymouth Street, Montclair, NJ 07042

All names and likenesses of interviewees used by permission

Printed in China through Colorcraft Ltd., Hong Kong

Book design: Rebecca Wismann & Matt Martin-Vegue
        The Studio WLV

Library of Congress Cataloging-in-Publication Data is available upon request.

ISBN 978-1-4803-4242-2

www.halleonardbooks.com

www.FenderRhodesStory.com

CONTENTS

Preface

One afternoon I received a call at home from my Sis, Terry Dexter letting me know that a friend of hers would be contacting me about a keyboard project. (God bless her heart; always connectin' folk).

Sure enough, Ben Bove called and introduced me to his ingenious idea of making a documentary – all about the Fender Rhodes electric piano. I was interested and we eventually met in-person. I was impressed that he is a collector and aficionado of vintage keyboards; specifically various models of… "The Rhodes"

As we talked more, he informed me that no one had yet made a film or written a book about the Fender Rhodes. I checked, and to my surprise, there was nothing. I was very curious, "Why?"

Like many, I, too, *love* the Fender Rhodes sound. I have used the instrument on many of the recordings I've produced and in numerous live shows over the years. Just then I thought…

"How cool would it be to do this?!"

So we made a list of interviewees. After our meeting, I started making calls and sending emails. I gave Ben my predictions of who would participate. ("Shhh… ") Roughly two weeks later came the first interview with George Duke. Then we continued on… "Down the Rhodes."

In early '09, I worked as A&R / Production Consultant for George Benson's "Songs and Stories" project. This gave us immediate access to some of the interviewees and made coordinating convenient. Several weeks following that time, it was Tavis Smiley who inspired me to "Immortalize the subject matter"… but, I'd never done a book before… and needed a great writer.

In mid '09, during a Christian McBride hit in Hollywood (where George Duke sat in, by the way), I ran into A. Scott Galloway. We had met years ago, but, I hadn't seen him in awhile. I told him about the documentary and he eagerly viewed a sample reel on my iPhone of who we had interviewed thus far. He "got it" and offered his assistance to do any writing we needed. (Man… he just didn't know).

In late '09, we interviewed Quincy Jones. I asked Q his thoughts about doing a book-version of the project. He thought it was a great idea! My gift was a signed copy of his book, *The Complete Quincy Jones*. Now, here we are…

What excites me most is how so many have embraced us in support of this project… living-proof that music connects us all.

As a proud member of the Musical Intelligentsia, I am honored to be part of this amazing tribute.

Musically Yours,
Gerald McCauley

Introduction
Rhodesways

I have God to thank for steering me straight into editing a book about the Fender Rhodes electric piano. Me – a drummer and wanna-be late night radio DJ who whistled while I worked and shopped in record stores and fell into music journalism by chance. Hitting my knees before a big picture window bathed in moonlight, I do confess the following: the sound of the Rhodes seduced me from youth – had me at "Hello" – and remains a sonorous enchantress within the soundtrack of my life.

The first I heard of her was on jazz records from my father's top-shelf collection – the opening Bob James bars of Quincy Jones' "Dead End / Walking in Space" medley, the Austrian gospel of Joe Zawinul on The Cannonball Adderley Quintet's "Mercy, Mercy, Mercy (Live)," Sergio Mendes exhaling a balmy breath of sensual cool on Brazil '66's "Scarborough Fair," Chick Corea chasing bulls and an enigmatic Flora Purim on "Spain," Herbie Hancock tucking me in to "Tell Me a Bedtime Story," and my mom's school friend Stanley Cowell giving me a glimpse of the Outer Limits on "Absolutions" – the closing composition of Max Roach's *Members Don't Git Weary*.

The Rhodes floated me thru my latch key / TV childhood, beginning with the transfixing aural bed beneath Blossom Dearie's soprano voice on "Figure 8" from "Multiplication Rock" and Bob James (again) settling me in for "Taxi" to Dave Grusin's flinty flares under Sammy Davis Jr. singing "Keep Your Eye on the Sparrow (Baretta's Theme)" and George Tipton tapping the black sheep in his genes for the soulful "Soap" theme.

I further recall the Rhodes on the haunting intro of Quincy Jones' inaugural production of "Everything Must Change" (from *Body Heat*), the arresting debuts of Dexter "Life on Mars" Wansel and Bobby "The Genie" Lyle and a powerful solo by WAR's Lonnie Jordan telegraphing humanitarian urgency on "Deliver the Word." I remember Billy Beck of the Ohio Players and Larry Dunn of Earth Wind & Fire defying anyone to ghettoize them as solely funk musicians with their jazz work on the all-too-brief "Ain't Givin Up No Ground" (from *Honey*) and "See the Light" (from *That's the Way of the World*), respectively. Ditto for Kevin Toney of the Blackbyrds with his lightning-fast Liberace-worthy flourishes on "Love is Love" (from *Flying Start*) and – perhaps most definitive of all – Ricky West providing the launching pad for an Arp Odyssey to ascend into the here-after on "Summer Madness" by Kool & The Gang (from *Light of Worlds*).

When I became old enough to drive Pop's Corvette, my essential night cruiser cassette was loaded with Rhodes, heavily rotating "Bumpin' on Sunset" by Brian Auger's Oblivion Express, "Life Moves On" by Rodney Franklin, "Feels So Good (Do it Again)" by Jimmy McGriff (cheatin' on his organ), "Grace" by Ronnie Laws (f/ Barnaby Finch) and "He Loves You" by the Christian soul-jazz septet Seawind (featuring Larry Williams on Rhodes).

Back then I was often mooning over some girl I'd placed on a pedestal beyond my reach. One song that got me through was the Rhodes-soaked "Time Waits For No One" by the Jacksons / Michael Jackson (personally sub-titled "For Lovesick Boys Who Considered Suicide When 'She's Out of My Life' was too damned'soft'").

Later still when a break up was imminent, I could always find consolation in the goodbye duet "Let Me Go Love" by Nicolette Larson and Michael McDonald.

It was a pair of live recordings that showed me how quintessential acoustic piano performances could be transformed with alternative renditions on the Rhodes. Compare Les McCann's album version of "With These Hands" (from *Much Les*) to the one on *Live at Montreux* that magically metamorphosizes the Swiss jazz festival auditorium into The Man's intimate wedding chapel. Then A/B Deodato's studio take on "Spirit of Summer" (from the pop-jazz primer *Prelude*) to the one he realizes on Rhodes *Live at Felt Forum* – both with orchestra yet dipped in singularly polar beauty.

Before "Forget Me Nots," pretty, pint-sized dynamo Patrice Rushen made her signature known on a title most apropos: "Stepping Stones" (from *Shout it Out*). (I can't even count the number of times I've heard some funky boom-bap beat in hip hop and felt in every fiber of my being that 16 bars of Rhodes by "Baby Fingers" was just what my inner A&R man ordered!) Before "Sun Goddess," Ramsey Lewis massaged his Rhodes into sweet submission on an album called *Solar Wind* that featured two Seals & Crofts covers: "Hummingbird" and "Summer Breeze."

Speaking of which, I find it suspicious and downright smacking of exploitation when you consider how the Rhodes suddenly made certain songs by rock and pop artists more "soulful" and Black Radio-friendly. The list of multi-million-sellers runs deep and wide, including the Bee Gees' "How Deep is Your Love" and Andy Gibb's "Don't Throw it All Away" (both played by Blue Weaver), Hall & Oates' "One on One" (played by Daryl Hall), Atlanta Rhythm Section's "So Into You" (played by Dean Daughtry), Billy Joel's "Just the Way You Are," Chicago's "Call On Me" (played by Robert Lamm), Steely Dan's entire catalog from "Do it Again" to "Cousin Dupree" (manned by many), all through the work of siblings Karen & Richard Carpenter (a.k.a. The Carpenters) and Peter Frampton's "Baby I Love Your Way" (beautifully rendered by Bob Mayo).

At Quiet Storm radio stations – for which I worked at the very best, KUTE-FM in Los Angeles – angels descended from Heaven with the Rhodes as the wind beneath their wings: Phoebe Snow ("No Regrets" w/ Don Grolnick), Angela Bofill ("I Try" w/ Dave Grusin), Brenda Russell ("In the Thick of It" w/ original Rufus keyboardist Ron Stockert), Randy Crawford ("Rio de Janiero Blue" w/ Leon Pendarvis), Phyllis Hyman ("No One Can Love You More w/ Jerry Peters), Lonette McKee ("Maybe There Are Reasons" w/ Patrice Rushen), Dee Dee Bridgewater ("Nightmoves" w/ Bobby Lyle), Barbra Streisand ("Guilty" w/ Richard Tee) and Roberta Flack (from "Feel Like Makin' Love" w/ Bob James to "Making Love" w/ Richard Tee, again, one of NYC's finest).

Which ushers me to the realm that most reminds me of the Rhodes – its hard-earned reputation for sexual persuasion: "With You" by The Moments featuring Harry Ray (keys un-credited), "Sensuality" by the Isley Brothers (f/ brother-in-law Chris Jasper), "Magic in Your Eyes" by Rufus featuring Chaka Khan (f/ Kevin Murphy and David "Hawk" Wolinski), "Feel Like Flying" by Gino Vannelli (f/ Joe Vannelli), "Harbor Lights" by Boz Scaggs (f/ David Paich), "Hello Like Before" by Bill Withers (f/ Clarence McDonald) and creamiest of all, "Inside My Love" by Minnie Riperton (f/ Joe Sample). Instrumentally, the notorious *Touch* Lp by John Klemmer (f/ Dave Grusin) was always a winning midnight persuader, Chick Corea's "Crystal Silence" has afterglow on lock and *anything* by Lonnie Liston Smith makes horizontal… transcendental.

I reflect back with fondness on *all* of this wonderful music because I'm sure you love a great deal of it too, or are at the very least familiar with it. You might not have ever considered that the Fender Rhodes is the coolest of common denominators.

On June 18, 2009, I bumped into Gerald McCauley at Catalina Bar & Grill. In the course of catching each other up on what we were doing, he trumped all of my precious liner note essay projects when he told me he had just begun collaborating on a Fender Rhodes documentary with a guy named Ben Bove. I was intrigued. When he "just so happened" to have video interview highlights I could see on his iPhone, Christian McBride on-stage took a backseat as I sat glued to a tiny hand-held screen on which legend after legend was casually sharing their story of this instrument. I told Gerald right then, that if there was any writing to be done in conjunction with this film, I would be happy to "handle it." Soon after, happiness (and a huge heaping of work) was granted.

When the term "book" sprang forth, my thoughts zoomed straight to one that has been a favorite since my parents bought it for my 15th birthday – "Jazz-Rock Fusion – The People * The Music" by Julie Coryell & Laura Friedman / foreword by Ramsey Lewis (Dell – 1978). I admire its fuss-free layout of introduction, Q&A and discography on each artist. I modeled my initial Bob James entry of this book on that. As I proceeded through the texts, Gerald and Ben expressed a preference for more linear chapters that made it read as if each interviewee were speaking directly to the reader – which was also cool by me.

Editing these chapters, I learned so much about the instrument and the individuals. This book is full of great gems that stretch from funny anecdotes to mind-bogglingly detailed technical breakdowns. There's something in here for everybody. You'll find many of the people saying similar things about their experiences with the Rhodes but – without fail – there are memories that belong solely to each of them. It is a fascinating read and reference not just for keyboard fanatics, but music fans, historians and anyone touched by the mystical mellow madness that is the Fender Rhodes electric piano.

I am most proud of having championed and conducted one interview myself – that of the legendary Les McCann. His testimony was profoundly passionate and adoring. He dubbed the Fender Rhodes a musical, spiritual and tactile extension of his very soul. Connection doesn't get any deeper than that.

Harold Rhodes is a healer.
"Float On."
(For Carlos Sanders)

A. Scott Galloway

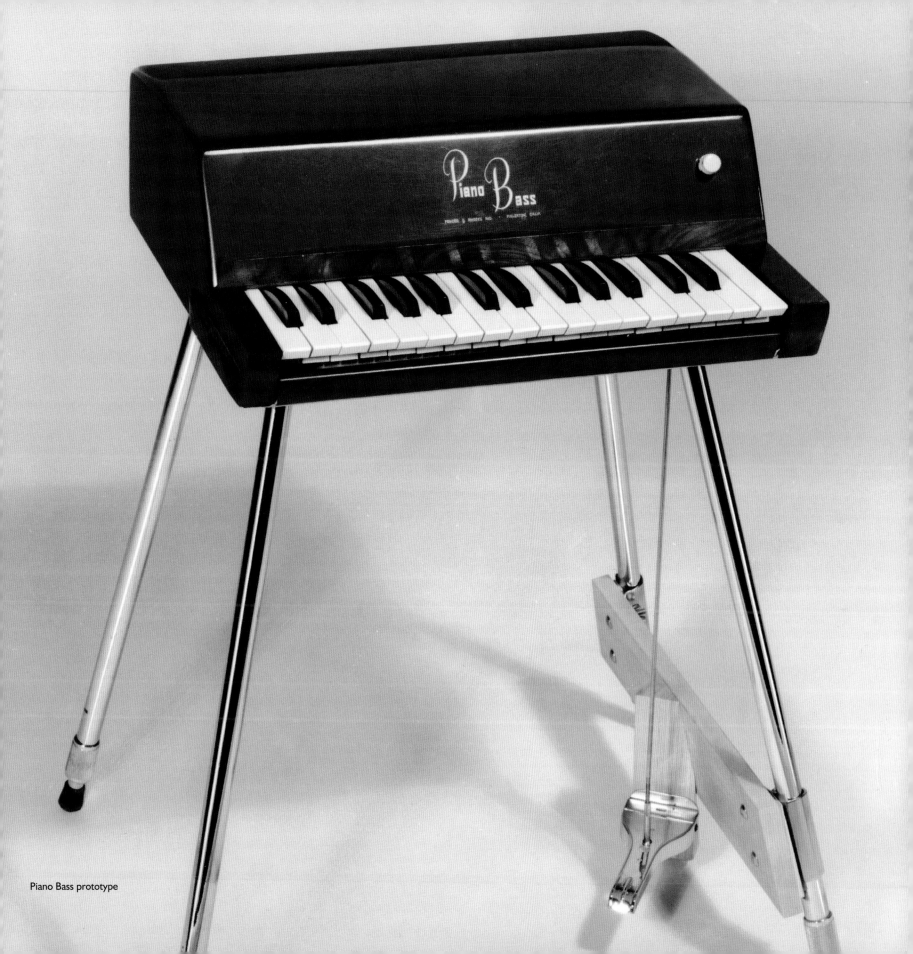

Piano Bass prototype

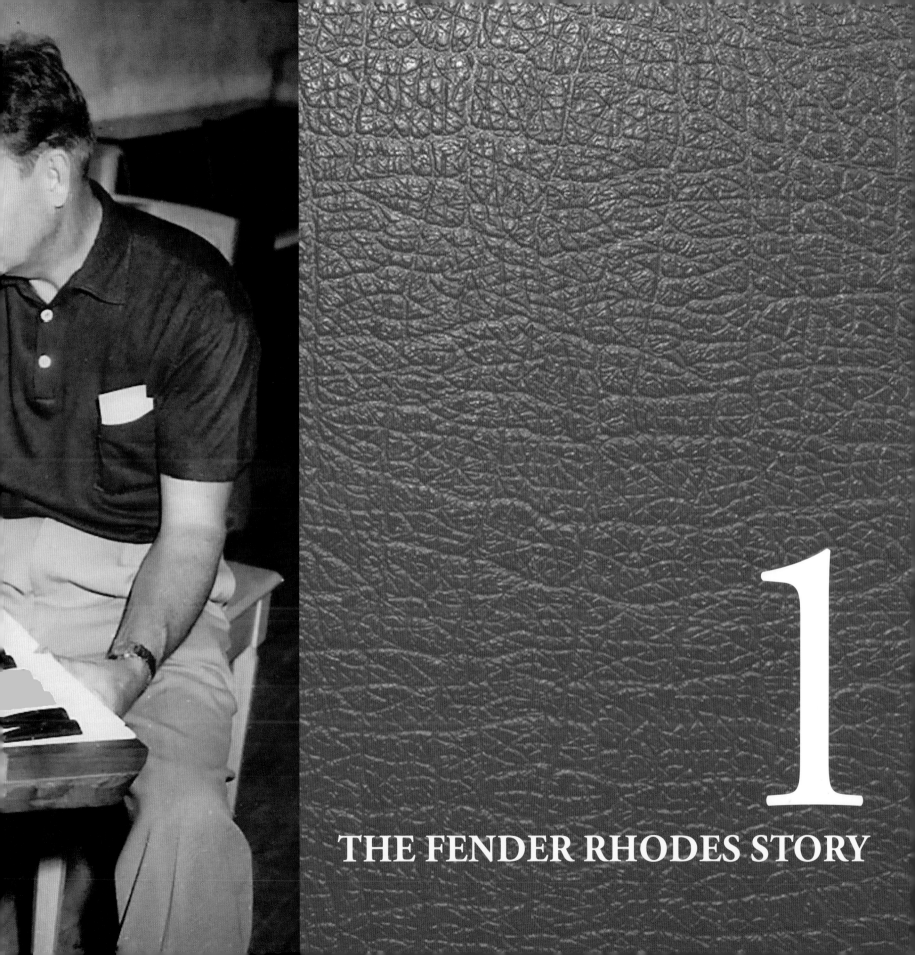

1

THE FENDER RHODES STORY

Harold Rhodes

Music Educator / Inventor

Harold Burroughs Rhodes is the inventor and namesake of the Rhodes electric piano. Born in 1910, he was a highly successful piano instructor going through Flight Instructor training on a military base when he invented the instrument in 1942 as a 29-note keyboard. It was initially called an Army Air Corps Piano or a Xylette – a lap-top piano that could be played comfortably by bedridden soldiers mainly as a means of emotional rehabilitation. Between 1946 and 1965, the instrument went through many modifications, during which time in 1959, the Fender instrument company (renowned for its electric guitars and basses) manufactured a popular 32-note Fender Rhodes Keyboard Bass. CBS purchased the Fender company in 1965 and took over manufacturing the Rhodes with still more modifications. Largely viewed as a "toy" by most musicians, the instrument got a second look once jazz great Miles Davis insisted that his pianist, Herbie Hancock, play the keyboard during a session for his 1968 album, Miles in the Sky. Their first recording: a song titled "Stuff." Not long after, the Rhodes had a run of over a decade as one of the most popular electric keyboards on the market.

The radio interview with Mr. Rhodes below transpired in 1985 or 1986, so some of the dialogue is with the intention of things to come – specifically The Mark V Stage 73 – the last piano to go into production before the Rhodes factory closed its doors).

Well, I guess my entire life happens to have been aimed at the job I finally wound up doing in the Air Force, WWII. We had no thought of electronics at that point. All we had were a great number of injured patients coming back from the Battle of the Bulge and they were trying to figure out ways of creating some type of musical therapy. We didn't use that word in those days. We were just having fun.

I happened to be wiling away my unused hours in my Air Force training program by giving (piano) lessons to my buddies – lessons in improvising. I wound up in a hospital in Greensboro and I was asked to see what I might be able to do for the patients there.

Pianos are big and uncomfortable. As I would walk across the air field, I would come across B-17s and other disabled planes. I saw aluminum tubing hanging out of the wings and I thought, "Maybe I could make a piano-like instrument out of this scrap material." So I took the tubing and cut it into Xylophone lengths, rigged up a crude little hammer of sorts out of wood I could find and made a keyboard. Then I set about to teach these fellas how to convert their telephone numbers into melodies and play simple chord accompaniments. It took off like wildfire!

I was called to the Pentagon and asked what I was doing down there. As a result, I was put in charge of the music instruction phase of the rehabilitation program in all of the Air Force Hospitals. The Secretary of War finally gave me a little medal and stated, "Do you know how many people you have exposed to music?" I said, "No" and he told me it was about 1/4 of a million people… patients.

After that, the question was what in the world do I do with this information now. I spent 30 more years developing the instrument you now call the Rhodes piano. Many, many mistakes I can tell you.

If you'd like a technical description, it's like an unusual tuning fork where one of the legs is actually a piece of piano wire. That's struck by a hammer, so you have a legitimate action – striking, which is like a piano… like an acoustic instrument. Then there is a little electric pickup that records that sound, much like an electric guitar.

Some of the advantages are, for instance, we can stretch tune. I remember Miles Davis wanting a very- exaggerated stretch tuning. To the technicians in the field, stretch tuning means that we go almost 22 points sharp by the time we hit the top note. It makes the sound more crisp. Also, we have a dynamic range because we have a hammer striking a string that's comparable to an acoustic piano and we have an action that's comparable to an acoustic piano action.

I must say that the company – in its quest for reducing costs – made many changes which were very "costly" in quality of performance to a great number of pianos that are out in the field. I'm speaking now as a sad inventor having to report that…

With the Mark V, we're back to a wooden key as we originally had it. I don't know whether you'll have a chance to hear a recording of Eddie Higgins. If so, he happens to be playing one of the first 100 pianos back in the days when I was in total charge. You'll hear the crispness in high range and the speedy repeat of the piano as it was built in those days. The Mark V goes back to that.

This recording of Eddie Higgins dates to about 1967. He was the house pianist at the London House in Chicago and did several recordings playing one of the pianos that I handmade for him. (One tune was Antonio Carlos Jobim's "The Girl From Ipanema.")

There are ways of changing the tonality by adjustment. The tonality most asked for today is more crisp and trumpet-like, but that's a musician's choice. These settings we had there were more like an acoustic piano setting.

The major thing that I notice is that all of the synthesized versions of what you might call "the Rhodes sound" lack a certain amount of individuality. Among them, I just told you earlier about the stretch tuning. Another is the wide dynamic range which the Rhodes possesses that is really impossible in a synthesized instrument so far.

The day may come when a musician feels the pleasure of having the total dynamic range normal of a piano. Until that happens, when the piano is played with a synthesizer, it seems to add that otherwise lacking dynamic range to his touch, particularly in a live performance.

Mr. (Leo) Fender said to me one time, "You ought to put my name behind your piano because it might help sell it."

That was back in the days when Fender was a very successful manufacturer of guitars. Fact is he's had nothing to do with the piano, except to be a money bags for me back in the days when I was developing the instrument. So that's why the name has been changed since to what it should have been in the first place – The Rhodes Piano.

The person first responsible for bringing out the Rhodes piano was Miles Davis. Back in those days, Miles Davis was the world's finest trumpet player. In his groups, he would have either, Joe Zawinul, Chick Corea or Herbie Hancock. He would point to this little box and say, "You're not going to play the piano you think you're going to play. You're going to play this!" So it got out to the public by way of Miles Davis recordings.

It really made its own way without much help from the company. I remember going to Ole' Miss University. The students had a stack of Herbie Hancock records and said, "I want to sound like that. What can I get to do it?" So the piano really sold itself and we grew along with it… very slowly… and made a lot of mistakes. It's still a developing instrument. There are still more things that can be done to this instrument, so it's not what you'd call "perfected." It has only those few years of background whereas a regular piano has (much more). {note: the piano was invented in 1709}.

Each person picked up the instrument and used it in his way and often asked for a particular voicing, that is, if you realize, if you have a screwdriver and a pair of pliers, you can alter the tonality of the piano to suit. Ray Charles did it in an entirely different way, as you could imagine, Ray Charles would.

Miles Davis wanted the pickups real close. In this case, there's one pickup for each tone. It can be adjusted to 1/4" away from the tone or 1/8", in which case, the volume doubles. Cut that little distance in half again and the volume doubles again – the closer you get; the more bite-y the sound is. This was to satisfy Miles Davis' particular likes. So you'll hear the piano being used in many different ways and sounding many different ways as a result of what (each) musician is looking for.

At first, it appeared that the (Rhodes) piano was going to go the way of the steam engine – just a relic – but, now there seems to be a movement back.

We are now making, a limited number – 600 as a matter of fact – of MIDI-type keyboards and if (I'm hearing) Chick Corea correctly… they're practically sold before we get them on the market because of what Chick and John Novello are doing. They have the only 2 that exist (thus far).

Above:
A young Harold Rhodes

Below:
Harold Rhodes in his
military attire

Opposite:
Harold Rhodes
Pre-Piano demonstration

Above: Fender Rhodes electric piano instruction systems bus

This Page: The CBS Musical Instrument van 1967

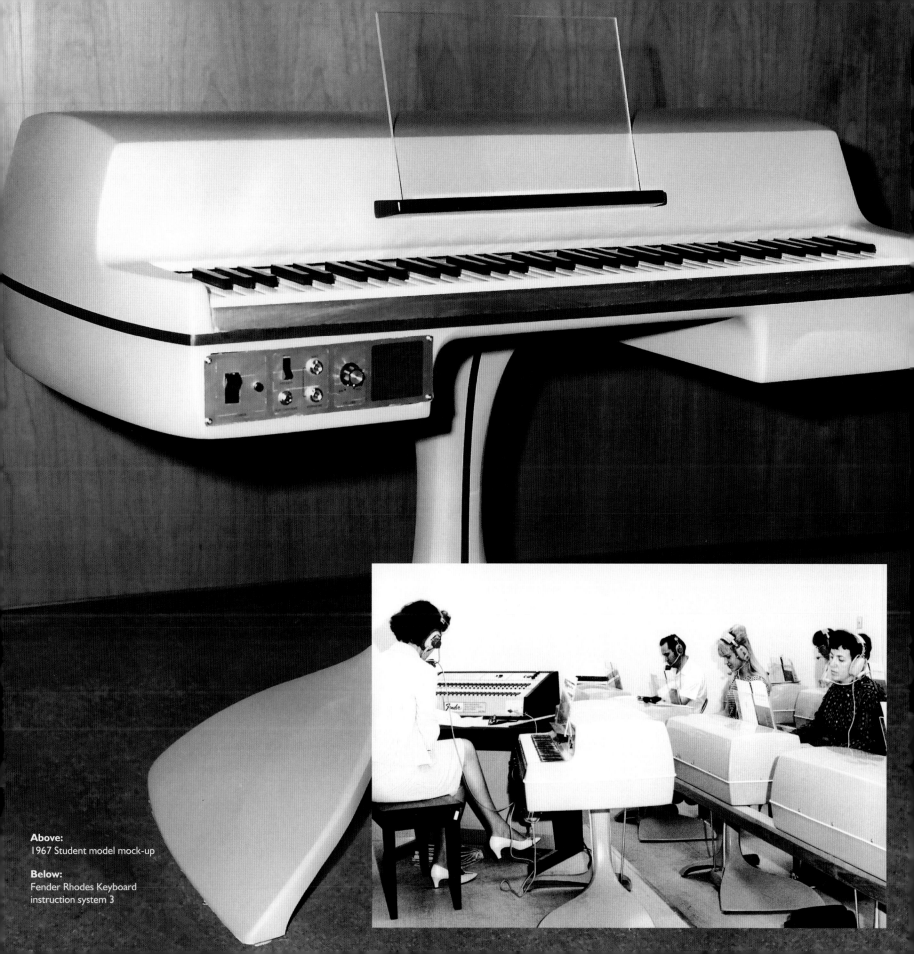

Above:
1967 Student model mock-up

Below:
Fender Rhodes Keyboard
instruction system 3

Harold receiving the NARAS President's Award

Top Row:
Horace Silver
Joe Zawinul
Ralph Grearson
Michael Boddiker
John Beasley

Bottom Row:
Harold B. Rhodes
Michael Greene
Angelia Bibbs-Sanders

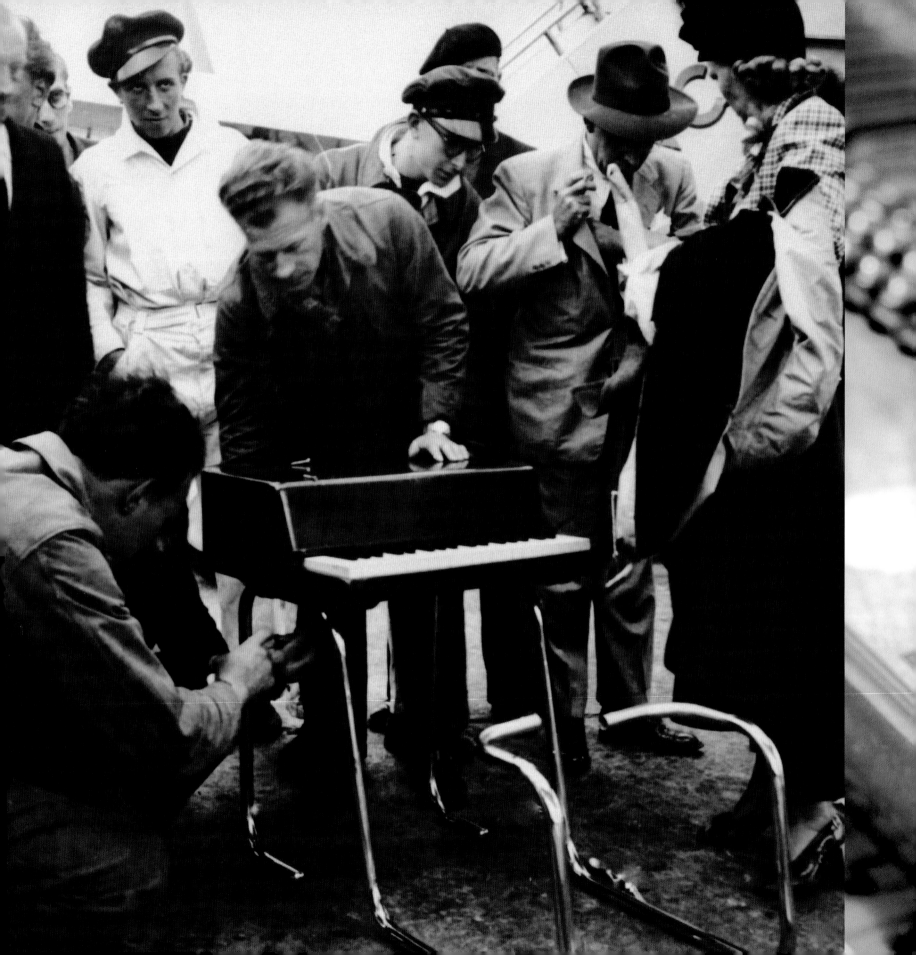

2

IN THE MAKING

Steve Grom
Former Marketing Director (CBS / FENDER)

I started with Fender in 1980. I was in the Quality Control department. I came in as a supervisor, which in the scheme of CBS back then, was the bottom rung of management – which meant I had to wear a tie! [Laughs] I was assigned to the Fender amp line and the Rhodes piano line. I had used the instruments as a musician, but had never been involved in the production of them, so it was a massive learning curve – especially with the piano. I played enough that I could sit down at one and go, "Yeah, this works" or "No it doesn't." It used to drive the guy that was the production supervisor *crazy* because he was a real nuts-and-bolts kind of guy. He was more like a car mechanic and didn't want to hear, "Oh, it didn't sound right." He would go into outer space when you'd talk like that, but that's what it was all about – it was being able to

hear it and there were enough subtleties in the way a Rhodes was put together that if it wasn't right, you could hear certain things; when it was right, it was magic. That was what I had to try to convince this guy – how to put them together so the majority of them were as good as they could be.

Being in Quality Control, I had the production world on one side and the Sales / Marketing / Research & Development people on the other side – the ones envisioning perfection. On the other hand, was the day-to-day hassles of manufacturing: how do you take something like a Rhodes piano that has so many parts, so many pieces, a huge amount of labor and a lot of different people involved – and make sure that every part and every person is 100% right? It was an interesting challenge.

During the time I spent in Quality Control, I got to see other parts of the company. I interfaced with the R&D department, the Marketing department and the Purchasing department. So I saw what was going on. What I saw from the Marketing department, I thought, "Ooo, I think I'd much rather do that than be a factory guy." That's where a lot of the creativity and product definition came from. It really wasn't up to Manufacturing to decide what to make. To a degree, R&D was under the direction of Marketing. They were the guys between marketing and sales – the ones that had to sell it. So, that was the hard part. I was fortunate that the Marketing guy in the early '80s wasn't what you would call a go-getter. He was more than happy to let this young guy who'd just come on and was full of energy – me – do a bunch of things that actually should have been his gig.

One day he asked me, "How would you like to go to Boston to do a clinic with Harold Rhodes?" First of all, I didn't know if I could say no, so of course I said yes. The next thing I know, Harold and I are flying to Boston to do a clinic at this very prestigious music store in Boston, E.U. Wurlitzer's. They were a huge Rhodes dealer. I didn't know what the heck was going on and I'm with Harold. I didn't know if I was supposed to carry his suitcase or what – and everybody was there to see Harold. I ended up doing a couple other things like that while I was still part of the Quality Control. One thing led to another and by 1983, the guy who was brought in to do marketing when CBS bought Arp and got more into the synthesizer side of things, went to work for Kurzweil when they first started. So they gave me the job as Marketing Director – for all the keyboards!

So I got in on the marketing side right at the tail end, but, I was involved a lot in the marketing of the Mark V because that was already in the design phase. Harold Rhodes was incredibly passionate about the piano. I mean, it had his name on it... and as passionate as he was, I don't think he really embraced that he had invented a completely unique musical instrument. He was so fixated on creating a new version of a piano. He had his Steinway action in the R&D lab that he was trying to recreate. It was funny that he was always looking for the next breakthrough... never happy with anything. From what I understand, Leo Fender was the same way. They were never satisfied. They were always working on it. So a couple of the times, especially as I got more into the marketing side of it, I dealt with Harold in a completely different way. It wasn't so much nuts-and-bolts because all through the '70s, Harold did a lot of the marketing. Yes, he would do some of the design, but he was the guy out there really pushing, really hustling that kind of stuff.

One day he and I went up to see Ray Charles. Ray needed a new piano, so Harold arranged for it and we put it in the back of my wonderful little Datsun pickup. We head up to L.A. from Fullerton where the factory was, to Ray Charles' facility. Once Ray knew Harold Rhodes was coming, he was all smiles and the nicest guy. We were bringing him this nice new piano. So he and Harold talked a little bit while I got to set it up. Then we proceeded to listen to Ray Charles play for 15 or 20 minutes. We did that another time with Chick Corea. It's pretty amazing watching guys like Ray Charles and Chick Corea play.

Driving Harold was fascinating too, because he'd talk about his teaching method. I had studied music, but he started talking about his idea of teaching people how to improvise very early as part of his teaching method. At that point, he didn't have much documented, but it was amazing the way he had thought it out. One aspect of his teaching method was instant gratification. We all know playing the piano takes a long time. You have to struggle and struggle. You're trying to read music and master exercises... His whole thing was to get people playing songs. Get them playing as quickly as possible, teaching them – almost without them knowing it – chord theory, how to play melody lines, how to improvise... It's too bad that he hadn't done more to document that.

In 1980, the gentleman who was president of CBS Musical Instruments – a guy named Bob Campbell who had been at Steinway – was going to retire. So CBS needed to find a new executive to run CBS Musical Instruments. At the time, CBS Musical Instruments was: Fender, Rhodes pianos, Rogers Drums, Rodgers Pipe Organs, Gemeinhardt Flutes, Lyon & Healy Harps, Steinway, and the VC Squire String Company. That was the umbrella of CBS Musical Instruments. They had decided they were going to bring in a gentleman who had been at Yamaha for many years. John McLaren was going to come in and take over for Bob Campbell and those two guys knew each other because they had both worked at Steinway, years earlier. Bob Campbell had stayed with CBS and then John McLaren had gone to Yamaha. So John came in – and John is a really fine piano player. That was his attraction to Steinway.

When he got to CBS, the corporate headquarters for CBS Musical Instruments had been in Deerfield, IL, a very nice suburb outside of Chicago.

Well, John was living in California, didn't want any part of living in Illinois and realized the Fullerton facility had more than enough room to relocate. So he decided they were going to close the operation in Illinois and bring the whole corporate entity out to Fullerton. That's where his office was.

The one production item John felt near and dear to, was the Rhodes. As the young supervisor on the piano line, I walked out on the floor one day and there's the President of CBS Musical Instruments in the little set-up booth playing one of the pianos. He's the biggest boss of all and though I had not really met him, per se, I knew who he was. I'm thinking, "Oh, my gosh – what's going on?!" As it turns out, to walk to his office, he had to walk right by the production line. He'd heard one of the set up guys playing; went over and wanted to play. Once I calmed down, we ended up having a great conversation. Then it became commonplace for him to stop by a couple times a month and say, "Can I play one?" "Yes sir, you can play as many as you'd like!"

He had a real enjoyment for the instrument – just wanted to sit down and play it; was more than happy to talk to a couple of workers. There were 2 or 3 guys that worked on the Rhodes line that were pretty good players themselves. One of the guys was about John's age, so they'd exchange tunes. It was cool to see one of the workers talking to the top executive of the company and the common denominator was the piano.

When John McLaren came in as President of CBS Musical Instruments, he brought Bill Schultz in to be President of Fender and Rhodes – it was all under that roof. John had the whole corporate structure to worry about – all the different company Presidents reporting to him – and Bill became the guy in charge of the whole Fullerton operation, of which Rhodes fell under that. John and Bill both came in right about the time that the infamous EK-10, was hitting the production line and then the streets. Like anything else, when you come into a new operation, you try to get as much information as you can and get a feel for what's going on. Neither John nor Bill were prepared for what they got when they came into the Fender world – at least the world of Fullerton and really, all of CBS Instruments.

There were a lot of problems going on – especially with Fender. Fender was the cash cow for all of CBS Musical Instruments. Fender brands, whether they were guitars or amps, literally generated enough income that whether the other ones were profitable or not, almost didn't matter. Fender generated so much revenue that Rhodes had some really-good years. Rogers Drums would usually about break even. Steinway would have a few good years but a lot of times they would break even. So from a business standpoint, Fender was the key to the whole thing. Well, Fender was starting to struggle. Fender had been doing a lot of export business that was starting to fall off, so they walked into the middle of that. They walked into a problem with a Rogers drum project that had turned into a nightmare. They walked into the EK-10. When I got there in 1980, they were working on developing that and the development took longer than it was supposed to.

Then when it was done, a lot of people were scratching their heads going, "Well, is this really what you want?"

When I was going to school, I studied a lot of electronic music. The school I went to had a very nice electronic music studio and I was really into that. The idea of a Rhodes piano with a synthesizer and what they came up with was really strange. It was a very odd instrument.

Not only was it an odd creation, it was a nightmare to produce. Just the design of it, the mechanical interface between the electronics and the piano was really touchy. So they walk into this.

Every time they turned around something else was going wrong at a horrendous level, the EK-10 being one of those.

As much of a headache as the EK-10 was for me having to deal with the production side, it became a huge boost to my career because I knew how it worked and how to fix it. So going back to my trip to Boston with Harold Rhodes, first time I ever traveled for the company on business, Harold and I are in Boston for this clinic. He gets a phone call. The guys at Manny's Music in NYC have two EK-10s that don't work. Harold's telling me this, like, "You have to go fix them." [Laughs] I mean, I'd never traveled on business before. I'd never been to NYC before. I had no idea where 48th Street was… but, I changed my plane ticket and went to Manny's Music during the hey-day of Manny's Music – a place jammed full of people yelling and screaming at each other.

MARK III

I go in and mercifully, I was able to fix one of them. We had seen that same problem over and over – "bend this a little bit, okay that one's fine." The other one I said, "Send this back to California." I was a hero! Henry Goldrich called Harold, "Hey, the guy came, fixed it and it was great!"

Again, as much of a headache as this EK-10 was, they had orders for them that were behind. I remember us working all one Saturday and all one Sunday because management said we gotta get X number of these done by the end of the month. They had all these orders and they had been sitting there for months and months. It was unheard of to work Saturdays and Sundays! They were Shanghai-ing guys out of the R&D department, out of the engineering department, like, "You will get these done!" It was money sitting on the table and they were tired of it not generating revenue.

The MIDI Mark V

There were a couple of those that were made. A company called Forte Music up in the Bay Area was working on a MIDI interface at the same time we were. The Mark V MIDI was just being discussed in its real early days. When we bought Arp in 1981, the keyboard that they had in development – the Chroma – had a computer interface on it, but, it was a parallel interface as opposed to a serial interface like MIDI. Even in '81, '82, the engineering guys that we had brought in from Arp were not convinced that MIDI was the way to go. They were saying it's got limited bandwidth and doesn't have the growth potential… but, the momentum by '81 '82 for the existing MIDI specification was starting to grow once some of the Japanese companies hopped on it –

Yamaha, Roland, Korg and all of those people – it sort of became the de-facto standard. We had to decide, okay, we're a long way down the road, development road, with the Mark V to go back now and start thinking, "how are we going to do this?" The technology was out there to do it, but there were mechanical issues. How do you mount the little membrane switches? How do you get them accurate? How do you get the same key velocity from note to note? Then there was physically packaging it. As we all know, there was a lot going on under the hood. It had to have a power supply to drive this. Are we going to put a preamp in it? Then it became a matter of… the term we would use was, "creeping features" – once you start going to that next step, now we can add this. OK, well now we can add that. All of a sudden, you've created this new monster that has its own series of issues. So, we were looking into that.

We made a couple and we gave one to Chick Corea and one to John Novello, a real fine studio guy up in L.A. They got the two that we made. Then there were a couple that these guys at Forte Music put together. It was a fantastic thing once it was up and running, but it was a fair amount of work and we were also concerned about the cost. We were really wrestling with a lot of the costs on the Mark V – as a product that had a lot of parts, a lot of labor, everything kept going up. With all the wood, all the metal, again, the amount of time a worker would spend just adjusting the tuning springs on an 88 – they had to do all 88 – so somebody would spend half an hour working on just that one little part of it, even after the assembly people had gotten them close. Well, close enough isn't right… it had to be there.

Every time we turned around, there was something else that was going to make it a little bit more expensive. In the day, the Rhodes pianos were never cheap, but they were a good value. By the time the Mark V came along, the super high-end synthesizers of the early '80s – the Oberheim OB8, a Prophet-5, the Rhodes Chroma – those keyboards were 4 to 5 thousand dollars. They were starting to run out of customers that had that level of money. All of a sudden, those companies started their second generation keyboards – nice synthesizers that were down to like $2,000. That was still a lot of money at the time, so we had to be real conscious that we had an instrument that had to compete at a similar price range. You bought your Prophet-5, it had a hundred sounds. Granted it made one really good sound, but, it was hard for us to say hey ours is going to be $2500.

So a lot of the things we were looking at on the Mark V were to make an instrument that answered a lot of the questions and solved a lot of the problems from previous models. But we were also seriously looking at how we could be more cost effective.

The fact that we went to a plastic case: we paid a little bit more for the actual plastic, but there was no labor. The wooden box was made in the same wood shop that did Fender guitars and necks, necks and bodies. So there was a lot of labor to make that big plywood box, and you know, all the tolex covering and putting on the hardware. Being able to remove that was a significant cost savings.

The fact that we made it lighter was a benefit. We made the thing look a little bit more modern – a little bit hipper than just the same old wooden box. So those were some of the things that we had to kind of battle with the Mark V.

The final blow was the Yamaha DX-7. Players finally said you know what, doesn't sound exactly like a Rhodes, but it's got a very cool sound that's in that vain. Yamaha was the first one to get over the barrier of the number of notes you could play at one time. The Polyphony of a DX-7 was 16 notes. Prior to that, even the high-end Oberheims were 8. For a lot of guys that were serious piano players or used to playing a Rhodes, were you could just grab a handful of notes and play as many as you want. You could play all 73 notes at once if you wanted to – put the sustain pedal down and they'd all work. Having only 8 notes, you've got these weird things.

If you tried to play runs up the keyboard, you got here and oh, those notes disappeared. Or they'd have odd algorithms in the software where every 3rd note would drop out. You'd play and think, what the heck's going on? There was something that wasn't musically satisfying to a lot of guys.

Then all of a sudden here comes the DX-7, you can play 16 notes. For most guys, that was a major breakthrough. Until you've tried to play piano kind of things on a synthesizer, you didn't experience the frustration, but the DX-7 – it worked great. That FM Synthesis Yamaha had developed did an interesting job of creating a sound that was, like, the next evolution of a Rhodes piano. It still had that ability to blend. That was one of the amazing things about the Rhodes… something that Harold I don't think ever realized how amazing it was. How an instrument that could have a very thick texture like a Rhodes piano, yet could be recorded, be in a mix and not get in the way. It would create this beautiful, mid-range foundation for things to be layered on top of.

It was a nice pad, just sort of sparkled and shimmered in different areas, but it didn't get in the way of guitar parts, it didn't get in the way of horn parts, didn't get in the way of vocals.

The involvement Leo Fender had in the early days was pretty significant. There aren't a lot of people that were around at that time to ask what it was, but some of the documents that we've found show that as early as 1959, Leo was getting involved with Harold, both from a design standpoint and a business standpoint. Helping with patents and things like that, Leo helped take Harold's creation and make it more "manufacturable." That was one thing about Leo Fender and his guitars – he had a great eye for looking at a part, figuring out how it was going to be made, how it was going to be made affordably and accurately and give the performance they were looking for.

They were using Fender parts to make some of the things for the Rhodes. On a lot of the early documents regarding patents, there was a gentleman named Dick Gausewitz who was a patent attorney in Santa Ana. We've seen documents as early as 1958 from Dick Gausewitz to Leo Fender – and I had dealings with Dick Gausewitz as late as probably '95 where he was still involved. He wrote a huge number of the patents for Fender and all of their various divisions. Dick and Leo: a very interesting pair. They worked on things for years and years, not only at Fender, but, Leo Fender used him in later years when he had CLF Research making Music Man Instruments, then G&L Guitars. Those guys had a long career in the musical instrument business.

LABORATORY

MR. FENDER ONLY

John C. McLaren
Former President (CBS MUSICAL INSTRUMENTS)

I spent 16 years with Yamaha and most of that time I was head of the music, audio and sporting goods division. Anything that didn't have an engine, I was responsible for. CBS had been talking to me for a year and finally persuaded me, that I should join them. Of course they had Steinway and they had Fender – legendary companies – as well as several other companies. So I was tempted and I did it. Becoming President of CBS Musical Instruments Division in January of 1981 was like being made captain of the Titanic just after it hit the iceberg – it was a difficult time. [Laughs]

There was a major recession and the dollar had been pumped up very high against other currencies to overcome inflation here. That meant our export prices as a manufacturing company –

Steinway, Fender and the others – our prices went sky high. In 1981 as I recall, the price of a Fender guitar in Germany, without us changing the export price at all, went up about 30% because the dollar had inflated so much against the Mark. So that was a very difficult time for us in many respects.

At the same time, I really enjoyed the experience – it was wonderful – great companies like Steinway, Fender, Gulbransen Organs, Rodgers Organs, Rogers Drums and of course the Rhodes piano. The Rhodes piano situation was very difficult then. Newer electronic synthesizers like the Yamaha DX-7 were coming in that were just awesome by comparison. The Rhodes was, technically speaking, primitive and sales began to decline quite sharply. So that was another challenge we had to face.

As this whole new generation of digital technology and synthesizers were coming in, even the earlier analog synthesizers were losing out – people like Oberheim were getting hurt. What that meant from the dealer point of view, if he's going to invest money in inventory, he wants to be very sure it's something that his customers want to buy, he could turn it over and sell it. The Rhodes became increasingly questionable.

CBS, which itself was having a lot of problems and their concept of a timeframe was quite different from what it would be in the musical instrument manufacturing business. That was a real culture clash because everything that we were trying to do in the musical instrument division was way too long in terms of what CBS wanted to see. So the EK-10 was put together with real haste by guys who were very talented people, but doing it far too fast, as they knew themselves. The EK-10 was an effort to introduce the new synthesizer technology combined with the traditional Rhodes electromechanical technology. If it had a few more months of development, it might have been a very, attractive instrument, but it had all kinds of problems. EK-10s would be on stage and the synthesizer portion would pick up radio stations from China and all around the world [laughs] didn't help the musicians do their thing. So we shipped out a lot of EK-10s as I remember in 1981, and I took over at the beginning of 1981. Most of those came back in '81, so it was a very challenging time.

Another part of the situation was that many people didn't understand the Rhodes as a musical instrument – the fact that it was technologically obsolete was not relevant to its position as a musical instrument.

If fine musicians found in the Rhodes a way of expressing their musical taste, whether it is 200 year old technology or 2 week old technology, doesn't make any difference. When all is said and done, a Steinway concert grand piano is still being made today, looks exactly the same as the concert grand piano of 100 years ago, so technologically it's like, mid-19th century. It's a fabulous instrument, that's still played. So I think many people didn't recognize that Rhodes had potentially a much longer life. It might not sell in the large quantities that it had before, but in smaller quantities at a higher price, there were enough people that knew what Rhodes could do for them, that no other instrument did in quite the same way. There could have been a continuing life for Rhodes, but this was the time when CBS was trying to bail out of the musical instrument business and a number of other businesses that didn't relate to its core businesses, so they sold off the whole Fender package… and Rhodes got killed in the process.

The Fender factory didn't close until CBS had sold off the business. They sold everything as a kind of going concern. The new ownership, with Bill Schultz as President – I brought him with me from Yamaha, he had been running the Fender division, and he put together a group that bought the Fender Company. Bill didn't feel they had the resources to really rebuild Rhodes. He was probably right, given the financial limitations and technological limitations that they had available. So he shut it down and later sold the name at least – and maybe the technology such as it was then – to the Roland Company in Japan. Roland made an electronic Rhodes as they called it, but it wasn't a Rhodes piano.

Fender then sold off Rhodes, which as a business decision was probably a smart thing to do because they didn't have the resources to rebuild the product, the engineering and its position in the marketplace. Roland, a Japanese company making synthesizers, is a very fine company. They came out with an electronic-style Rhodes piano – didn't catch-on too well.

I met Harold Rhodes before I joined CBS because Yamaha's offices were in Buena Park, which is just 10 minutes down the road from the Fender offices in Fullerton. At trade shows, meetings and even sometimes in restaurants, you'd bump into each other. I knew him as a very dedicated musician and educator. He never thought of himself as an inventor. He thought of himself as a teacher. He invented, if that's the word we should use, the initial Rhodes piano because he was working for the War Department with guys who'd been injured, badly, in World War II. He wanted them to have an instrument that he could put on a bed; a guy could play around on and learn something. So he invented this little mechanical device, for that purpose – something that would give these terribly wounded men some inspiration. From that idea, it grew into the full Rhodes piano.

I found Harold a handsome guy – full of charisma – loved music and played well himself. When I joined CBS, we got along very well for an odd reason – I was one of the only other keyboard players in the Fender location there in Fullerton – everyone else played guitars and so forth. So, we were a lonely couple of guys who liked playing piano.

Harold was devoted to the Rhodes piano. He wanted to make it absolutely as good as he possibly could. It frustrated the hell out of him that he couldn't get the resources out of Fender people or out of CBS to take the instrument to the point he felt it could be taken to.

The other thing was, as the sales of the Rhodes declined very sharply in the couple of years before I joined the company, his income declined very sharply too, because he had made a deal with Leo that he would get paid based on so many pennies per key of instruments sold. As the quantity of instruments being sold declined and he was still getting the same number of pennies per key, his income declined very sharply. Even though the price of the instruments might have gone up quite a bit, he still got so many pennies per key so there was no consideration of inflation built into the deal that he had. When I came in, he was very vocal in telling me and anyone else who would listen, that he was going bankrupt. So I made a deal with him. We gave him $50,000 in cash to help him over an immediate hump he was in and I changed the formula on which he got paid. So at least, it recognized inflation and so forth. As you might imagine Harold and I got along even better after that.

He was a very likable guy, a very smart guy and his passion for musical, mechanical, artistic perfection was very endearing.

Before World War II, he had this radio show teaching people how to play piano. He met a young lady, a student. Many years later, just a few years before he died and he had several wives in the interim, which was maybe part of the reason he wasn't very well off when I met him, but he met this lady again, Margit. They came over here and we had lunch a couple of times. Really delightful lady and she took care of Harold when he was… you know he was very healthy, he played tennis and everything, but he had an accident, his van rolled back in the driveway, the door opened, it knocked him down and it broke his hip. That was the beginning of the end for Harold. He lived another few years but he never regained the health that he enjoyed up to that point.

Another wife he had – the wife that he had when I joined CBS – was a charming young lady, quite a bit younger than him. They split up and she went her own way, but then she came down with Cancer and Harold – loving kind guy that he was – took care of her in every way that he possibly could until she passed away.

There were several years when almost everything you heard in popular music had the Rhodes in there. The Carpenters might have done more to make that Rhodes sound popular than almost anybody else and they did a marvelous job with it. One of the things Harold used to say when the new synthesizers were coming on stream, they would try to copy the Rhodes sound. They'd have a tab on there – "Rhodes Sound." Harold laughed and said, "If they knew how hard we had worked to try to get rid of that 'Rhodes' sound and make it sound like a real piano, then why would they be copying us now!" [Laughs] There again – that is the nature of music. What is a poor reproduction of something to another guy because he's got a different musical taste and perception – my God!

I can do all kinds of things with this, you know, but he was amused by the fact that these synthesizer guys were saying that "this is our Rhodes sound."

To the people at Fender, Harold was a pain in the rear end. He would come in ranting about anything that he wasn't satisfied with and he'd make no bones about it. We had a Steinway upright piano that Harold insisted on sending out to be rebuilt; then he wasn't happy with it, never used it for anything we knew about. But he insisted on having that piano – spent tons of money on it! He was a perfectionist and he wouldn't compromise. He'd write letters – 3, 4 and 5 page letters expressing his outrage to whoever was running Fender or CBS. My predecessor, Bob Campbell, had several of Harold's letters. Bob, by-the-way, was a very fine pianist and organist himself. So Harold felt he had a more sympathetic ear from Bob and then from me, because we both played piano like he did.

I think Harold was an employee, but the form of compensation was unique. I think they wanted to make sure he had the necessary health insurance and things like that. So I believe in that context he was an employee. But Harold – no matter what technically he was classified as – was a free spirit and his job was to make sure the Rhodes piano was protected and improved and enhanced as much as possible. Of course, he got paid based on how many keys they sold so, he had a financial interest that was very clear. He made a lot of money in the early years… but, I think that was always a secondary consideration for Harold. He spent a lot of money on all kinds of crazy – he owned a ranch up in the hills behind Fullerton, he had old Fire department engines and all kinds of stuff like that. He was a collector like that.

The division headquarters when I joined the company was in Deerfield, IL. I really didn't want to move my family to Deerfield. My family thought it was a good idea, but I didn't. I had spent a winter in Chicago and they hadn't. So I went to New York. Bill Mendello who is now President / Chairman of Fender, was my CFO. I called him in the office and I said, "Bill, how would you like to live in California?" "Oh, God," he said, "I'd love to." He came from New Jersey. I said, "Bill, here's my plan. Show me how much money we can save with this plan." 20 minutes later, Bill came back and showed me we'd save 8 million dollars with this plan. What I was doing was getting rid of this big fat corporate overhead at the division headquarters, and putting these key guys out to run the individual companies within the division. They needed leadership and lacked it.

Then I went to NY and met with then chairman of CBS Tom Wyman. Bill and I went in and I started outlining to Wyman my plan for moving the division headquarters back to Fullerton, where it had been located some years before. Wyman says to me, "Hey John, it's your division – you want to move it to California, go right ahead." I was out of there in a flash [laughs]. We moved back to California and I didn't have to move my house, sell my house, or anything. In fact, I was closer to my office in Fullerton than I had been when I was with Yamaha for all those years in Buena Park. So, from that point of view, it worked out very well. Needless to say, Mendello was thrilled to bits to move to California.

Frankly, I never really liked the Rhodes as an instrument… you know, I play piano. In my house I've got a Steinway Concert Grand piano. That is a piano to me. The Rhodes was interesting. It had portability if you were an 800-pound elephant it was portable, but relative to conventional pianos, it meant guys… pianos, were suffering all the time. You get a gig and if you play saxophone or guitar, you take your stuff with you.

But if you're a pianist, you go to a club or venue and you have to play whatever piece of crap is there. A lot pianists end up in loony bins because of that. So the Rhodes was a terrific thing for those guys. A couple of guys shove it in the back of a station wagon and at least you know what you have to deal with when you get there. In some ways, the Rhodes was fun to play, but it was not my favorite piano. It did have some unique colorations and sounds you could get. Listen to some of the guys that used Rhodes and they do some terrific percussive effects with it, but, overall, I didn't much care for it. I certainly didn't care for the EK-10. I'm the manager of the musical instrument division of CBS and we had problems all over the place, but one of the biggest was the EK-10. So, in terms of my professional, angst, Rhodes, the EK-10 particularly, was a big part of that.

But I must say – Harold was a delightful guy. I loved the guy. I loved him for the things I said before. He cared deeply about music. He also thought I played very well, so I liked him right away. I play by ear and he was fascinated I could do all the harmonies, chords and so forth that I do without knowing what the hell I was really doing. Harold thought that was fascinating.

John R. McLaren
Former Research & Development (CBS / FENDER)

The first time I met Harold Rhodes was in the old CBS buildings. They were Leo Fender's original buildings, all run down and everything. That's where Harold would hang out, where Research & Development (R&D) was at. The first time I saw him, I knew he was somebody special. My father had said, "You're going to meet Harold Rhodes, a very famous man." He came in beautifully dressed – a very stylish guy. When he'd come in you'd light up. He'd just bring life to wherever he'd go. He was the star – and he wanted to be the star, okay!

I started there in '80/'81 and worked there for high school credits. My father was able to do a deal so I could take a couple periods off and spend the time in R&D. I had seen the Rhodes lab – Harold was in there, Steve Woodyard and everything – and I was told prior to meeting him that he had his own teaching program. He was heavily into teaching. We had a number of those old student pianos around – the "Jetsons"-green, avocado color things.

He told me that this is part of the student program and as I got to know Harold, it was funny – very caring man he had patience to teach you anything. I was 16. He'd call me in the office and say, "I'm going to show you how this works." He'd have either a new tone bar generator tine in a 1-key module and he's showing me how it works. I had job assignments, but with Harold it didn't matter who's in charge – he's in charge! He was very concerned for many years with the quality of the pianos. It drove him up the wall. He was always writing inter-office memos to everybody to straighten out the quality. He was a very good engineer and an artist.

Harold was part of the music program for the Army, he had a couple of his buddies and he did some charcoal sketches of them – incredible. They were-beautiful. It was just a sweet thing to see because you know Harold had interests in all kinds of stuff.

My first assignment at CBS in the original building: go find Harold's car! What happened was Harold had some dealer problems with his pianos. Usually we would send somebody out from the service department and they would handle it, but, Harold just hopped on a plane, went over there and did his work. When he came back, he didn't know where his car was. I said, "Mr. Rhodes, what're you doing with this banana-colored Aries K car?" He said, "Oh, I lost my car." So orders came down to go to LAX, find his '79 Oldsmobile 98 Regency Diesel and bring it back. Sometimes Harold was absent-minded about trivial things he just had no time for. The big thing he really cared the most about was the student program.

After he'd made his first crude piano, he thought, "Maybe I can make an improved version." So he came out with the Pre Piano. This is about 1948, '49. It was introduced in Hollywood at his music studio where children and adults would take piano lessons. It was a very exclusive program.

He built these actions into the piano and did most of the work himself. The action is fairly crude but it worked. He had a friend named Osbrink, I believe, who owned a foundry in L.A. He made the castings for the tone bar rail.

This Pre-Piano, interestingly enough, has a piezo pickup in it, so when you play it, you're actually hearing it right from the casted frame. I don't know how many he made of these, but they were troublesome – parts would break… but he had a piano.

In 1959, Harold went to visit Leo Fender at the old buildings. Just prior to that, Osbrink had invested with Harold $50,000 to make a working piano, but it didn't quite happen. So Harold found Leo.

Now Leo had an amp line which is cabinets. He was a wealthy man – had dealer structure and everything. So Harold and Leo worked together on this, but it wasn't actually part of the Fender Company. It was their little side-business that went into the Fender building. They had a full machine shop, for instance, so Harold could make different tone bars or whatever he wanted and the company was founded called Cleftronics. Leo had this company where the purchasing, tooling and everything were funded. I think it was in August of 1959 that it became Fender-Rhodes. I have somewhere when they opened in the Fullerton Bank, the first deposit for $5,000 – which was an incredibly large amount of money back then. I have some invoices that say Cleftronics on them.

So they started it – and there was a lot of engineering. Leo was a very good engineer and Harold was too – very creative… understood the piano, so there was a bonding there.

The next step that they took was the Piano Bass because they had an action going now – a wooden action, not very complex but it worked. They had problems with the other octaves, so they kept the Piano Bass. I'm just guessing on this, but when Osbrink found out that Harold was hooked up with Leo and the Fender Company, he wanted his money back. He didn't tell Leo about this, so it was kind of a problem. So they had to eventually come to an agreement to give him his money back. At that point, it was like he's out of the way, let's move on. So the Piano Bass came out and did very, very well, but it was troublesome too. It still had the casted tone bars [one piece unit, broke, replace whole thing], it had a piece of piano wire, it wasn't a tine it wasn't tapered down or anything, it was piano wire and they would break. You couldn't replace the wire. You had to replace the whole piece – the tone bar, everything.

By about 1963/65, they made great improvements in the action. They were developing new tines that were durable. The tone bar now was separated from the generator and tine, so if you broke a tine, you didn't have to buy a new tone bar. The Doors really put the Piano Bass out there in the late '60s. They were also playing one of the earliest Rhodes piano 73 key. The bell-like sound in "Riders on the Storm," that was a Rhodes.

Harold really wanted to have a teaching program, though. They struggled with that and came out with a couple of different versions of the Console, which wired up 6 to 12 pianos. The instructor would sit at a desk and the student wore a headphone and microphone combination. He could talk, listen to any of the students and help them out. It was a very impressive program, but financially CBS wasn't too interested in that… so it was short lived.

The program was, let's go for the Mark I [portable stage piano without speaker]. It went through several different transitions, but when it came out, it was extremely successful. In the '60s/'70s, everybody had a Rhodes. You heard Rhodes in everything all the way up to '85.

Now you're hearing it again with the way the kids are buying these things. They're retro and they gotta have one. It's 120 lbs. to carry around, but, you cannot replicate a Rhodes piano.

I had a joke for a while. One guy says, "You know, every Rhodes plays differently." I say, "Well, first it depends on who's setting it up," because we had these sound booths – there was a little air conditioning thing in there and they'd test them or whatever.

There were time periods where they had keyboard musicians that were good techs, but they tended to have other hobbies on the side that they would bring in – "chemicals," let's say – and that could definitely change the quality from one piano from the next! Harold was always overseeing the quality – that was so important to him. It was so popular that by 1978, we produced 16,000 pianos. I think that was one of the largest years ever!

When Rhodes was sold to CBS, prior to that sale, Leo had to buy the one share of stock from Harold that was 76 cents to have complete control over the company. Columbia Broadcasting Systems were concerned about Rhodes because, with some legal issues and it not quite fitting in – it was sort of Harold and Leo's side project; the deal almost didn't go through. So they had to do all this stock / paperwork transactions and everything. Then it was transferred all to Leo and Leo transferred it to CBS. There was always a rumor that Harold got a royalty. He did get a royalty, but, I've heard so many people say it was a penny a key. So, he would make 73 cents on a piano. That's not the case. Harold was paid much more – however the deal that he cut with CBS was not really a good deal. As the price of the pianos went up, Harold's royalty didn't increase. So a piano that was sold in '72 for something like $600, by 1980, was a considerably higher amount – almost twice as much – but, Harold still got the same royalty.

For a while, he was in charge of Marketing, drawing a salary and did quite well. Actually, Harold was making quite a lot of money in the '70s – a very wealthy man making tons of money with this piano.

A friend of mine lived two doors down from Harold in Anaheim before he came into the money with CBS. The door was always open and people would just come and go. Harold had his workshop in there, door wide open, didn't care – wasn't something he needed to worry about. He had a couple of attractive daughters and the neighbors liked to hang out with them. All of a sudden there was no activity going on in the house, nobody around. So, they were wondering what was going on because Harold always had you know, people coming and going. Four days later, a big stretch Cadillac limousine pulls up with the windows down. I was surprised to see this limousine in this area. Then the girls' heads pop out sayin', "Daddy's rich! He did a deal with CBS, he's making all these pianos and he's rich now!" So they all hopped in the limousine and just had a good 'ol time.

One of his wives, Delores Rhodes, would do the PTA meetings and everything. She was very flamboyant, very similar to Harold, but a very sweet lady. When Harold moved, he had a very large home – about 4 acres of land with orchards and fruit trees on it. He didn't realize that having that amount of land, he had to become part of the Grower's Association and they would monitor his land. So, Harold went out and got a little John Deere Tractor.

I remember hearing people say, "What are you going to do with this tractor?" and he said, "I don't know I just like to drive it around." So he'd be driving it around and had a childish side to him which was fun.

He had a 1930's fire engine he would drive around, which I believe was fully functional and a 1930's police car – he was really amazing with some of the stuff he collected. During the gas shortage in the '70s, he put in his own pump for diesel and gas and lived on top of

These gas trucks are making it up a winding, narrow road to fill his tanks. One of his sons put diesel fuel into a gas car, or the other way around. Harold had to put a whole new engine in the car and he was really upset about that.

The end of the Rhodes piano was a very sad thing. We had the EK-10 piano which was a major disaster. We had produced all these instruments that had all kinds of different faults. This was supposed to be the saving grace for Rhodes – going to keep them on the map. They ran 3 shifts to make these EK-10s, and shipped them out as fast as they could. Some of them went to Yamano Music, the distributor in Japan, and they were having problems in nightclubs because of radio interference and the PAL system with the TV networks. It was a very bad thing. We didn't want to pay the shipping charges back so he threw them in the ocean, in the Japan ocean, as a... what do you call it, a reef project.

I remember the EK-10s coming back and being destroyed on the dock. They couldn't salvage anything – it wasn't worth it. You could smell the new pianos – the tolex, the shiny parts – and they were just destroyed, run over with a forklift, then scooped up and thrown in a 40-foot dumpster. I saw this daily... They just kept coming in. The Rhodes piano – the Mark II – had plastic keys now, not wood and theywere troublesome. They broke. It was hard to ship them without them breaking, so that collapsed, and the tooling was worn out.

I saw this big wonderful factory slowly dying. People were given their pink slips and left. It was very hard to see that because some of these people had worked there for 20 years. Their parents, mom or dad worked there.

I remember seeing Harold look very ill. He was out of money. My father had issued him I think $50,000 to help him out. Then he broke his hip, so he was getting into very poor condition. We put a huge amount of capital into R&D to try and come out with a piano that we could be proud of – the Mark V – but after the EK-10, all these plastic keys, all of the synthesizers, the DX-7, which clobbered every other synthesizer, pretty much took the Rhodes off the map.

I remember the last few days of the Rhodes pianos. There was one lady working in a poorly lit area, and one supervisor who was not a working supervisor. He was union so he supervised this one poor lady… and she was very, very depressed. I would go talk to her and she just knew it was a matter of time. When she was let go, it was left vacant… parts everywhere.

You've got to remember, this company – Fender, Rogers, and Rhodes – had 1,300 employees, a factory 350,000 square feet, not including the old buildings as well, it was like a college. It had a gym, it had its own post office, a nurse's office to stitch people up – it was a huge place. To see it get reduced to 90 for Fender and nothing for Rhodes…

The problem was, since there were no sales, there was no budget. They kept trying to infuse money. They were getting the harps assembled in Mexico – bringing them back and forth – and the piano had been off the market for about 2 years. When the Mark V was introduced in '85, people that were used to playing the Rhodes liked it. They liked the feel, the new improved action, but, that's it. They already had Rhodes. They still had Rhodes pianos and then all the synthesizers. So it was the end of it. They just didn't sell.

I watched those R&D guys work so hard – dedicated people like Mike Peterson and Steve Woodyard – trying to make everything happen, but there's no way of repairing this. The last 600 Rhodes we had in inventory, they retailed at $999. I think dealer cost was around $600 – a B mark is what they called it – they were sold for $300 and shipped to Yamano Music. We just had to get rid of them. We didn't have the warehouse space. He MIDI-equipped all the Mark V's and I asked Mr. Yamano – Mike Yamano's assistant – how the Mark V's were doing. He said, "Not good." I believe he still has some inventory.

Then the auction came. Everybody was gone and they decided to auction the machines, tables, benches, drafting tables, cafeteria stuff – everything. It was almost like this wonderful factory was being stripped and raped. I saw the Rhodes stuff go in a package – it was so cut-n-dry and cold. These guys would buy the sound booths and everything for next to nothing. I remember this one lady's bench… it was like she'd just went to lunch. Her coffee mug was still half full. It had mold in it, but she had all her personal pictures out and a poem she wrote on there. She had all the Rhodes stuff / tools all laid out and she didn't work there… but, there was a union book called "The Brotherhood of United Electrical Workers." Strangely enough, the book was opened to a page that read, "When you join this union, you have a job for life." I thought, "How sad… " When I saw everything that I loved so much being hocked off, it was just traumatic.

Thank god there are plenty of Rhodes pianos out there. People that want one can still get one.

Mike Peterson
Former Engineer (CBS / FENDER)

I had been pretty much building things ever since I was old enough to pick up a tool. In junior high, I met a bunch of musicians, started hanging out and building things for their band. They were overjoyed to have me because stuff always breaks in the band. Somewhere along the line I met a fellow named Paul Rivera. I don't know if everybody knows who Paul Rivera is, but he has become a tube-type guitar amp guru, who later in his career became "the guy" for custom modifying guitar amps for the heavy-duty guitar players in Hollywood. At the time I met him, he was in the corner of a little place, in kind of a run-down part of San Diego called Meatball Speaker Repair. We were walking down the street and saw this fairly interesting looking drawing of the meatball from the underground comics and thought, "We have to go in there!"

Sure enough, in the corner was Paul Rivera with his amplifier repair business and who knows what happened – I just kind of decided here's a guy that I need to spend more time with. I can learn something from him and he decided here's a guy that probably could be useful for me some time in the future. So, we ended up collaborating on some small projects.

Later as my musical hobby turned into a profession, I opened a custom manufacturing company in San Diego. Paul Rivera rose up through the ranks of custom guitar amplifier tweaking and finally ended up being the President of Pignose. I started making things for him – custom speaker cabinets, hardwood speaker cabinets and custom pedal boxes. Another thing led to another thing and after two or three jobs, he ended up becoming the Director of Marketing for Fender guitar amplifiers.

He called me up one day, as the company that I was in didn't seem like such a good fit and he says "Hey, you want to work for Fender?" I thought, "That sounds like a really cool idea," because – like many guys like me – I would look at musical equipment that my buddies had paid thousands of dollars for and think, "Wow, this is incredibly poorly made stuff… and you paid how much for it?" Of course, later on, I found out why the stuff was the way it was. I discovered that even if you are in the music business, you can't always do better.

Paul introduced me to Harold Rhodes and to the Fender Company. My first assignment was to work with Harold – I think they probably thought they were hiring more like a shop tech just to build Harold's ideas. They didn't realize that they were actually hiring a guy who had his own ideas and probably was going to move them in a direction that they may not have anticipated.

The first project was supposed to be Harold's idea for a dog-leg key. Dog-leg, I guess, is a golf term. Harold played golf, among other things. The idea was that the top of the piano is fairly high off the surface of the keyboard and if you put another instrument on top of it, which was really popular among the multi-instrumentalists of the time, you end up playing like this (hands separated). Even though you can do it, it's not conducive to proper playing technique. So the idea was, "Wouldn't it be nice if you could lower the top of the piano a little bit so that you could put another instrument on top and keep your hands closer together?" Harold had cobbled-together a crude, not-quite-playable, early incarnation of this key bed laying around the lab. I looked at it, we talked about it a little bit and that was the beginnings of the whole thing.

When you're approaching a classic instrument and you're hired as an engineer and you're a young creative guy who is just overflowing with ideas, how do you approach it? Do you simply salute it and say, "Beautiful instrument Sir, it's a total work of genius," or do you systematically go to work and attack its weaknesses while trying to preserve the things that made it a classic? As the project evolved, it wasn't a decision, it wasn't the CBS management coming to me and saying, "Your job is to design a completely new Rhodes piano." It was, "Your job is to go work with Harold and come up with some stuff." The idea to develop a completely new piano was pretty much mine. It was based on trying to solve several problems.

What are the strengths and weaknesses of the piano? Obviously, the strength is it has a classic sound that's unmatched by any other instrument and it just plain sounds great. The weaknesses are it's really heavy, it's hard to manufacture consistently, it's hard to keep adjusted and tuned so that you get that perfect magical sound. The other thing is a little bit more technical of a question – the Rhodes action is a very simplified action. The grand piano action has many moving parts and it's evolved over hundreds of years to do what's actually a fairly amazing thing – to play a very, very quiet note and a very, very loud note. In order to do that, the action has to be able to control the rebound of the hammer as it hits either string – or the tine in the case of the Rhodes – control the rebound and not hit more than once. The Rhodes action being a very simplified action, there are a lot of compromises in it. One of the downsides of the traditional Rhodes action is, you could adjust it to play a really gnarly loud note, but when you did that, you couldn't get a soft note.

You could adjust it to play really, really delicate, pretty notes, but if you stomp it, then you'd get multiple hits – the hammer would hit the tine multiple times and bounce; it would produce a really, really awful sound which we called a spud note. So, those were the three major goals we were trying to accomplish – reduce the weight, make them more consistent, and improve the dynamics.

At the time I was working on my ideas that would later lead to the Mark IV. Harold and Steve Grom were trying to keep the production line running and they were having enormous difficulties. The Rhodes is a lot more complex instrument than you think. If the Stradivarius violin didn't have the reputation that it had, you brought one to a master woodworker and said, "Can you make one of these," most master woodworkers would look at it and say, "Yeah, that's simple." Well, the Rhodes may not be a Stradivarius violin, but it's got a lot of complexity built into it and a lot of secrets that are hidden in the various minds and shops of the part manufacturers. When you take a drawing that is missing all of the secret information and give it to another vendor who says, "Sure, that's easy, I can make those and I can make them for half the price," it turns out that somebody missed a secret. All of the secret information was not written down. Some of the processes were worked out by Harold and the master craftsman at the shop. Once they had it right, it was just something they all remembered until the master craftsman died or retired or the job was given to a different shop.

So Harold and Steve were constantly fighting fires. There would be reports coming in from the field like, "This batch of pianos is un-tunable!" "This batch of pianos sounds horrible!"

So they would bring in some representative samples, analyze them, measure them, play with them and find out, "Oh, look at that… this part that's supposed to be a really tight fit is loose, or this part that's supposed to be drilled perfectly straight is drilled crooked." Their work in production monitoring and control naturally led them to their further research and understanding of what makes a perfect Rhodes. It kind of surprised me that the inventor of the piano, Harold himself, didn't really know all the answers – that, obviously, he must have known most of the answers because he invented the instrument and made the magic that happened, but there was still a fairly good amount of mystery going on in the action. None of us really knew exactly why the magic ones sounded magic and the bad ones sounded bad – why some could be tuned and some just plain couldn't be tuned. So Harold and Steve spent a tremendous amount of time studying one-key models, looking at parts under the microscope and even sending parts out to metallurgists – trying to understand what it is that made the good ones good and the bad ones bad. Meanwhile, at the same time, I was over in my corner of the lab coming up with all sorts of crazy ideas for alternate actions, alternate packaging, alternate action rails, alternate case designs. That's kind of the way the labor was distributed at that time.

The Rhodes action is a very ingenious action, in that it accomplishes quite a lot of the magic of a grand piano action with 2 pieces. It's got a key back with felt on it, a plastic hammer with the back end of the hammer having a little curved section and a little flat section. As you press on the key, you make contact with the curved section and accelerate the hammer upward.

Then as the hammer reaches maximum velocity, you bring the flat part in contact and immediately apply the brake. So the action basically is accelerating the hammer, then at the moment when it's going as fast as it's going to go, apply the brake. The brake is to prevent bouncing, which we've determined is the sound killer if, ideally, you want to have one and only one precise, clean strike. If you have more than one strike, those strikes will never be in phase, they'll never reinforce each other and you end up deadening and killing the sound.

The traditional Rhodes action does this in a kind of a smooth way. You've got a smooth transition from the curved part of the action into the brake part of the action, so you smoothly transition from accelerating the hammer and as you're accelerating, you're moving the point of contact. The point of contact is getting closer to the axel, the action is a non-linear transfer, so the action gets progressively heavier as the hammer is accelerated, up until the point where the brake is applied, but the brake isn't applied perfectly, instantaneously… it kind of slides into it.

My idea was, "What if you separate the two? What if you separate the brake from the accelerator, basically making the accelerator geometrically identical to the jack on a grand piano, then at the end of the stroke, abruptly apply the brake." A few one key models were put together by carefully tuning the resilience and rigidity of the various different components. It turned out to be a pretty critical tuning to get everything to work, but when it was tuned correctly on the little one-key model, it actually behaved in an almost magical way where it would self-adjust to automatically reduce the distance between the tine and the hammer tip at the end of the stroke when you were playing soft and as you would play louder and louder, the distance would increase – kind of "auto-magically" did the right thing.

Everybody that saw it was very excited about it and because of the excitement over these one-key models and ideas, even Harold was saying, "Maybe we should come up with a completely new piano based on this idea."

So there really was no plan to build a Mark IV. There was kind of like, "Well, let's hire this guy, put him in the corner and see what he comes up with." It had Harold's dog-leg key, the low-profile top, it was in a plastic case, it had a lighter weight frame and all the other things we were trying to accomplish at the same time.

The reason the Mark IV didn't cut it is, the magic that made the action do its thing, was not perfectly well understood. It turned out that it was a very careful balance of "stiffness and resiliencies" – energy-absorbing foam here and special felt there. It wasn't completely reproducible. The one-key model felt really, really good, but when we actually built a full-size piano, players noticed that it did have the dynamic improvements of being able to play hard and soft, but it also felt a little weird. Whether "felt a little weird" was, "it feels different from a standard Rhodes," or "felt a little weird" was, "it had a cancer that made it unusable as a musical instrument," my main concern was the magic was insufficiently well understood to put it into production.

I think we all decided – there was a market report produced which recommended enthusiastically that the piano go into full production. This was produced by the crack marketing department and I don't mean that in the terms of drugs. I mean we who were critical, fairly serious about this and wanted to make sure that we put out something that was really good.

The more that we played with it and the more that we looked at it, we realized it was a harder problem than anybody thought – kind of like everything else with the piano – and it was going to take a indeterminately long (but not a few weeks of extra work) to finally perfect it. Because we were operating in a tight time window and CBS was nearing the end of its involvement in the musical instrument business, they pretty much said, "One more try and we'll see if we can make this work." Little bit by little bit, the weeks were ticking off and we had to have something. When the news was given that we don't know how long it's gonna take to perfect it… we switched to plan B.

Plan B was the result of Harold and Steve's research into what makes a Rhodes sound good. It was partly just going old-school; it was partly just undoing the mistakes that had been made over time in the Mark II. The stroke of the hammer was reduced – not for any musical reason, but because the "marketoids" and management thought, "We can reduce warranty claims due to broken tines if we don't allow the player to hit the thing as hard." Of course, hitting it hard gives one of its classic magic overdriven-kind of growl sounds that everybody loves. Taking that away really is a great loss to the musician.

So, simply going back to the longer hammer throw distance helped a lot of things. Going back to the original Mark I hammer throw distance helped a lot of things, going back to the classic wooden key bed helped a lot of things. The plastic key was an attempt at cost reduction, but it turned out it wasn't. It turned out that it was exceptionally difficult to injection mould a piece of plastic that was, what, 16" long or something?

It's a hard part to mould. It's a hard part to keep straight. You don't get very much yield out of your injection mould, you can't just pop them out, the mould has a slow cycle time, the development cost was horrendous. Fortunately, we had a superstar mould maker and injection moulding shop owner that we worked with who was able to make the things work, but, when purchasing tried yanking the job from them and giving it to the lowest bidder, the lowest bidder said, "Hey, that's impossible. We can't make these!"

So, part of it was just going back to the tried-and-trusted designs. As Steve and Harold were studying the Mark IV action, they observed some things they could do on the Mark V action. They observed that if we slightly adjust the shape of the rounded portion on the hammer, maybe if we extend the braking surface a little bit out the back end to give a little bit more braking, maybe the kind of mythical bump (action modification) that started out being added by technicians and later as we started studying it, the bump turned out to have several very interesting properties, we studied how big a bump and where to put the bump. You might say that the Mark IV action was one absolutely enormous bump!

So, the Mark V was basically Harold and Steve trying their best to perfect the piano. The parts that I worked on, well, I designed the case, the stand, a lot of the little internal packaging details. Yes, yes, I did the graphics! I actually was one of many who observed that the Rhodes was labeled "input" [laughs] and the reasoning, I guess, was, "Well, that's where you plug the cord in isn't it?" So it was correctly labeled output – it was a cleaner, more modern graphic.

I admit that I'm not much of a graphic artist so it is a little lean, mean and minimal – but, the idea was to try to reduce, as much as possible, the weight of the thing. Unfortunately, in pretty much all of engineering – not just the Rhodes piano – everything comes with a tradeoff.

Kind of getting off-topic for a minute and drifting back to the Mark IV, one thing that we discovered after making this thing very light, is that now you had this effectively hollow cabinet; a hollow enclosure with some thin, vibrating membranes. It was kind of like an acoustic guitar that was really good at amplifying all of the non-musical noises that the piano made while you were playing it, so all the keys sliding against things and bouncing and hitting things – the non-musical part of the sound – became fairly objectionable. Depending on who you talk to, it was either, "Oh, my God, that's horrible," "I hate it," or "what noise? I can't hear it." Depending on how loud the amplifier was turned up, whether or not you had the headphones on in the studio where there was an open mic nearby and somebody else was trying to sing quietly and there was all this clicking and clacking going on.

So, the compromise that we came up with on the Mark V: any grand piano technician would probably recognize the construction of the key bed as being kind of a traditional piano key bed construction. It turns out that having that amount of wood in the plastic case damps the unwanted sound sufficiently that we could get by with it. The big old-fashioned wood case actually damped the unwanted sounds even more.

However, many people have complained, especially when they had to carry it up the stairs to the second and third floor gig... didn't have roadies, had to carry it themselves and then had to play after carrying it. Probably our biggest complaints and requests for change were, "Can't you make the damn thing lighter?"

The semi-interesting side note that fits in to all the history of this was the Arp musical instrument company and the Arp 16-voice electronic piano. Anybody that follows the music industry knows that Arp has had some great successes and some not-so-great things as well. Somewhere along the line in the last stages of their life, the Arp Company was bought by CBS and we started working with them to try to see what we could do with what was left of their company. The reason CBS bought the Arp Company was to get the Chroma synthesizer, which was one of the very first polyphonic analog synthesizers – right around the time of the Prophet-5. They had also built a warehouse full of these 16-voice electronic pianos that were put into a black tolex case. The marketing department thought that they looked really ugly, so one of my early diversions from, "hey can you take a few minutes away from working on the Rhodes piano and go try to make this thing look a little better," I came up with a kind of cosmetic rework for what was then to be called the Rhodes electronic piano, the Arp 16-voice. Unfortunately, the thing didn't sound very good and Harold was very angry that they called it the Rhodes piano because he was thinking, "People are going to think I did that!"

However, the original ideas – the larger kind of wood sides and the kind of overall graphic concept of it – was first used in the electronic piano, then later expanded and hopefully, done a little bit better in the Mark IV. The parts of the case that seemed to work well were then translated over into the Mark V. The stand was originally designed for the Mark IV.

For all of you suitcase lovers, you can all hate me because I was the one that advocated that change (no suitcase cabinet). There actually was some reasoning behind it. You've got to remember the times. This was the era of the multi-instrumentalist – this was the Rick Wakeman era, when people were starting to pile up stacks of multi-keyboards and a lot of it would be fed into a mixer. We weren't thinking of it as a stand-alone piano that would be played solo. We were – or primarily I was – thinking of it as a part of a multi-instrumentalist's kit. A guy would have a mixer, probably some effects, probably a fairly good sound system, possibly even going through the house PA, possibly not needing the speaker on the ground, it was heavy and… it's kind of a personal thing. Some people really love it. There was a certain amount of resistance, but in the end, Harold agreed, Steve agreed, management agreed and we went forward.

The speaker is probably a better design for the player sitting in front of it and playing it. Otherwise, it's probably a less good design… I remember going to see bands and sometimes they'd have a suitcase Rhodes and I'm going, "Is that thing turned on?" Because, depending on how loud the band was, how disciplined they were, how out of control the drummer and guitar players were, in many cases it didn't get out into the audience in a way that really made it cut through the rest of the instruments.

For a guy just sitting in a piano bar, low volume, solo piano jazz club kind of thing, it was probably great. The biggest defense of the suitcase that I've heard is from the guys who play it and love sitting in front of it. They say, "It makes me feel like I'm in the middle of the music… the sound is all around me… "

The company at that time, we were in the mentality of "this is our last try." The original Kurzweil sampled piano had come out during the development. We noticed people standing in line at the NAMM show to hear it, then walking away from the display going, "That's going to change everything."

The Yamaha DX-7, the Prophet 5, even our Chroma, was kind of showing that the future was maybe possibly not going to be so friendly to the old electro-mechanical instruments that only made one sound. I didn't make the decision. If you would have left it up to us in the R&D lab, we would have said, "Let's go ahead and make 73s and 88s in the first production run." We all knew in the lab that the 88 really was a compromise – that the sweet spot of the piano was the 73. As you extend the bass notes down and extend the high notes up, they work but they don't work quite as well and they don't have quite as magical a tone. We found some of the upper notes to be more "clicky" than tonal, but I suppose some people really love it. The decision basically was we can barely afford to do one piano – give it your best shot. Then if there's another production run and if it sells well, and if we're still in business, and if and if and if… but, the one and only Mark V 88-Key prototype.

I hand-made the mould for the plastic case and in the process of molding the plastic case, the plug mould was kind of difficult to remove from the plastic part and it ended up being destroyed in the process of pulling the first part, so only one prototype was ever made.

The harp, which was the hardest part to make, was from a production 88 Mark II. It had the enhancements that we came up with; a lot of the grommet tine and tonebar enhancements. It had the new keys, the new hammers, the wooden key bed and the new geometry keys that we have one custom made prototype done. So it was effectively a Mark V, but, we never did tune it, tweeze it and get all the bugs worked out to the point where you could look at it and say, "Wow, that's really something."

In regards to MIDI, marketing said, "Can you put MIDI on this thing?" We looked at a variety of tech-niques and technologies at that time. It turns out that, especially with the facilities we had, with the technology we had, with the knowledge we had, with the state-of-the-art at the time we had, it turned out to be a harder problem than we thought. The problem with putting key switches on an electromechanical piano is you don't want to modify the feel of the piano. You want it to feel like a Mark V and many of the key switch technologies – assuming that you don't use something exotic like a beam break or a light sensor or something – you're going to be pressing against a spring of some sort. We looked around at various different mechanical springs and we looked around at a variety of conductive rubber springs. We finally came up with a dual concentric conductive rubber dome switch where you press it down a little bit and one part makes contact.

You press it down a little bit more and the next part makes contact and by measuring the time in milliseconds between the first contact and the second contact, you can kind of crudely assess how fast the key was pressed. When I say crudely, I mean, crudely. The MIDI spec allocates 127 gradations for the so-called velocity signal. We had trouble getting 16 reliable signal-above-the-noise measurements because of the scanning speed of microprocessors of the time and the small distances involved, but we managed to get it in and to work. I basically hand-built the 2 or 3 MIDI Mark V prototypes Chick Corea used with his Elektric Band.

The company wasn't as profitable as CBS wanted it to be. CBS was losing interest and starting to think, "Maybe we should get out of this business." They had a labor dispute in the last days of the factory where they basically offered the union employees, "Accept our contract or we'll close down the factory" and the union voted against the contract.

Philosophically anybody who cares about music – really everybody – knows CBS never should have been in the music business. Everybody knows pre-CBS Fender is the classic Fender. Unfortunately, there was no pre-CBS Rhodes, unless you count some of Harold's really old prototypes. However, the Fender Rhodes piano was pretty much produced by CBS and suffered from the manufacturing shortfalls and cost cutting that they forced onto the production line. Even though those of us down in the trenches wanted to make the thing sound really good, it's a complex, expensive, beast to produce. I think if they realized how difficult it was, they would have run away screaming a long time ago.

People probably told them, "Oh, it's really easier than you think. These problems that we're having, they're just temporary. Once we get this worked out you'll probably make a ton of money… " Probably a thousand different reasons… but, we all could see the end was coming. It ended up that Fender went back to their basics – guitars and amplifiers – and the piano was just allowed to die.

The whole experience was very enjoyable most of the time, when I wasn't arguing with manufacturing about tolerances. One thing that was odd, but, in a good kind of way, is that John McLaren – who was the CEO of the entire CBS Musical Instruments mega-group, including Steinway, Lyon & Healy, Gemeinhardt, Gulbransen and the whole thing – would frequently come down to the lab, pull up a chair and just talk to us… for hours. Sometimes about the piano, sometimes about business, sometimes about music, sometimes about philosophy, but he wanted to just get a first-hand account of what things were like in the lab and especially what Harold thought about the way his piano was being treated. It was really refreshing and kind of surprising. Of course, we all used it as an oppor-tunity to push our own political positions!

When I worked with Harold Rhodes, he was 73 years-old. I forget which number of bypasses he'd had, but, he had an interesting medical history, yet, so full of energy and enthusiasm. The thing that many people don't realize is Harold had no formal position in the company whatsoever. He wasn't an employee, he was not the leader of the group and at least on paper we all outranked him.

The fact is because he was the inventor of the piano we all respected him so much and treated him as if he was the leader of the group – except when I went off on my own and came up with some crazy idea that he would be screaming at me and going, "Why did you do that? That's the most awful… " but, that was a rare thing – most of the time we got along exceptionally well.

What I remember most about him is his energy and his refusal to grow old. He had this enormous compound up in the hills of Fullerton. One day we went up there to pick up something and he locked himself out of his house and so, no problem – I'll just climb the fence. I'm thinking here's a 73 year-old guy with heart problems climbing an 8 foot fence and thinking nothing of it.

That's Harold. Every day he came into the lab, excited, ready to go. "What problem can we solve today? How can we make this thing better?"

Steve Woodyard
Former Engineer (CBS / FENDER)

I remember Harold Rhodes telling me about how he got started – he was a kid in L.A. and would go to this piano store that had a shop upstairs. He was more interested in the guys working on the pianos than he was down on the sales part of it. I remember him telling me over the years that he had his own piano studio – his teaching studio – and that his best student turned out to be his girlfriend. He wanted to marry her – asked her father and her father said, "No way." Then the War happened, so he went off and they went their separate lives. He reconnected with her later and, of course, he married her. He'd tell those stories to me very infrequently because usually his conversations with me were over the product and the piano.

Harold had the ability to focus on what he was concentrating on and literally zone out everything else. When I would tell people these stories about how he would lose stuff, you know it was an ongoing thing for him to… park his car, walk in and leave his keys in the car after he locked it. The secretary at the front desk had a Jimmy Stick, just because of Harold. When he came down to the lab, one of my hidden responsibilities was to track his stuff that he put down. Because he'd leave it and then there'd be a frantic call later on, "Where's his sweater, where's his glasses?" People asked me, "What… is he senile?" No – Harold was sharp as could be. He just focused on one thing. I told people they could drop a bomb next to him and if he was concentrating on something he wouldn't notice it. He was somewhat eccentric in that regard.

He was a really nice guy, but very demanding of his surroundings and the situation. You were a part of that team to make those things happen. He was working just as hard to make it happen too – whatever it took. You know if he had to talk to managers up at headquarters, then he did. You never felt like he was dumping on you – more like he was dragging you along with him... INCLUDING when he went into the hospital for a heart attack! I thought for sure he wanted me in the next bed for surgery also.

There were a lot of people who didn't like that kind of environment. You know... it was very stressful, but, that's really a part of the music industry and it's a part of the creative industry. You've got to make product, you've got to make new product, you've got to satisfy customers and you've got to satisfy very unique customers – because artists are what market your product, so you have to make something that the artists wants to play. If he wants to play it, then it sells. If he doesn't want to play it, then it sits. That's what that environment was like.

The origin, as he used to tell it, was a situation where he would go into the Officer's Club. He'd sit down (at the piano) and teach the guys how to do things – to make simple melodies with their girlfriend's phone number or something. Apparently the base medical officer got wind of this and talked him into producing a whole training program for rehabilitating the GIs. He said that the tricky part was they had to make the little piano in addition to learning how to play it and make sounds with it. He pretty much spent the War years developing that program. He did finish it, introduce it and it was a very successful program.

He got a medal from the government. I remember him saying it was the most successful rehabilitation program they had at the time.

Then he tried to adapt that piano on a larger-scale to the home market. That was the Pre-Piano, I guess in the early '50s, but there were some quality problems with that. He had a problem with a vendor that wanted to do certain things their way and he didn't have the resources to contradict him. It failed as a result – it broke and it was easy to see why that could happen. It was like a xylophone. The flexing reeds were long and they tapered into a little generating block and would break there.

Harold became a farmer for a minute and sold farm equipment, but he always fiddled with his keyboard parts in the shop in his garage. He never discontinued it. It just took a back seat for awhile.

Leo Fender wanted to develop a piano to add to his product line. Harold was just too far ahead of him. The way Harold simplified the story is that Leo basically took what he had and went from there instead of reinventing the wheel. He didn't talk about that much... However, he said Leo put his name on the product, but, didn't do anything for it. I don't know if that's true or not. That's how he felt about it, but, he was grateful. He said when CBS bought the company, they saw enough of what he was doing to make it part of the company. He said Goddard Lieberson liked it and wanted it with the package.

The way I got to Fender is I needed a job, so I applied there. I actually had four careers there. I started out as a guitar technician. I stayed with that a number of years, but I went to school the whole time. As I progressed through the school I changed jobs within the company. I was taking a class on electronic technology – a certificate – and I was also taking math classes at the local college. So I transitioned from the guitar line as a guitar tech to the inspection department where I was a receiving inspector. I used drawings, measured the parts and confirmed the parts. The factory service center had shut down years earlier. When it reopened, I moved in as an amp technician for about a year.

Then the gentleman who worked on the Rhodes pianos – I think his name was Jack Smith – left to work somewhere else; because the Rhodes piano is both a mechanical device and an electronic device, they wanted somebody that could do both. I was mechanical, I could play the guitar, I was electronic, I was a technician, repaired the amplifiers, so I inherited it. I started working as a Rhodes technician and an amp technician. Harold would come down pretty much every day for quite a period of time and show me stuff – worked with me on developing my skills and technique.

Our building was adjacent to the Research & Development department with our one engineer, Horst Absmann. When he needed an extra hand, he came over and got me. After doing that for a number of years, they decided to have a permanent assistant to Horst, so they moved me from the service center to the R&D department and I became one of the engineers. Again, I was taking classes all the time – science classes, physics, calculus and all that wonderful fun stuff. Then after a period of time, Horst was promoted to Engineer over the factory, which left me pretty much on my own.

One benefit I got from all those years was that, because I worked with so many of our sponsored artists, I developed a sense of touch that was very articulate. I also had to develop an ear to hear and feel all the nuances per note – not just on a group of notes, but all the way per note… through the field. As you push down different levels, there are different resistances and responses. I became very articulate in how to feel that. I didn't realize that until later but that's what allowed me to develop the Mark V… and the Mark IV. When Mike Peterson would design stuff with the Mark IV, I'd come over, play it and try to translate how it felt to him in engineering terms so he could go to the next step. We worked very well together on that.

Harold was still a consultant, at this time he was retired. He wanted something in the existing keyboard range to promote also. So I started off working on the Mark V pretty much on my own and the major thing I focused on was the interaction between the key, the hammer and the tine – 'cause that's it. I developed the Mark V action, I changed the hammer curve, I changed the pedestal size, I changed the fulcrum points and I changed how the hammer swung – how far it swung to hit the tine. I noticed years earlier that some pianos that were not properly adjusted, once they were, still had an amazing feel and a good sound. What it boiled down to was that the existing Mark I and Mark II had two basic sounds – a soft and a hard. When you hit soft you get one sound, when you hit hard you got another, but, I remember some of the old ones had a third sound. I noticed that he had a larger hammer swing. That meant that, in this way, the pushing of the key, you go from point 1 to point 2 – top to bottom.

In T1 or in a certain time and the time is controlled by the player, and if the hammer swings through 2" during that time, then it strikes with so much impact force, but it if swings through 2 1/2" or 2 3/4" or 3", it's gotta be doing something faster, because still time here is the same. So now it's traveling a larger distance in the same time. That means it's gotta go faster. So it strikes the tine harder and produces a third sound – "the dynamic sound." The downside is that it's more abusive to the tines and the hammer flanges – the pivot pin. But the piano felt better. It offered just a touch more resistance to the performer, and that resistance gave them more control. It had a different dynamic sound range. In the lower-mid range where it was muddy, it was a little more active.

We took one of the prototype Mark Vs over to Victor Feldman to let him try it out and within 10 minutes he was playing it differently. I said to him, "You are doing more things down in this range of the piano than you normally do." He said, "Yeah, you're right." He just automatically downshifted when the piano could do it. It meant that the piano gave him more dynamics, more harmonics, more attack, so he played differently – he used more of the keyboard.

Mike was developing the Mark IV and we just couldn't make it play as well as we wanted. Harold felt like the sound followed the touch… which is sluggish. We gave up on the Mark IV – which was Plan A – and went back to Plan B – which was the Mark V. Mike designed the cabinet, modified the action rail, and designed the stand. The stand is outstanding. I felt we should be in the business of selling stands based on his design, but, that didn't go anywhere. So it was definitely a collaborative effort.

There were no 88s for the Mark V because we ran out of time. The most popular piano has always been the 73. A lot of people who bought 88s bought them because they thought they needed 88, not because they used it. For every 3 pianos sold, 2 of them were 73s, so we did the 73 first.

We intended to produce an 88 – we made the prototype – but, things went bad with the company and it never made it to market.

The MIDI Rhodes was actually out of my area, but, MIDI was very popular by then anyway, so it was a natural progression. I had been laid off. They did it to see if they could do it. They designed a Mark V – retrofitted nipple-switches in it and made electronics – but, it was bad timing. It would have been a wonderful instrument and a big hit if the market and the company had been ready… but they weren't.

Amplifiers Over The Years

The first amplifier was from Jordan Electronics. It appears that we tended to call the name of the product based on the name of the designer. The Jordan was a mono amplifier with mono vibrato in it. The preamp was really good but the power amplifier was weak and self-destructed easily. I guess Harold got in touch with the gentleman at Peterson – Mr. Peterson – who is the Peterson strobe tuners. He had a design apparently for a stereo vibrato system and Harold thought it was wonderful. Everybody else thought Harold was crazy! They didn't understand. So the amplifier became the Peterson system, which was stereo vibrato, which really made the suitcase.

It was a wonderful product, but it had the deficiency of having Germanium Power Transistors in it. So when it went bad, it went bad in a big way – caught fire and blew out the speakers!

Delco was the supplier of the transistors and apparently they notified us that they were discontinuing that product, so we had to design a new amplifier which, at that time, was given to Bob Haigler, who was the amp engineer. Bob designed a new 100W power system. The Peterson system was old and had low power supply capacity, so it could easily be driven into distortion. Bob's design – with monster filter caps – didn't go into distortion and played wonderfully. It's reliability was tremendous. Even to this day, pretty much all of them work. If I see one that's bad, it's because the solder connections have gone bad. Just touch up the solder connections to the terminals and off it goes again. That was the last one – Haigler's.

The only problem with that one was the vibrato. The Peterson system used a light bulb and a light-dependent resistor. The light bulb had a turn-on time and a turn-off time that was slow. The vibrato system in the 100W system used an LDR and LED package and the turn-on time and turn-off time was fast and sharp. So, one of the good things about the Peterson system was that the stereo vibrato had a Chorale effect to it. Turns out, it was those light bulb turn-on time and turn-off times that caused that, whereas, the LDR LED system was so fast that it was more abrupt – less popular sound-wise. Bob had some ideas about changing that but never got to it.

The biggest disaster across the years was the tines. When I was still in the factory service department, they switched from Torrington tines to Schaller tines. Torrington is in Connecticut and the process for making tines is called Rotary Swaging – the same process used to make sewing needles.

It's like a press that rotates and hits as it rotates. The needle shapes the tine. The taper from where the tine was pushed into the generating block to where the tine reached its vibrating size was 1/2".

Miscommunications between us and Schaller in Germany allowed them to make that down to 1/4". When you played the tines quietly it worked fine, but when you hit them hard it would deaden out. The hammer tip has to make contact with the tine at such a point where it sends the tine in maximum swing – without flexing and without jamming the tine. Literally, that's called "the strike point." It's a range on the tine that's maybe 1/8" or 1/4", depending on tine length. If you hit the tine too far down the wire, the wire flexes and the hammer tip doesn't really get out of the way of it. If you hit it too close to the block, it thuds and doesn't produce maximum transfer, so you've got that sweet spot – which is called strike point. This is why the harp has got a curvature to it so that you present that sweet spot to the hammer tip because the hammers are straight and the sweet spot on that Schaller tine moves out of range. So when you played it softly it worked fine. If you played hard, it'd just thud. They got a lot of parts and used a lot of parts before they realized that. That was the biggest problem.

Naming The Mark II

Horst was designing a new action, he was designing the plastic key action and we had a number of other things coming together at the same time. Harold wanted a control panel that had a shelf on it for a music rack. Up until that time, the panel was flat. So we got the prototype panel in and we put the logo strip on it. In the previous editions the clear aluminum name rail had the faceplate over on the left-hand-side with the little black plastic and chrome logo in the center. We went away from that to the new one, which was a lexan strip that went across a slotted area and the lexan strip said Mark II. Harold walked in and was looking at it – we always had him check out everything we did – and he started to laugh. It was just Harold, Horst and I. He said, "You know, isn't it about time we changed the name from Mark I to Mark II?" We cracked up said, "Yeah, you know, it has been 10 years and we've changed the piano like crazy!" So we called up the vendor, changed the printing and that's it. So the difference between a Mark I and a Mark II, technically, is just the change on the printed logo strip.

The reason the quality varied so much in the early '70s is because it was manually assembled and manually adjusted. The pianos produced in 1970, '71 '72 '73 were dependant on the assembler. The harp support blocks were hand-mounted, the harp was hand-mounted and hand-located, the pickup rail, the tone bar rail were mounted in the frame by hand. So the operator had a lot of discretion. That means that pianos could be very different from point to point. One of the things they did to the action rail was that they put spacers underneath it.

Depending upon how many spacers they put in, that would raise the action rail up and down and that would cause the hammers to hit the key. Horst spent a great deal of time designing repeatable manufacturing capabilities into the process that would minimize the operator's ability to undo what the design was.

The hammers were modules of 12 mounted in the extrusion. The extrusion was a specified height – didn't need spacers or shims. Support blocks were pre-drilled and the harp was framed and put in with a jig. Horst made a lot of jigs to do things, so as the years went on, the pianos got more consistent.

One of the things Horst did that he and I readdressed later, is that the key pedestal had a bump on it. The hammer would roll across that bump, then come back and cradle between the bump and the edge of the key pedestal. He thought that that bump required you to be too precise so he took the bump out. In doing so, he also put the felt on the underside of the hammer, so you had rough wood surface dragging against felt. That caused a lot of friction and the key became harder to play and more sluggish. We went back to the bump eventually, which improved the feel, but it still had a short hammer throw – which I fixed with the Mark V.

They were working on improving the tine to cut back tine breakage. Horst was actually striving to improve that with the Schaller tines. I made a tine striking machine that we would mount a tine to and let it hit and it hit and hit. The Torrington tines would break easier than the Schaller tines. Horst did shorten up the throw but he never indicated to me that he was doing it for any other reason than manufacturing capability.

Harold Rhodes was fascinated with the art of improvisation. He made pianos in order to supply a vehicle to train. He didn't talk about that a whole lot, but, he was always interested in teaching methods. He wrote books, he designed student pianos to teach in the schools. There was the gold student piano, then the green modular one, then the walnut cabinet one. I always thought he was a teacher first and a designer second – and the designer supported the teaching. He didn't intend these things to be performing pianos.

Harold had a big house on the side of the hill. In it he had two grand pianos – a Yamaha and a Steinway, I believe – but, he didn't have a Rhodes in his house. At best he had one of the student pianos to test it out and that was it. He admitted one time that he didn't like the sound. His goal was always to produce a piano that played and felt like a grand piano. We actually made a prototype that put a Rhodes hammer-throw action underneath the strings – that was a real screwball thing! Yeah, he said he wasn't very fond of the sound and wondered why everyone liked it. He felt like he got 3/4 of the way there then everybody said, "Stop! We love this." He's like, "I can do better!" "No, you've done great already. You're done!" So, that was one of his goofy things. He was definitely a character.

We had strong relationships with a number of artists and Harold had personal relationships with a couple of them. The most prominent one was Herbie Hancock. Harold's relationship with Herbie was far more extensive than even I imagined. He'd go over there, they'd have dinner and Herbie was very active in testing out new parts – more so than any of the other artists.

We would bounce ideas off the other artists, but, Herbie would actually suggest ideas. One of his suggestions was the two accessory jacks on the control panel for the Peterson amp system, which he asked me to install. He suggested it, I modified it, we installed it into the piano and it became a standard idea. So Herbie's relationship with Harold was very well developed.

Then we saw Cannonball Adderley, Ray Charles, Joe Zawinul and Chick Corea. Horst had a very good relationship with Joe Zawinul – [laughs] – the Austrian and the German were a natural! Harold had developed a strong relationship with Patrice Rushen, as did I. So, we worked close with them. That's the music industry in general. The performer is the heart of your marketing team.

The DX-7 was the new kid on the block. It sounded good, it was selling well, it was definitely biting into Rhodes sales. So they decided we needed to have a product that was competitive. The first attempt at that was the EK-10, which was a strange device. It generated both a mechanical / acoustical sound and an electronic sound triggered off of generators. Roger Balmer in the marketing department thought the DX-7 would take over the business so he put an end to the Rhodes MKII production, which he decided was to be about a year after this time period. Then he wanted the Mark IV developed up until to fill in when that time happened and the Mark IV didn't make it. So we had a time period between that of almost 3/4 of a year where we actually had some product in the warehouse to sell.

Basically we weren't making anything, so that put it out into the market that we were out of business – that the DX-7 killed us. It was just bad timing. When we were ready to produce product, the company was going through some serious economic problem, so the product was killed.

I'm amazed at the fact that they said it was going to die and it hasn't. The sounds of a Rhodes are a major part of a keyboard artist's repertoire – whether it's produced by a Rhodes or produced synthetically. Most players prefer the mechanical sound, but to protect their mechanical instruments they're playing their electronic instruments on the road, but, it's as popular now as it was before – if not more so.

When I see it on TV, I say, "Oh, there it is again." I see Justin Timberlake playing it, I just saw Alicia Keys playing one and Patrice Rushen is still active, you know... So, it's amazing that it's gone from being a product to becoming an icon. I feel that – in a very strange way – it's "domineered" my life. I've had the luxury and good fortune of being associated with an icon... which not very many people get to do.

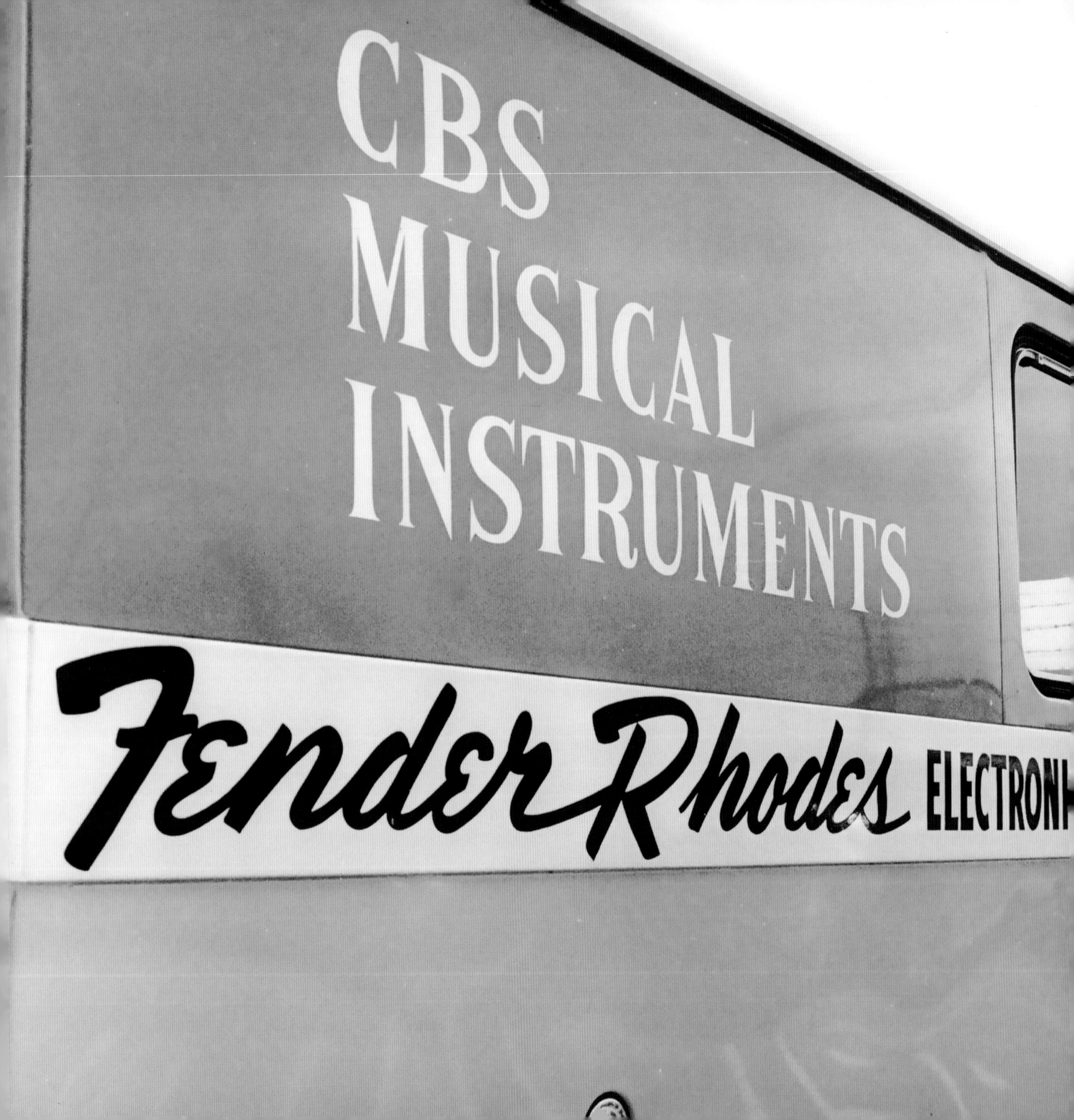
CBS
MUSICAL
INSTRUMENTS
Fender Rhodes
ELECTRONI

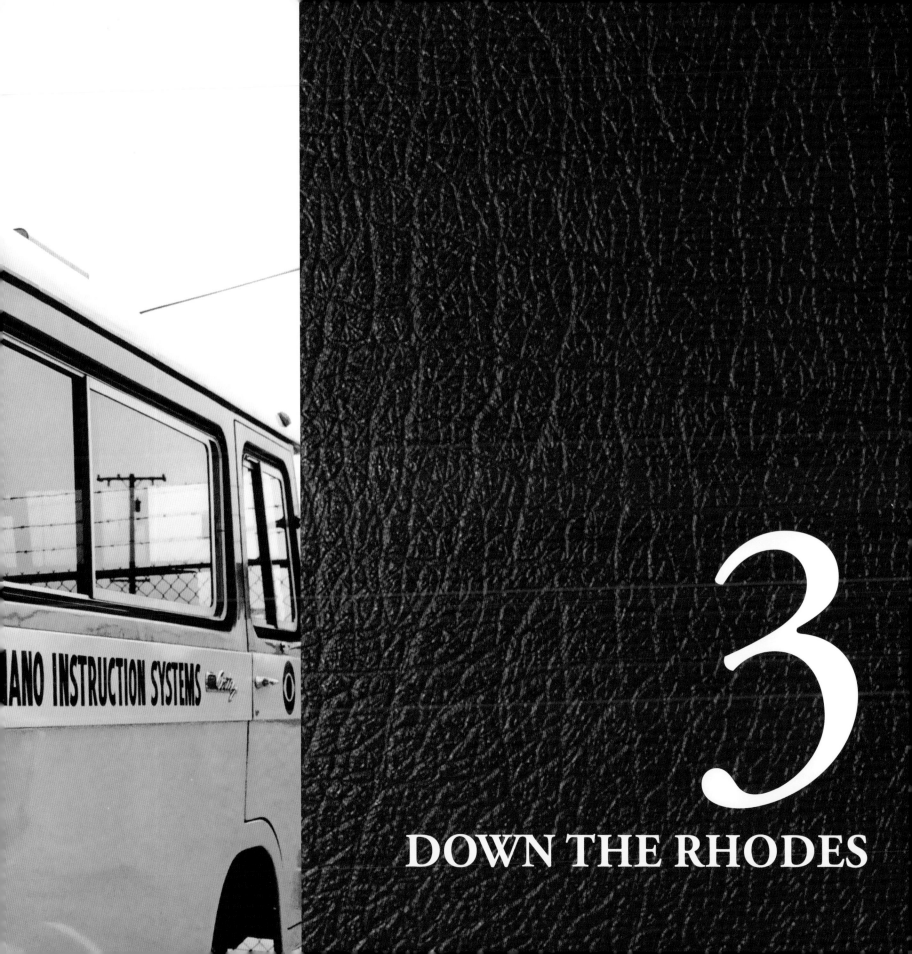

ANO INSTRUCTION SYSTEMS

3

DOWN THE RHODES

Benjamin Bove

Musician / *DOWN THE RHODES* (Film Director)

Well, I guess my story is a little different than most of the other Rhodes players. Being a younger guy, I didn't grow up with the Rhodes. The first piano I ever played was a digital keyboard. I actually never played an acoustic piano. We didn't have one in our house. So, at 7 years-old or so, I was playing a keyboard... and there were all these buttons, like, "piano," "electric piano" and "organ" – but, it didn't compute that those related to real instruments somewhere. I mean, my piano teacher Larry Eason had an acoustic piano, so I knew the acoustic piano patch referred to that, but it didn't quite click that an electric piano button meant the sound for some real electric piano.

It didn't happen until high school when my Jazz Director, Niles Dening, brought out this piano-looking thing and it was called a Fender Rhodes. We were playing Woody Herman's arrangement of Chick Corea's "La Fiesta" (from the seminal Fender Rhodes album Return to Forever – ECM – 1972). I sat down to it, played a chord and I was like, "Oh... That's what that electric piano sounds like." The sound was so much better on this Fender Rhodes. That's where the breakthrough was – the day I learned that this digital keyboard is just a jump-off point for real instruments like this that exist. Then I went to the Hammond organ, then the Clavinet and I'm like, "Wow," finding all these real instruments.

My passion for the Rhodes really began however when I went to purchase my first Rhodes, to recapture the sound of the Rhodes I played in high school. When I bought a 1980 Rhodes Mark II-style suitcase 73, I was very intrigued as to why it didn't sound like his 1972 suitcase 73 – not bad one way or the other, but quite different. So I then became heavily involved with them inside and out for years, figuring out which Rhodes sounded like what. I've been through hundreds of them for sure, and feel comfortable in knowing what makes them sound great and customizing them. Besides using a custom preamp on my main Rhodes, I like having the outside customized as well to really demonstrate that it's not like any other piano you'll find.

I do have to say, a testament to how these Fender Rhodes pianos were made – all these years later, if you find one, usually it still plays and that's pretty amazing. It's important to know though that every one of them still in existence needs work; sometimes a decent amount of work. You can't expect to find a classic car parked in a barn for a long time, then expect to buy it and boom – turn the key and drive it out of the barn like you're driving it off the showroom. On top of that, at the peak of their success, CBS Musical Instruments was producing thousands and thousands of pianos each year, and you can't imagine that each single one was lovingly maximized to its fullest potential before it made it out the door. So my biggest thing for Rhodes owners is to get the thing serviced by someone who knows what they're doing. A Fender Rhodes you find on the side of the road needing work is no comparison to the true potential unlocked by a knowledgeable technician. It's a different experience and you can't go back after you've played a great one.

I'm always amazed when someone says, "Ah, yes… the Fender Rhodes. That's old." I'll tell you what's old – the acoustic piano. That's over 300 years-old! Antique! People still use the acoustic piano in music and they don't talk about how old it is, and if the acoustic piano can be used in new creative ways over so many years, that tells me the Rhodes has generations of music to go. With all the increasing electric-based technology in music, Rhodes is still a relatively new and relevant technology.

It's difficult for a keyboard player because you have a big acoustic piano, a big electric piano, a big Hammond organ – all these BIG instruments that keyboard players are asked to play, and it's hard to always take them with you either due to weight or space, so a digital keyboard that can have those sounds in an all-in-one device is very convenient. You can pick up a digital keyboard, put it under your arm and take it with you. There is also an expectation sometimes for the keyboard player to be sort of a sound orchestrator – a band looks to the keyboard player first to generate all the additional sounds. So digital keyboards are versatile and serve a lot of purposes, but it's also great to have the real mechanical instruments as well. I see more keyboardists using both keyboards and the real mechanical instruments together in their music, which is a great harmony.

When you're talking about the Rhodes piano, you cannot forget Herbie Hancock and "Chameleon" (the funk-jazz fusion classic from the 1973 album Headhunters). The sound of the Rhodes on that track is what a lot of people strive for in their Rhodes piano sound. It set the standard for a lot of people today.

The compositions that Chick Corea was writing for the electric version of Return to Forever were just powerful. It wasn't just so much that the instruments were turned up – there was a drive to that music. A lot of bands were taking that on at that time, but the power of RTF was especially cool. Cuts like "Space Circus" (from *Hymn of the Seventh Galaxy* – 1973) and "Song to the Pharoah Kings" (from *Where Have I Known You Before* – 1974) make you look up and go, "Whoa!"

Stevie Wonder's music is surrounded by the Rhodes piano. Along with the Clavinet, Stevie is most at home behind a Rhodes. "As" (from *Songs in the Key of Life* – 1976) where you've got Stevie playing the Rhodes with Herbie Hancock playing fills and taking a solo on the Rhodes is just heavy.

I met Gerald McCauley through a friend of mine, Terry Dexter, a phenomenal singer. I was talking to her one day about my passion for Rhodes pianos and she said, "Oh, you should meet Gerald." I couldn't tell you exactly how we started talking, but eventually we did meet up and we kind of had a rapport about us.

We started talking about this and how there had been no in-depth projects done about the history of the Rhodes. It seemed like a great idea because rather than being a project about a specific singer or musician, using the instrument as a common link between so many different artists was a creative way to do something. He thought it was a great idea, showed me support and felt that it would be good to do a documentary project. He said, "I'll set up an interview" and away we went.

You know how it is when you talk with somebody you don't exactly know very well and they say they're going to do something fairly phenomenal for you… just because? You're like (halfway sarcastic) "Oh, okay. Sure. No problem." Then I get a call, "O.K., I've got the first interview set up with George Duke for this Friday." I was like, "OH – he's serious business!!"

Gerald – with his connections, his music knowledge, and his establishment in the music community – is just amazing. He's my true brother; a wonderful human being.

I'm just excited that we're bringing this phenomenal story to the public because it needs to be told. It didn't start with Harold Rhodes being a man that was trying to make a couple of quick bucks by inventing some popular new musical instrument. The Rhodes sprang from the heart of a man wanting to help people and educate the world through music… I hope that's what we're doing with this project.

Gerald McCauley

AKA "The Mayor" (Producer)

The Fender Rhodes is used in many forms and cultures of music. If it weren't for Harold Rhodes, I shudder to think what music would have sounded like...

The first album I owned was a gift: *That's the Way of the World* by Earth Wind & Fire. There was lots of Fender Rhodes on that record! Even the album cover was cool... to see all the band members in their costumes... That inspired me to wear my *funky haberdasheries*; emulating what I saw on album covers. In the music, the keys stood out: "What tone, sound is playing the chords? What is that!?!" I found out it's the Fender Rhodes. I'd see performances on "The Midnight Special" and "Don Kirshner's Rock Concert" where musicians would play this instrument onstage. Once I identified "it" as that sound, I totally fell in love with it.

Ronnie Foster, a long-time good friend, has been a huge influence – the first keyboardist I met. My trumpet tutor took me to an incredible free concert in the park sponsored by Stevie Wonder's radio station, KJLH in Los Angeles. Ndugu Chancler was on drums, Byron Miller on bass, Bobby Lyle on piano, Ronnie Foster on keyboards / synthesizers, Azar Lawrence on saxophone and guitarist Wali Ali. Ronnie performed a popular jingle "Radio Vision" using the Vocoder. I was so enthralled by the keyboards! Afterwards, I approached Ronnie at the side of the stage and said, "Man... I love what you did!!! I want to call you." He said, "I'm in the Union Book." I put my hands on my hips and said, "I'm 12 years-old... Do I know what that book is?" He gave me his number, I pestered him {laughs} and finally he answered the phone.

He invited me to the first recording studio I had ever been in. At the time, it was Yamaha Research & Development Studios (Glendale, CA); owned by Yamaha Corporation.

Ronnie was producing lots of much music then. One of the artists I met at the studio was Brazilian superstar Djavan. I also met many of the top session players: Harvey Mason, Nathan East, Paulinho Da Costa, Greg Phillinganes and Jonathan "Sugarfoot" Moffett.

I was 15 years-old. It was a remarkable experience to meet these artists and be a fly-on-the-wall at Ronnie's sessions with Dorian Harewood, James Ingram, Bill Withers, Stevie Wonder and Michael Jackson.

I'd see the group Toto, including David Paich, come in to play Yamaha instruments, so I developed a rapport with many of them seeing me as this kid around the studio. Watching Ronnie work is where my interest in keyboards grew. Seeing how synthesizers and samplers make every instrument and sound available in the keyboard domain was fascinating to me.

Growing up I attended Locke High School. Patrice Rushen (a Locke alumnus) did a noon-time concert at our school auditorium. It was the first time I saw someone play Rhodes in person; in a live setting. She performed a beautiful ballad called "Settle For My Love" and hits like, "Haven't You Heard." Her use of the Rhodes made Patrice my hero on the instrument.

One song in particular that has beautifully haunted me over my lifetime is "Maybe There Are Reasons" by singer / songwriter Lonette McKee (from her album Words and Music – 1978).

Many remember her as an actress in films like "Sparkle" (with Irene Cara and Dwan Smith), "Which Way is Up" (starring Richard Pryor), Spike Lee's "Jungle Fever" (as Wesley Snipes' wife) and "Honey" (as Jessica Alba's mother). My favorite role was the nightclub singer in "Round Midnight" (starring Oscar-nominated saxophonist-turned-actor Dexter Gordon). However, as singer, songwriter and recording artist, "Maybe There Are Reasons" is her finest hour. What a vibe! I've never gotten over that song and a big reason for that is Patrice Rushen's Rhodes performance on the recording.

Some other great records that featured the Fender Rhodes: Kool and the Gang's "Summer Madness"… the eerie chords and the Arp synthesizer (played by Ricky West and Ronald Bell, respectively) made it haunting. The Ohio Players' "Skin Tight" ("You're a Bad, Bad Mrs"… "Groovy Billy Beck y'all." – on Rhodes) Bill Withers' "Lovely Day", The Memphis Horns' "Just For Your Love" and Hall & Oates' "Sara Smile"… each song with very tasteful Rhodes playing by Clarence McDonald. Norman Connors' records "You Are My Starship" (featuring Michael Henderson) and "Betcha By Golly Wow" (featuring Phyllis Hyman) showcased Onaje Allan Gumbs on Rhodes – an incredible keyboard-to-voice accompanier.

"Sun Goddess" by Ramsey Lewis (with the recurring vocal line "Day-o, D-ayo") and the dynamic live version that featured Larry Dunn on Earth Wind & Fire Gratitude album. Maurice White produced the song "Free" by Deniece Williams and Jerry Peters played the beautiful, ethereal introduction on Rhodes.

Raymond Jones keyboard player in the band Chic, which had a sophisticated sound with strings and acoustic piano, always layered their music with Fender Rhodes underneath on songs like "Good Times" and "My Feet Keep Dancing" (from Risque' – 1979). It was prominent on a Dexter Wansel production with The Jones Girls, "Nights Over Egypt"… Rodney Franklin "Song for You" (featuring vocalist Howard Smith from Destiny – 1985).
So many phenomenal recordings… So many players have singular touches on Rhodes: Herbie Hancock, Bob James, Richard Tee, Dave Grusin, Don Grusin…

George Duke – so awesome was his work with Frank Zappa and the entirety of his own albums Don't Let Go, Reach For It and Follow The Rainbow.

Larry Williams (of the group Seawind featuring singer Pauline Wilson) played Rhodes on Al Jarreau's version of "Spain." Al had previously written lyrics to Paul Desmond's classic instrumental "Take Five" (first recorded with The Dave Brubeck Quartet) and did it again with Chick Corea's "Spain" – an amazing record. "I can remember the rain in December…" Al was killin' it, and the Rhodes solo that Larry Williams took on that song was landmark, (as was his whole This Time album filled with incredible uses of the Fender Rhodes).

Then there's The Crusaders with Joe Sample. I was so blown away with his technique and style of playing the Rhodes.

Joe also played Fender Rhodes on "The Lady Wants to Know" (from Sleeping Gypsy – 1977) and a lot of the early records by Michael Franks. Steely Dan's Aja (1977) album, a phenomenal production, let alone the use of the Rhodes in its arrangements, with guest keyboardists like Joe Sample and Paul Griffin. My favorite Steely Dan song, "Babylon Sisters", with Don Grolnick on Rhodes is one of the best recordings I've heard of the instrument sonically.

Another artist synonymous with that instrument was Minnie Riperton – her angelic voice and the Fender Rhodes is heaven, as-well-as, the songs she co-wrote with Leon Ware and her husband Dick Rudolph ("Inside My Love") or Stevie Wonder ("Perfect Angel") – some of the best Rhodes tracks ever in my opinion and, Michael Jackson – particularly Off the Wall with "I Can't Help It" written by Stevie Wonder and played on the record by Greg Phillinganes.

George Benson's "Give Me The Night" album featured Herbie Hancock, Greg Phillinganes, Richard Tee and George Duke playing Fender Rhodes on those great songs (most of them written by Heatwave's, Rod Temperton).

On projects, my role is usually as producer – to conceptualize; but I play keys and Rhodes too… some niiiiice Rhodes tracks on a group project I formed called Groove Metropolis.

The Rhodes makes our music Groovy!

For entertainers who are image-conscious, the Fender Rhodes is cool because of its size. You can dress it up to match your stage décor and all that, like I do.

The Rhodes has never really gone anywhere... not when you have bands like Incognito (led by guitarist Jean-Paul "Bluey" Maunick), Sade (named after their British Nigerian lead vocalist, Sade Adu), the Brand New Heavies (featuring N'Dea Davenport) and Jamiroquai utilizing the Fender Rhodes in their sound, influencing similar groups all over Europe and the world.

D'Angelo – was playing the Rhodes long before he became famous. Erykah Badu came on the scene big with the Fender Rhodes on songs like "Other Side of the Game." I saw her during halftime of an NBA All-Star game performing (just voice w/ Rhodes accompaniment) Carole King's "You've Got a Friend." Singer Dwele is in a McDonald's commercial chillin' behind a Fender Rhodes.

Hit-making producers James Poyser, Robert Glasper, Mark Batson and Big Jim Wright keep a Rhodes in their recording and touring arsenals. In Mariah Carey's movie "Glitter" (2001), she plays a singer that receives a Fender Rhodes as a birthday gift later used in concert by her band. (Note: Dorian Harewood, narrator of our documentary, played the record executive "Guy Richardson" in "Glitter").

So the Fender Rhodes is everywhere... impossible to escape!

Progressive technology – from equalizers and filters to plug-ins and soft synths – are all modeled after and / or emulating something vintage. It's amazing to have these great tools, but there are times when the music requires *classic*...

I'm grateful for this opportunity to bring together so many *classic* musicians to share their information, their knowledge and their experience of this important instrument in music history.

I've learned a great deal on this journey "Down the Rhodes."

Benjamin Bove and Gerald McCauley

Donald Fagen signing the Rhodes from CBS studios

Top Left: Steve Cohen, Gerald McCauley, David Paich and Benjamin Bove

Bottom: Gerald McCauley and Quincy Jones (The Mayor & The Dude)

Opposite Top: Herbie Hancock and Benjamin Bove

Opposite Bottom Left: Gerald McCauley, Bob James and Benjamin Bove

Opposite Bottom Center: Gerald McCauley, Ramsey Lewis and Benjamin Bove

Opposite Bottom Right: Gerald McCauley, James Poyser and Benjamin Bove

Top: Miles Davis' Rhodes

Bottom: Robin Lumley segment
Melbourne, AU

Above Left: Gerald McCauley and Robert Glasper

Above Right: Dorian Harewood narration session

Bottom Left: Boney James – session on Bob James segment

Bottom Right: Robin Lumley and Jeff Brownrigg

4

RHODES SCHOLARS

Michael Bearden

Michael Bearden is among the most valuable Musical Directors and keyboard players in the business, having worked with everyone from Ramsey Lewis and Rod Stewart to Madonna and Michael Jackson. In fact, he was working as Musical Director for what would have been Michael Jackson's glorious farewell series of concerts, "This is It." He shares some invaluable notes with us as they pertain to the Rhodes on the road. It's an instrument to which he extends profound respect and lovingly refers to as, "The Truth."

It's an expense to carry keyboards that have so called "Rhodes sounds" in them, but in my dues paying days, a Rhodes was the standard. My dad let me upgrade my Wurlitzer – matched me for whatever gig money I could save. He said, "If you can save half of what the Rhodes costs, then I'll buy the other half." So I did all kind of little tea parties, block club parties and bar mitzvahs to get the money and I finally got one. It was just amazing the sound of it. Everything I was hearing on records when I was coming up and the stuff that I wanted to play, the sound I wanted to have – it was all right here. I was so happy. My mom used to get mad. "Why don't you go outside and play with regular kids?" I'm like, "I'm not a regular kid… I got a Rhodes!"

Back then I had a stage model so I had to have an extra amp to carry. I was working a lot. I'm from the south side of Chicago. One night I was doing a gig and I was coming home at like, 2 in the morning and it was snowing. Where I lived was a walk up and I got the Rhodes all the way up to the top of the stairs by myself. I reached in my pocket to put the key in, then, I slipped and fell right down the stairs with the Rhodes on me. I survived! I just had to get up and take it back again. That's my dues paying days with the Rhodes – falling down stairs, setting it up myself, gigging in a cab – whatever you had to do – but, once you set this up and started playing, it was just magic.

Some of the first players I ever heard were Herbie Hancock – a mentor of mine since I was a kid – and Ramsey Lewis, since I was maybe about 15 or 16 years-old. I used to hang out with Herbie and just learn simple stuff. I'd also known about George Duke for awhile and had heard Chick Corea on some things.

When I first started playing, I did a lot of gigs with Ramsey Lewis. He really liked to just play piano, so my job would be to play Rhodes. I had a little Clavinet thing on the top and another little synth. One of my early second keyboard playing things – at 19 or 20 – was playing with (jazz and world music flautist) Herbie Mann. I would have a piano, but, I would always have a Rhodes. They would have to cart it around or I would have to cart it around – the days of tipping skycaps to get it on the plane and that kind of thing!

I've never used a real Rhodes and a digital Rhodes on the same track. I've never been in a controlled environment where there was the truth and then there was the copy. The Truth always wins for me. That's not knocking the copy because there are some good copies out that sound amazing, but, when you have this here, it's just so organic. The way we feel and how we play "pianistically..." if you really want to have some expression (plays a note), that's just beautiful right there.

The Resurgence of the Rhodes definitely lies at the feet of D'Angelo, in my opinion. I was his Musical Director around the time that Brown Sugar came out and helped him craft the show. We did a big show in New York – standing room only – Prince couldn't even get in – CRAZY! We only had a Rhodes and another keyboard that D really liked to program to get his signature sound. For the longest time I couldn't even get him UP from the Rhodes. He would just sit there and play all of his stuff. Nobody knew that he was the dynamic performer he turned out to be while he was anchored to that Rhodes.

It's amazing how much sitting behind this instrument feels like home. When you're in front of a crowd and you got this in front of you, you feel like you can do anything... invincible! What an amazing gift this was to D'Angelo. Obviously he heard records coming up where this was prominent and wanted to infuse that into the music he was doing. All of a sudden, it was like a new generation of musicians who had never heard this, saw it in a different light. Technology is just technology and doesn't mean anything without the human part... especially the heart part. So, that was the great thing that D did. I'm lovin' that Justin Timberlake is doing that same thing – has it prominently in his show and can play it too.

I don't like when young artists, or artists in general, see something as beautiful and elegant as a Fender Rhodes and call it "old school." If you're a new, young creative artist, make it new again – show me what you can do with it! A car in its concept is old school, but, you still use it to get to where you need to go. It's the same thing with the instruments you use. They don't have to be new and flashy all the time. A Rhodes is what it is. When you sit behind a Fender Rhodes, you know it's gonna sound amazing!

Greg Phillinganes is a dear friend. When I was growing up, he played a lot of that with Michael Jackson – on *Off the Wall* and records before that. I grew up listening to that and idolizing that. When I got a chance to work with Michael on his "This is It Tour," my name was on the short list of Musical Directors… which is awesome to me. So I went down to see Kenny Ortega, who was our director of the tour. I had an interview with him and he said, "Man, what're you doing in like a couple of hours? I need to get Michael to come see you now." I've done gigs with Michael before, like the whole 30th anniversary concert, in 2001 right before 9/11 at (Madison Square Garden) and some record things. MJ would record and record and record a lot of stuff. Some of it made the records, but, a lot of it didn't make it. I've known Michael for a while.

So I said, "When I come down, have some keyboards in the room." So he put a keyboard in the room. I was already playing when Michael walked in and (snaps his fingers), he just started dancing… singin' like that… lookin' like that! I hugged him and we started talking – we hadn't seen each other in a while.

We talked about what he expected from the tour and so on. Then I started just taking advantage. I said, "MJ, you gotta sing this for me!" So I just went right into "I Can't Help It" (a song from *Off the Wall* co-penned by Stevie Wonder and Susaye Greene). I was like, "OH, MAN!" The brilliance and the blessing of music is how it can just transport you right back to how you felt when you first heard a song or first started playing it. I instantly went back to my childhood… I can never get that moment back, obviously, but, it was something I'll never forget. Because he had so many songs, we never played that song again. I've known Stevie since I was about 18. Greg and I have played with him in various configurations over time in a lot of concerts. It's amazing how that connects us.

Stevie thought MJ sang "I Can't Help It" better than he did… told me that the first time he heard it coming back to him through some speakers. He was like, "Wow… " Michael was just a stickler for having that sound. Before we went to London, I was looking at the new configurations of the Rhodes and seeing how I could get one into my rig on the tour because MJ really loved the sound of it. "I need to have that sound," he would say.

In one of our earliest meetings, he had gone online – which means that his son, Prince, took him online – and showed me a list of songs the fans wanted to hear. Then he showed me his handwritten list. He puts his glasses on – which was really cool… just humanized him to me – and says, "Look at that, Bearden.

What do you think?" I said, "Well, this is cool, MJ, but you have no J5 and you have no *Off The Wall*." He was like, "I know!" He would look at it, then just ball it up and throw it down like, "Ugh!"

We were going to use a real Rhodes for MJ's tour, depending on what I felt and how the production end could handle it as far as setting it up. The good thing about what we were about to do in London was we would have been stationary – in the same arena the whole time. That was to my advantage in getting a real Rhodes in there. My bassist, Alex Al, and my other keyboardist, Morris Pleasure, came over and they liked the idea of a real Rhodes. Everybody just loved it.

Once you hone your skills on an instrument, if you're used to that... if it ain't broke don't fix it! The Rhodes has its own touch and its own sound; this is home for me.

As MD for "Lopez Tonight," George Lopez's show, every night, 4 nights a week. Most of the artists that I work with – Jennifer Lopez, Madonna (9 years), Whitney Houston (2 or 3 years including "I Will Always Love You" at the Super Bowl) – anytime I'd get on the Rhodes or something that's The Truth, they all like it and gravitate towards it. On live shows and in the studio, they've gotta have it. Mary J. Blige – no different!

Musicians of a certain taste – young or old – who have come up listening to The Truth, want nothing BUT the truth around them at all times. I was walking around NAMM. There are a lot of new gadgets that are shiny, flash and do a lot of things, but, the biggest crowds were at the places that had standards: B-3 organ and piano.

People want to see how they can do stuff cheaper and faster on their laptops while they're on the subway which is good – I do it, too – but, the people that stayed the longest were the people that wanted to play the Rhodes. I sat and played for a minute... then, everybody wanted to get on... to know what was going on with the Rhodes. Madonna uses a lot of synthesizes in her music, but, when "Vogue" comes on (plays chords) just that alone... The thing about the Rhodes is, it's melodic, it's lyrical and it's percussive too.

We did a benefit and Maestro Arturo Sandoval came on and he played with us with Andy Garcia – the great actor who is also a great musician. They wrote this piece for the Haitian benefit that we just did at the Nokia Theater. He played a montuno (a staple rhythmic groove within Latin music) on the piano, but, I hit him on the Rhodes with (a sick percussive Latin counterpoint). The best instruments give you options – color choices and layers so you can create a palette. Even though it's electronic, the Rhodes is an organic extension of expression.

When I played on the scores for John Singleton's films "Four Brothers" and the "Shaft" remake, I had a Rhodes – the authentic sound of the period. I did a record with Rod Stewart called *American Soul Book* where he sings – and quite well – a lot of soul classics. (Producer) Steve Jordan had me on a real Rhodes. We used some other instruments, but they were all real – no synths anywhere on that record. I actually played some vibes on it too. When Rod heard it, he loved it so much that Clive Davis put the record out immediately and they're already talking about doing a second one.

So this was integral in the part of making Rod's record. It was an amazing thing to be able to go in the studio and sit with musicians. The way we usually record today, I'll record a track then Greg Phillinganes will come in and record a track. We don't even get to see each other. We just find out that we're both on the record later, but, on this particular album, me and Greg were there at the same time on some things.

We were all sitting in the room – Steve on drums, the great Bob Babbitt from the Motown days played bass on a couple things, Ray Parker Jr. played guitar on the session and nobody had anything that wasn't real – real guitars, real drums, real basses... real instruments. I had my Rhodes. As soon as I walked in and saw, "Oh, you got the Rhodes," we were cool!

Gerald McCauley, Michael Bearden and Benjamin Bove

Chick Corea

Chelsea, Massachusetts-born Chick Corea spent eight months preparing for an audition at Julliard, but quickly became dissatisfied with "formal" training upon his acceptance. So he returned to New York City where he'd studied at Columbia University for two years prior... for an education of "the third kind." The formal music world's loss was the thrilling gain of progressive jazz music and beyond as Chick explored the limitless possibilities of it all as a player, composer and band leader. Though he is associated with a wide range of electric keyboard instruments, he is a pioneer of popularizing the Fender Rhodes.

His early work on the Fender Rhodes piano specifically birthed timeless classics that include "Crystal Silence," "Spain," several "Children's Songs," "The One Step," "Melody Maker" (w/ Dee Dee Bridgewater), "View from the Outside" (with his Elektric Band) and many more.

The '60s were very memorable for me. I wanted to get to New York City after high school and I did. I cut my teeth on so many things there. That's where all my heroes were – Miles was there, Coltrane, Ornette Coleman, Thelonious Monk and Art Blakey & The Jazz Messengers with Horace Silver. That was a great time for me which culminated in the call from Miles in '68. Just prior to that, I was working with Sarah Vaughan.

I worked with Sarah for a year and a half, which was a great experience, but, when Tony Williams called me to join Miles Davis' band… I couldn't say no to that! So I scrambled to get a replacement for me. Fortunately I found Bob James, who had been Sarah's accompanist just before me, so he knew Sarah's tune book. I pleaded with Bob, "Please cover for me!" He was reluctant at first because he'd just left and was doing something else, but, fortunately he did… and I thank him for that.

For the first 3 or 4 months with Miles, I played only acoustic piano. Then the eventful night arrived when Miles threw an electric piano in front of me. We were playing a club – I believe it was the Jazz Workshop in Boston – and that quintet was Tony Williams, Wayne Shorter, Dave Holland and Miles. Dave Holland had joined the band just shortly before I did. I will never forget this: I was behind Miles walking toward the bandstand. I was headed toward the acoustic piano and Miles just turned around and said, "Play that." That was it. I hadn't even seen the electric piano! So I sat down and started to grapple with it. I absolutely hated it at first. It didn't work well, notes were missing and it was out of tune. You have to take care of this fella – learn how to maintain it, tune it and so forth, which I learned later.

It took me a while to warm up to it. The first thing I noticed about the instrument was the fact that I could play louder. You know, at that time, Tony Williams was one of the first drummers, in an acoustic small group, to play really… I'll use the term *vigorously*. I mean really play a lot! He could develop some power. The acoustic piano and the acoustic bass were no match.

Even before that, if you heard Coltrane's quartet with Jimmy Garrison, Elvin Jones and McCoy Tyner, when the dynamic was real easy in a ballad you could hear the piano and the bass, but, once Elvin got going – Elvin and 'Trane turning the energy way up – the bass was the first thing you couldn't hear anymore, then the piano would go dim! There weren't monitors in those days.

So when I had this electric piano, there was this knob that I could go, "BRRRIIP." I thought, "Wow… now I can sort of match Tony's level!" That was the first thing that I liked about it. It was practical in that way.

However, I still didn't like the sound and I didn't know how to engineer it and maintain it to get a good sound. Plus, every night a different piano would appear… usually a Rhodes, sometimes other electric pianos. Sometimes I'd get a relatively decent one, but, usually they would be very badly prepared. Most of the rest of the gig with Miles was like that… I never had my own Rhodes at that point.

It wasn't until a couple years later when Dave Holland and I left Miles and formed an acoustic band called Circle – which blended experimental music and free music. Then I wanted to put together a more melodic and rhythmic group. That's when I put Return to Forever together. That's when I got my first Rhodes and started to learn how to get a beautiful sound out of it.

When I started RTF, it really didn't have much to do with the sound. It had more to do with the concept of what I wanted to put across. I had experienced quite a variety of ways to play in the '60s. Starting out, I had about a year and a half with Mongo Santamaria's band. I worked with Herbie Mann's group and some more Latin things.

I worked with Kenny Durham in some quintets and then with Joe Henderson. I worked with a group we used to call The Sister Sadie All-Stars – me, Blue Mitchell, Junior Cook, Jean Taylor and Roy Brooks. That was Horace Silver's quintet at that time. Horace would take some time off and they wanted to keep working. I don't know how I got that gig, but, it was glorious for me to work with that group. Then I worked with Stan Getz, which is when I first played with Roy Haynes and Steve Swallow. Right after that, I asked Roy to join me on my first trio record, *Now He Sings, Now He Sobs,* with Miroslav Vitous. Then I backed Sarah Vaughan, then Miles.

Then Dave Holland and I started Circle and took our musical experimentation "the whole way out" with (saxophonist) Anthony Braxton and (drummer) Barry Altschul. By the time Circle was done, I wanted to communicate my music to audiences and have them experience the pleasure that I do. That led me to also want to have a singer in the band, so I wrote some songs – "Some Time Ago" and "You're Everything." I got together with my great friend Neville Potter – we roomed together for a while. He wasn't a lyricist – he was a great artist and poet – but, he began to put lyrics to my songs that were just perfect.

What happened was I had a gig in Philly for a week working with Joe Henderson's sextet and Stanley Clarke was the bass player. Stanley was playing his upright bass and had this huge rig behind him. It was the first time I ever heard an acoustic bass played that loud and that rhythmic. I had my Fender Rhodes working with Joe. So, Stanley and I became mates right away and started to form trios. I continued writing music until we had the quintet version. Actually, the first horn player in Return to Forever was Hubert Laws playing flute.

Flora Purim was coming over providing the vocals and Airto would be with her. I knew Airto because we had played together with Miles, but I didn't know Airto was a trap player. I knew him as a hand percussion player.

So we'd be at rehearsal and Horacee Arnold was playing the drums at that time with us. When I started to pull out my Samba-like tunes, I asked Airto one day, "Man, can you demonstrate for Horacee how you do a Samba on the kit?" So he sat down and played, and "BOOINNGG" – that's exactly what I was looking for! We played a couple of gigs where Airto joined us on percussion and play kit drums on just the samba tunes. Then there was a break in gigs.

That's when the actual group formed with Airto playing all the drum parts and Joe Farrell joined us on flute and saxophone. That was the beginning of Return to Forever.

I played a little bit of piano with the band, but I really enjoyed the melodic sound of the Rhodes and how it blended with the way Stanley was playing acoustic bass. It was light but had an impact that just worked for my music.

We had this first group going and then when we made a change out of necessity because Flora and Airto couldn't make it… Flora was having her first child.

As a pianist and as a member of a modern rhythm section with a vigorous drummer, the epiphany was that I could play an electric instrument and make the volume a bit louder. I had the sound right there with me when it was a suitcase.

I very quickly learned how to plug a non-speaker'd Rhodes into an external amplifier. Some of them were pretty big in those days. So my volume matched the drums and that was the first breakthrough.

The night that Stanley and I both remember is going to the Felt Forum in New York City and hearing John McLaughlin and The Mahavishnu Orchestra. That was it! I had never heard a guitar played like that before. I wasn't just looking at the band and hearing the guitar. I was looking at the audience and seeing this music being received as if it was hip, new and modern. Even though it was loud and electric, it still seemed like Jazz to me, but, the fact that it was causing an effect on young people and rock-and-rollers interested me because I wanted to communicate with them like that. I thought, as a composer, I can write for a sound like that if I could find a guitar player that played like John McLaughlin. Of course, no one has to this day, but, that was the idea.

Stanley introduced me to Lenny White who was his long-time friend. Lenny was working with Azteca at the time on the west coast and we did a trio engagement at the Keystone Corner in San Francisco for a week specifically to audition guitar players and that's when we found Billy Connors [note: Connors is the guitarist on the first electric RTF album, Hymn of the Seventh Galaxy (1973). He was soon followed by a teen-aged Al Di Meola who recorded the final three albums of the electric RTF: Where Have I Known You Before (1974), No Mystery (1975) and Romantic Warrior (1976)].

That whole period of Return to Forever is very memorable. Stanley and Lenny and I are doing a bit of nostalgia these days being together now… talking about the '70s.

It was a real interesting lifestyle at that time because we pretty much stayed on the road. We had apartments in New York, but our focus was just the music and continually playing on the road. Everything was new and exciting to us and audiences really liked the music. I encouraged them both – Stanley especially – to start writing music. It was just a very creative period.

I remember walking out on the stage playing a free concert at Central Park, to I don't know how many people, but I couldn't see the end of the crowd. By then, the way we were delivering the show had a lot of force and was loud too – like rock – so the response from the audience was wild. It was like a rock concert.

Herbie Hancock and I are like brothers… or mirrors. Every time we meet it's like, "BING!"

Before I really got to know Herbie, I was listening to what he was doing with Miles like everyone else. He set a new standard as far as playing jazz piano and his writing. I admired Herbie so much. One time when we were over at my house, I had two grand pianos. We started tinkling around on the pianos and that's where the idea came from to do a two-piano project together.

On the road, we discovered a lot of things. Two musicians working with one another is the microcosm of how bands or orchestras work, because it's a rapport between musicians and how to play together, how to create together. Because most of our music was improvised, it was all very direct communication… very of the moment.

We had to develop and we discovered the joys of making the other musician always sound good. We learned that when an offering comes to you from your fellow musical partner, you accept it whole-heartedly and make something of it. When we played duets, Herbie's attention was never on him-self, it was always on me – and vice versa. That worked incredibly well.

Early on, Herbie had his way of writing and making music that made people happy. I mean he started in on that right away. His compositions have always been incredibly lyrical and sing-able. It's interesting: when we had RTF, Herbie had Headhunters, Joe and Wayne had Weather Report, and John had The Mahavishnu Orchestra. We actually didn't see each other a whole lot because we were out on the road constantly. At the time, I wasn't even listening that much until we would play opposite one another on a show and we'd go check out what he's doing. Everyone had their own direction – all of those bands had a complete area of music that they were creating. It was a very rich period musically.

With his intention to make an educational instrument that could be duplicated easily, Harold Rhodes came up with a machine that to this day has been the most fulfilling to pianists that like to play electric instru-ments. It's not acoustic in the sense that if you pull the plug out you can't really hear it, but if you get close enough you could. It is "kind of acoustic" be-cause of the touch of it. There's this piece of metal called a tine which the hammer comes up, hits it, then it vibrates. The action itself is much less compli-cated than an acoustic piano. It's very simple the way the key is thrown – a very simple mechanism – but, it gets a sound that is unique. It's very useful.

It's too bad, currently speaking, that the instrument organizationally wasn't able to just continue to be made.

Like when a computer company creates a new application, if that company really does its job, they keep improving it and improving it. You come to rely on that tool. The Rhodes somehow went, "POOF!"

The model I have is a stage '73 that's been tweaked, maintained and upgraded by Brian Alexander, my keyboard tech since the Elektric Band in the '80s. It's almost a different instrument because he replaced and upgraded stuff. He did what a company would have done to improve it on the inside – everything except make a new case for it. So my Rhodes is really special. It's a gorgeous sound.

Because the dynamics of touring these days, it's difficult to carry equipment around, so I've always been looking for a way to digitize the Rhodes. I have a confession to make. I took my Rhodes – with my sound – and we made an amazing sampling of 15 different recordings of one note, starting from very soft to very loud. We also sampled the off key and other technical things, so I do have my Rhodes now captured in a "digital photograph," which I can play with a digital keyboard.

One suggestion for companies that are interested in making keyboards: talk to the musicians who play the instrument. It's an omission that instrument companies have made through the years.

They make the instrument out of their R&D guy's head without talking to the musicians who are going to use the instrument. I think everyone would be happy to see well-built keyboards with improvements that maybe myself and my friends who play the instruments could very well enumerate what should be done.

[A note about "Spain"]

The way I wrote the tune was by studying Movement #2 of "Concerto de Aranjuez" by the Spanish composer Rodrigo [note: made famous in jazz as the opening song of Miles Davis' 1960 Lp *Sketches of Spain,* as conceptually arranged by Gil Evans]. The solo introduction is from the piece by Rodrigo, *then* it goes into "Spain."

Chick Corea and Benjamin Bove

Lenny White, Stanley Clark and Chick Corea -- 1973

D'Angelo

Michael Archer (D'Angelo) stands tall at the forefront of being a force that brought the Rhodes sound back into prominence through his music that had one foot in the soul of the '70s and another in the gritty hip hop R&B of the late '90s. Though he has only released two albums and a handful of singles, EPs, soundtracks and stellar cameo appearances, he is among the most influential singer-songwriter-players of his generation. In the rare admissions below, "D" lets us in on a lil of his voodoo.

"Africa" is the first song that comes to mind as far as something I composed on Fender Rhodes, but ummm – there's been a lot of them. We did a lot of stuff on *Voodoo* (2000) with the Rhodes. I single out "Africa" because the actual sound of the Rhodes is what made the song what it was. My engineer at the time, Russ Elevado, took the top off of the Rhodes and mic'ed the bells. When the hammer strikes the bells, the mic was going straight to that, which gives it that xylophone sound at the beginning of the song.

When I was a teenager, around like 16, I would be lucky to find a Rhodes at a church. It was just called an electric piano or whatever, but I was in desperate search for one right after I got signed because the whole aesthetic of where the sound was going – back to "Superfly" and Curtis Mayfield – the Rhodes was an integral part of that sound.

The sound of the Rhodes is just very, very warm… it's great for "color clusters" I would call it. Playing in church, it was just me – no bass player, no drummer – just me. The low end on the Rhodes is perfect because you can emulate a bass guitar with it. I've done gigs where it was just me, a guitarist and a drummer and I'm playing the bass with my left hand, but, no one would have been able to tell the difference. Part of it has to do with my playing, but the big part of it is the sound of the instrument. No one even missed the fact that we didn't have a bass player up there. That's the thing I loved about the Rhodes.

Stevie Wonder, Herbie Hancock, Chick Corea and Joe Sample are the obvious ones that influenced me…

We did a lot of things with the instrument… especially on *Voodoo*… so much experimentation with just the sound of it – putting a wah-wah to it and different effects. I love the tremolo thing on the Rhodes. It's a unique thing that I don't think any other electronic piano has ever had… that little switch that's kind of equivalent to a tremolo on a B-3 organ… but, it's uniquely Fender Rhodes. We would play with it… like when you go to chorus from Tremolo on the Rhodes, it goes to stereo, we would only mic one half of the stereo so you only get it coming out of one side of the speakers. It's an old trick from back in the day too… but, now I'm givin' away secrets.

We had it in the studio and I was dying to get to one. I think my first one I played was a 73 key Fender Rhodes. That was great, but I think the first one that I owned was a suitcase 88. I took it on the road with me for the Brown Sugar tour and kept it.

Eumir Deodato

Rio de Janiero, Brazil's Eumir Deodato Almeida first rose to U.S. prominence as an orchestra arranger for pop and jazz greats. With the release of his first solo album, Prelude, on CTI Records in 1972, he became one of the most commercially successful progenitors of jazz-rock fusion thanks to his smash hit arrangement of Richard Strauss' powerful classical piece "Also Sprach Zarathustra" (which had become popular in the Stanley Kubrick film "2001: A Space Odyssey"). Though he is quick to claim he is not a "great" keyboard player, his use of the Fender Rhodes was uncannily intuitive in the way he wove it through his musical amalgam of Brazilian Orchestral Big Band Soul Pop.

From the eerily rumbling introduction of the Strauss piece and the majestic stride of his take on Gershwin's "Rhapsody in Blue" to the lovely tasteful melodic work on the live rendition of "Spirit of Summer" (in contrast to the acoustic piano studio version) and the deep funk of his live take on Steely Dan's "Do it Again," his love and respect for the instrument is ever evident throughout his work as both a performer and producer (from Tania Maria and Gwen Guthrie to Eliane Elias and Bjork). Deodato takes an enthusiastic "Super Strut" down memory lane for us here.

The first time I got involved with the Fender Rhodes was when I started working for Creed Taylor. He had a label called Creed Taylor Productions with A&M Records. Later he got his own company called CTI Records. I did a lot of projects with Creed Taylor, including Jobim, George Benson, Stanley Turrentine and Astrud Gilberto. Eventually I did my own records.

At that time they had a 73 Fender Rhodes, I believe – a stage model. Those pianos are funny because some of the notes don't come out really great. One of those notes was "C" so, on purpose, I used that note to start "2001," which begins kind of open and free. That sound it made, *blaaaagh*, a broken note. That's what it was!

It was a funky piano with an interesting touch as opposed to the classical or grand piano. I did one track, that I remember – a string orchestra and one classical piano. That was about it. Every time that I tried the regular acoustic piano, I missed this guy (Rhodes). He's very addictive. You can sell me on the whole action, the microphone, the way the sound comes out and even its own little problems like the distortion you get when you really go crazy on it – but, it still has a sound of its own. To me, this is still the best.

This is what I miss on my module – the true ping-pong vibrato. Only these older guys have it. On the new guys – the flat top – it's not the same…

When I played with Jobim, he would play regular piano and I would play Rhodes… or he would play Rhodes and I would play guitar… because I used to play a little guitar too. With Astrud we had acoustic and we had the Fender Rhodes.

I did most of the charts for Astrud for a long time, at least 4 or 5 records with her. I also worked with Luis Bonfa.

One very significant work was the song "Let Me in Your Life" by Aretha Franklin (title track of her 1974 Lp on Atlantic Records).

I did the arrangement and had a couple of nice guys there – Stanley Clarke on bass and Rick Marotta on drums, who is very well known in California. I have a tremendous respect for his thinking – a different thinking about drumming. In those days there was no overdubbing, especially on Aretha Franklin's albums. We did everything "live" – at once – and I played the Rhodes. I did certain things in that track that really feature the Rhodes… this piano has so many possibilities… so many different effects, sounds and textures. Not only that, you have a little bit more control of highs and lows; the intensity of the vibrato – less intense, more intense. It's really unique.

Some people know me for playing, some people know me for the records, some people know me from concerts, but, I'm basically an arranger. When I left Brazil to come here, I was an arranger. I was already working with different people. I had worked with Tom (Antonio Carlos Jobim)… and for either luck or, thinking of what to do, all these arrangements created history – such as Jobim's song for the Sabiá do Brazil festival. He and Chico Buarque de Hollanda composed a song called "Sabiá" which won the Grand Prize. That is what created the opportunity for me to work on the future projects we did. I did a movie in London, we did a record with Creed Taylor (*Stone Flower*) and I did a movie in Brazil ("The Girl from Ipanema"), but mostly arranging.

The arranger is someone who has to look at what is there and come up with something that's much stronger and better than what is there.

To this day, the Fender Rhodes has been my best companion. Whenever they have a good piano in the studio, whatever I wrote, forget about it... I want to add the Fender Rhodes! The Fender Rhodes has been with me ever since I started. I think '71 is the first time I played it because in Brazil they didn't have it.

After the *Prelude* album and "Also Sprach Zarathustra" (subtitled 2001 for the classical song's use in Stanley Kubrick's movie "2001: A Space Odyssey") Zarathustra existed, by the way. Zoroastra, I found his tomb in Baku, which is Azerbaijan. It's a country right above Iran and unfortunately, I had just one day in Baku, because I wanted to go visit it (it was 2 hour ride). This tomb is lit by natural gas. They have a lot of oil in Azerbaijan, and natural gas. They had just a hole in the floor. The gas comes up and that flame has been there forever.

The record was very popular so everybody wanted me to go play and of course, this was the baby to take, but, because these are very delicate instruments sometimes especially for traveling, I had to buy a bunch of them because sometimes they would break. I would have them ship one back and ship a new one in... At one point in the mid '70s, I had at least 16 of these pianos. Some were modifications such as the Dyno-My-Piano. I had two of them. Chuck [Monte] did one in the studio and the other one I bought from somebody.

So then I would travel. On one occasion in Boulder, Colorado, my main C note – the note I start "2001" with – was broken. I started telling the people, "Hey, the note is broken! Watch – *paah paah paah*" – and they say, "Oh..." don't worry about it: I took the cover off and [laughs] I had all the tools that I needed to fix it – tines, the tuning fork, the wire cutter, screwdrivers for this one... The passion for the piano went a little out of control when you go to that extreme to fix a piano in front of an audience. He gave me half an hour, then I had only 15 more minutes to play. "That's it. Thank you, good night!" We used the piano for a long time... until the airlines started charging so much money for transporting these pianos. Then I had to give up... I had to!

"Super Strut" is still my favorite song on my second album, *Deodato 2*. "Rhapsody in Blue" is a favorite too, but, "Super Strut" is the one that gained the most notoriety because my charts for those records are very simple.

"2001" was like that too. I had nothing. I just showed the musicians what it was, then, we rehearsed. As we rehearsed, I was waving. I had no idea what to do, so I was waving everybody in. Stanley Clarke was doing a solo and I said, "Uhh, okay," then I did a solo. Then, I waved at John Tropea to do a solo. Once in a while I nodded at Billy Cobham and he would do a fill. I said, "Alright, we're ready for Take One!" Creed Taylor called from inside, "What do you mean, 'Take One?'" I said, "Yeah, we're going to record it now!" He said, "We already did!" I said, "No! That was just a rehearsal! My solo is no good!" Creed says, "No, no that's great! Don't worry about your solo."

I said, "Yeah, don't worry about my solo?! Of course I worry about my solo!!" He wasn't going to let me do another take! The only reason he let me do it again is because I insisted, but, the other take was not as spontaneous as the first one... which just goes to show you. It has a lot to do with vibes. Vibes were great that day. It was a beautiful spring day. He always started recording at 9:30 / 10 o'clock in the morning... always and at 5, boom, that's it. Out, no more. So we used that and I just added some coloring – strings, horns and whatever. He chopped a little of my solo which was fine, but, it was still a [10-and-a-half minute track]. Pop radio stations wouldn't play more than 3 1/2 4 minutes, so I thought, "Well, that's it for that!"

So I went to Brazil to go to the beach and stayed for awhile. Then Airto & Flora (married Brazilian singer / percussion duo) started calling me saying, "Hey, your record is on the charts!"

I said, "Yeah, okay, what number?"

"65."

"65? So what!"

"No, you gotta come!"

"Gotta come for what? What am I going to do with a number 65 record? OK."

They called next week. "Deo, the record is 35."

I said "35? Yeah, so, he's got records before that were #35."

"Yeah but..."

"I'm not goin!"

Then it hit number 15 and when it reached number 10, I'm thinking, "O.K., maybe you should go back. Bye-bye beach!"

So I went back to NY, they called me in the office with a lot of people – booking agent and all that – are saying, "You've gotta tour!" I said, "Tour, why?" "No, we gotta tour!!" It was all a little strange. He says, "Deodato and others." The others are 300 other people – all his catalog people and all good friends of mine, including George Benson. For me, the problem was that the concerts were so long. By the time I went on to play, everybody was so high that they didn't even know what was going on! They were just sitting there like... like zombies. I said, "I can't continue doing this, it's not good." So I stopped. I had a fight with (Creed) and left the company... for other reasons too. I end up going to another company (MCA).

I turned to production after the late '70s because there was a lot of demand. The guys from Kool & The Gang had heard a record that I did for Warner Bros. called *Love Island* (George Benson plays a beautiful solo on the title track, by-the-way). They really loved the record and I knew them already because they had fantastic stuff. "Open Sesame" is a favorite, as-well-as, "Summer Madness" and funk stuff like "Jungle Boogie." I said, "Are you sure you want ME to produce you?" I was finishing another record for Warner Bros. (*Knights of Fantasy*, featuring "Space Dust" and the disco hit "Whistle Bump"), so they had to wait.

They started the record on their own, but, they were not happy with something. They really wanted me to do something with them. I said, "Give me another month and I'll be able to."

When I started working with them, we used the Fender Rhodes too. Sometimes I would play it; sometimes we had another guy do it when I had to be in the control room producing... listening to what was going on. When you play and have headphones on, you lose... You cannot judge because you have to use the same speakers for the whole record. I would not dare change speakers, with either the big JBLs or the small Yamahas. It's the same problem with being a young producer – playing and being your own producer. You have to go in-and-out... it's very tiring... very complicated.

The first album (1979's *Ladies Night*) didn't do too bad... it had "Too Hot" and "Ladies Night." Then, of course, the usual comment: "It's an overnight, fly by night success." So when I do the next record and it has "Celebration" – another "fly-by-night" success? [Laughs] Everybody says, "Eh?" I said, "Yeah! OK."

I did one more record with them (1981 *Something Special* which contained "Take My Heart" and "Get Down On It"). Then, of course, everybody knows what to do, which radically changed my position. I understand... but, they had life for a long time after that. When you get to certain point, then you start fighting, it's typical. Every group has that problem, but, still they're all my friends. I still talk a lot to George "Funky" Brown, the drummer – a very good friend of mine – and the trombone player Clifford Adams.

I went on to build my own little studio in Manhattan, in Tribeca. I produced a few records... Chuck Mangione and I did something with Roberta Flack, who I had worked with before as an arranger, but, this time as a producer. The Dazz Band (*Rock the Room*), One Way (*9*), Con-Funk-Shun (*Fever*), Kleeer (the wickedly seductive "Intimate Connection")... man, there were a lot of other groups that I produced, but, by all means, Kool & The Gang was the biggest seller, especially "Celebration."

The Donato – Deodato album was a favor because I used to know Donato. We did a record before in California for Blue Thumb.

Sergio Mendes was an old friend back from Brazil. There was a place where you have four jazz clubs one next to the other called the "Corner of the Bottles." It was where high society people went to drink. Scotch is very popular in Brazil. Sergio came to the states and hooked up with Herb Alpert at A&M Records. Herb Alpert did a record with him and they had the money to promote, boom-boom-boom, that's it. After that, anything he did was a big hit! I just ran into him by accident in Germany. We were playing on different days in Straubing and I knew he was there. As I was leaving, he was sitting at the coffee shop reading a newspaper. I came up to him and said, "You want more coffee, sir?" He said, "No, I'm okay" Then he looks at me and says, "Waaaauuh!! You crazy!!" [Laughs] We spoke and he's doing great. He's done great forever. Sergio is very well off because he had a lot of publishing companies and this and that. On his records, he controlled all the songs, so he's fine... just fine.

This basically goes back to our roots in Brazil. Sergio was totally into Horace Silver. I never really had a specific pianist that I could say this is the one… I used to like Martial Solal (the French jazz pianist). I liked Oscar Peterson. I even listened a little to Dave Brubeck and say, "What is that? It's not really my thing but, okay!" That one song did it – [sings "Take 5"]. In Brazil we didn't have much of anything, so I had to start it by myself. I got an Italian book of arranging and it was a pain-in-the-neck because you have to translate everything. It was very traditional too. Then, guitar player, Luis Bonfa, changed my life completely. He was a good friend. Luis Bonfa wrote many songs, but, the song you would remember him for is [sings then plays "Black Orpheus" – "Samba de Orfeu"]. He gave me "Sounds and Scores" – it used to come with a 45 RPMs to give you the example. I couldn't believe this. It was Henry Mancini!

I was already a fan because in Brazil they were playing (the TV crime drama) Peter Gunn. This is how he got started in pop music: "Peter Gunn." It was amazing. How he got to that point I don't understand. If you knew him, you'd say, "No, not possible. This guy cannot write that music!"… but, he did.

Then I started working with Luis Bonfa. I did the arrangements for him for the same festival – Rio Festival – every year. I repeat: I am an arranger. I'm not really a pianist. I never studied piano in my life. I just play "arranger's piano" and I fool everybody – they really think I can play! [whispers] "Shhhh… don't tell anybody." Arranging is a different story. Arranging is just writing and I'm very well known for what I DON'T write. I only do what I think is absolutely necessary.

Then Bonfa invited me to come to New York. I also played a lot of Fender Rhodes on his records. Fender Rhodes was the hottest thing in those days… in the studios, everywhere.

The problem was concerts. You try to get one of these pianos abroad that works good, it's a disaster… A DISASTER! Because I play mostly in Europe, transportation is a serious problem; especially within Europe, like, if you're going from Germany to Italy or from Italy to Portugal or whatever. You can't even dream of using these guys. It's delicate. The position of the pedal is very delicate. There's no automatic nothing here! This is all manual, one by one. You let this thing fall, boom, you're finished. You break the tines or the microphone (pickup) gets dislodged… These microphones are one by one – every note has a microphone. The microphones have to be completely adjusted to the same volume for each note. These resonators have to be adjusted and the only way is to do one by one. So, you have to make sure it's screwed properly. If it's a little loose… I played a lot of Fender Rhodes where the notes were completely uneven.

I still had to play them because in those days, there was no substitute. This guy has a touch all its own. It's very unique. You think it's a string – it's not a string, but it sounds like a string. If you look at a grand piano it's the same principle.

I was at Manny's Music in NY one day buying something and I heard the sound of the Fender and I said, "Oh, Fender Rhodes. I haven't played that in such and such." So I went to see and it's not a Fender Rhodes. It was another digital keyboard called a Yamaha Motif-8. I said "excuse me! No, are you joking me?!

I know this sound! Come on, give me a break."
To my surprise, it was possible. With the digital, the chips and all the circuits are much sturdier, so you can travel with it. So I had a big case built for it and was taking it on the road. Then you get to a place and where's my keyboard? I don't leave the airport until I see my keyboard. Because what're you going to do, you're going to go and end up playing what, an accordion or?? Can't do that! It's heavy like hell. So when they came out with the keyboard module, I said, "Oh, my goodness! This is what I wanted" because you can use a MIDI controller. With the controller you can find Korg, you have Roland, you have Yamaha, you have all this nice action with the weighted keys and you get a little MIDI cable.

The sound comes out of the module and the box is about this size. I tried it and said, "It's like the real thing... and reasonably priced."

You can also do a little bit of the ping-pong vibrato, but, it's not the same. Nothing beats this ping-pong sound – nothing – but, it serves a purpose. People want to hear "Rhapsody in Blue" and "2001." They don't care about the pong or the ping! The problem with the module is coming out with new models. You find one thing that works very well, then they change it and you cannot get it anymore! Why is that?

M-O-N-E-Y! But listen to me – the Rhodes... is a beauty. This thing is at least 75% responsible for my career.

Benjamin Bove, Eumir Deodato, Gerald McCauley and Onaje Allan Gumbs

George Duke

Born in San Rafael, California, George Duke holds the distinction of being able to say he has literally worked with everybody from A to Z – Cannonball Adderley to Frank Zappa specifically. His classical training prepared him for a journey into jazz, rock, funk, gospel, pop, Brazilian and everything else under the sun. Early gigs included a residency in San Francisco with a then unknown Al Jarreau. Progressive recordings as a leader on the European MPS label led to an American association with CBS' Epic Records where he released a couple of key albums titled Reach For It and Brazilian Love Affair.

He formed indelible duos with both bassist Stanley Clarke and drummer Billy Cobham and produced an eclectic number of recordings by Miles Davis, Flora Purim, Deniece Williams, Christian McBride, Take 6, Jeffrey Osborne, Hiroshima, A Taste of Honey, Angela Bofill, Rachelle Ferrell, Dianne Reeves, Seawind and Chante' Moore. Today he records on his own BPM label... and owns no less than three Rhodes.

The first thing I remember, there was this 73 key Silver-top Rhodes when I joined the Don Ellis Big Band, which I think was like 1968. I came down to L.A. and joined his band. They had a piano and they had this other thing... I didn't know what it was. I thought it was a toy!

It had this lamé-like finish… silver and sparkly… and this little keyboard. I hit it, it went PLUNK, and I was like, "I don't know about this thing man." I wound up trying to play mostly piano, but, there were certain songs that Don wanted the sound of the Rhodes, so I wound up playing it. That was my first experience.

I didn't warm up to it really until around 1969. I did a gig in L.A. with Jean-Luc Ponty, who is a violinist. Richard Bock, the producer of Jean Luc's records, thought that it would be good if we played in a rock club. Jean Luc says, "I'll do it if George does it." So I said, "I'll do it if you have a piano," because someone told me it was a rock club and they wouldn't have a piano. So Dick Bock said, "Don't worry, there'll be a piano there and it'll be cool." So I told Jean-Luc, "Cool, let's do it." We did the gig, I got down there… there was no piano. They had this Silver-top Rhodes! [Laughs] I said, "That's the same piano I played with Don Ellis! What a drag…"

Then I looked out in the audience and there was Quincy Jones, Frank Zappa happened to be there that night, Cannonball Adderley, Gerald Wilson… all these musical heroes of mine. I said, "Uh-oh, I gotta play this rascal!" It's all I've got. When I started playing it, I discovered, "Oh, there's some knobs here. What does this do?" I turned this knob and thought, "Oh… you can turn it up! I can play louder than the drummer!" I liked that! Then I found, "Oh, vibrato… wow!" I started experimenting, playing with my legs… I did everything totally extroverted I could think of on this piano. Eventually, somebody noticed it and said, "He's crazy!" Then Frank Zappa asked me to join the band.

That was the first really crazy experience where I noticed there's something about this instrument. Weeks later, I went in the studio and did a record called *King Kong: Jean-Luc Ponty Plays The Music of Frank Zappa* (1969). That's where I really used the Rhodes and really learned to love it. On Jean-Luc's album, we did a lot of Frank's more crazy – you know, I shouldn't say more crazy material – but, stuff that would lend itself to being played instrumentally.

I was at my mom's house. It was a Sunday afternoon and I was there for dinner. The phone rings and she says, "There's somebody on the phone named Zoopa." I said, "Zoopa? Who the hell is Zoopa? Oh… Zappa!" So I take the phone and say, "Hey Frank, how you doin'?" I had played a gig with Frank – did the album and did a gig with him at UCLA with an orchestra. I thought, "This cat's kinda got some interesting music." He says [imitates frank], "George I want you to join the Mothers." I said, "The who?" because I knew Zappa… I didn't know anything about the *Mothers of Invention*. He goes, "No, not The Who, The Mothers!" I said, "I don't know who the Who is." He goes, "Nevermind. I want you to come to L.A. and play with the band – see if it works." So I went to L.A. the next week and that's how I joined the band. He had a Fender Rhodes there – not a piano.

I joined the band in late '69 and played with him all through '70. The last thing I did with him was the film "200 Motels." Then I joined Cannonball Adderley around '73. I picked up with him again until 1976. I was "gone" then. I knew that there was something else going on here.

Quite frankly, other than the piano, it's the last great innovation in an instrument that I can think of. The Fender Rhodes is an amazing instrument. It has affected jazz, pop, everything. There was something about it that made me think, "I can make this mine." I liked the idea that I could turn it up. That meant a lot to me 'cuz I was working with drummers who – when they started laying on that cymbal – I'd get lost. My fingers used to bleed. Man… you have no idea! With this I could kind of lay back a little bit and I found that I liked the tone of it. All the notes weren't even in the early renditions of the piano, so depending on how hard it was played and how abused it was, each piano had a different personality. You had to learn how to play with that. I used to learn how to play with broken tines. I played with it and the audience would dig it.

Eventually I wound up using other effects… at the time, ring modulators, which Tom Oberheim made. I used to just play around with the thing and I found that you could get a lot of interesting personalities out of it.

You could pick up a record and hear Herbie Hancock play it, I was playing it, Chick Corea was playing it, Keith Jarrett was playing it. There were a lot of us that began playing the instrument, so it became the instrument of choice. Quincy Jones used it on his records too. On a lot of sessions, they would have a piano, a Fender Rhodes and that was it; maybe a Clavinet, depending on what they wanted to do. Certain producers actually began writing with it on the scores – it was the Fender Rhodes sound that they wanted (on specific songs or passages). That meant that this was a legitimate instrument.

In terms of the '70s, there was the piano, the Fender Rhodes, the Wurlitzer and the Clavinet. That was the arsenal. Now whatever you did in terms of wah-wah pedals, choruses and all this other kind of stuff, you could plug right in there, alter your sound and make it your own.

The worst part about playing a Fender Rhodes was carrying the doggone thing. When I was with Cannonball, I used to have to schlock this thing around and to tune it, it had these little springs and I'd be in there trying to tune the sucker up… It was a nightmare, but, it was worth it. I was young then. I would not want to carry that rascal around now!

Getting into the area of problems with the Rhodes, I was in Pori, Finland – when I first met Stanley Clarke, by-the-way – and my Rhodes got messed up. It came in off the plane and I don't know what happened. The metal sticking through the thing, it was just gone – a disaster. So I asked Chick Corea if I could use his piano. I didn't know Chick at the time, so the promoter asked Chick. He said, "Yeah, okay, use the piano but be easy on it." I was playing with Cannonball… Man, I beat the stew out of that piano so bad, notes stuck… Like when they lay flat. This was the only Rhodes in Finland at this Pori Jazz Festival, so Chick was pissed off at me. He had to play with Return to Forever with four or five keys sporadically across the keyboard not working. He was livid! I said "I'm sorry, man. Is there anything I can do? …hold it up while you're playin'?" That was terrible, but, it's a true story – my introduction to Chick Corea. Hope he doesn't remember it!

The Mahavishnu Orchestra opened for Frank Zappa on some shows and I was digging what they were doing. I really loved what Jan Hammer was doing… he was playing the Fender Rhodes as well. Billy Cobham and I started talking. He would say, "If you ever leave Frank, we should get together and form a band" and I said, "Well, if you ever leave Mahavishnu, I'm down to do that." So we mutually decided that on THIS date we're gonna depart and form our own thing. We stayed together for about a year.

By late '75, a lot of fusion players were just coming in playing a lot of notes and it didn't seem like they were playing any music. It was just as fast as they could play and as complicated as the time signatures could get. I said, "We need to bring some music back into this thing. Let's try to put a little comedy in here." Frank had opened me up to comedy and bringing other forms of music into what I do. That increased my musical arsenal to where I could have anything from R&B to doo-wop to rock n' roll to classical music to Latin, all in this stew. So that's what I began to do. I talked Billy into it. "Let's make this a little funny – bring the humanism back into this music 'cuz if we go over people's heads, we're gonna lose." Only a select set of people are gonna dig it and our audience is gonna go down.

So I wanted to bring in the R&B element and that's kind of where that started – fusion going a little more R&B – and it was definitely heavy Fender Rhodes oriented.

The record worked and it was absolutely amazing. I didn't like the record, to tell you the truth.

We did a thing called *Live On-Tour in Europe* in 1976 that came out on Atlantic Records. It's still selling – that record went in the black a long time ago.

A Fender Rhodes with a Minimoog and an Arp Odyssey on one side. That was my arsenal along with whatever else I could play. That evolved into wearing things around my neck and playing real funky!

One interesting thing I did with my Rhodes when I was working with Billy – who's a loud drummer – was give it more level. I started getting outboard stacks! I had subs, the speaker then the tweeter on top, stereo with a mixer and was turning it up as loud as I could to get it clean. I decided to try something. I got this guy and said, "What if we split the harp into three segments. Let's take the lower third, bring that out of one output, the middle out of another output and the high third out in a separate output." That gave me a totally different sound – true stereo on stage!

I stopped carrying the Rhodes after awhile, because it just got to be a trip… carrying it to the airport. There wasn't a lot of what they call "backline" today, where you pick up your equipment where you go. All musicians carried their own equipment. So I carried what I had which was the normal stock Rhodes. Personally, I liked the Rhodes that had the speaker on the bottom. I like to hear the vibrato do its thing. Maybe it's just because I grew up listening to that. What I always called the stage model piano was not my favorite. I thought the Dyno piano had some bite to it, but, I never really played it a lot.

I'm a piano player. I started on the big boy over there – Steinways, Bosendorfers, whatever. I have a hard time getting promoters that want me to say, "We're going to provide you with a piano." They want me to play a Motif ES8. That's not the same as playing a piano. It's weird… you go to concert halls and they don't want you to play their best piano. If they want you to play a piano at all, they say, you can bring one in. That's when you got these DX-7s, especially when you can gang four to eight of 'em together (with a TX-8) and have them, like, wobbling around and get that kind of phase between the instruments. It had another kind of vibe… It seemed like you had more than one instrument in a box. It was less to carry, so everyone became enamored with sound and they weren't thinking about music as much. Music suffered a lot during that initial synthesizer age. They forgot about writing a composition.

Things have come back around now. Maybe the rappers brought it back. They said, "There's value in vintage sounds." I'd hear 'em because I was Musical Director of the "Soul Train Music Awards" for many years and they'd say, "How come you don't use those instruments you used to use?" Of course, it was easy to change and save your sounds. This is basically one sound – unless you add some effects – but, there's a personality there that was not being captured in those digital instruments. There's something valuable about analog sound that digital has not captured. They've gotten very close, but, I don't think they have captured this real instrument… not yet.

There's a virtual instrument I love that's as about as close as I've played to this thing. It's called the Scarbee Rhodes – in a 24-bit format.

"The Vibe" of The Rhodes is the depth of this instrument… the layers. What they've begun to do with virtual instruments now is to go deeper… because there are a lot of layers to this instrument. The velocity level is quite broad, so if you dumb it down or make it smaller, you're only getting a snapshot, not a photo.

The problem for some young producers or players is they don't know what the real sound is supposed to be in the first place. It's no different for an engineer who's never recorded a live drum set – they don't know what it's supposed to sound like!

A few years ago I found out that Joe Sample had three or four Rhodes and three or four Wurlitzers in a warehouse somewhere – brand new… still in the box! I said, "Joe, take me down there right now! I'm using them on my next record"… 'cuz mine was in the shop!

I own two Rhodes today. I have another Rhodes down in a locker which I put in plexiglass – the one that I split the harp into 3 areas.

Most producers – if they have a studio – they've probably got a Fender Rhodes laying around somewhere… whether they use it or not. On-the-other-hand, I've done some records where I really wanted an electronic sound and I would go for that… something just right in the middle that fits in the track like that, but, if I'm playing some fusion or something with a hard edge or something that's soulful – man, without the bite, it really inhibits what I do. There's no difference between a Fender Rhodes and a piano to me in terms of playing electronic instruments – no substitute for the real deal. To be perfectly frank, it's just like sex – there's no substitute for the real thing.

I'm not sure when I first met Harold Rhodes. When I played with Cannonball Adderley he might have come to a show and said, "I want you to come down to my factory and look at this instrument." He did invite me down. He would tell me that Herbie Hancock came down, so I said, I better go then. That's when I was still fighting the whole idea of a Fender Rhodes. I wanted to just play the piano. I didn't want to play synthesizers either, same thing. Then Tom Oberheim said, "Come here, I want to show you something… show you the possibilities." I remember going out to Anaheim and playing around with this thing. I would see Harold, he would call me over and he'd say if there's anything you think might need to be altered, we talked about it. It wasn't just me – it was with Herbie, with Chick, whoever was playing the instrument – and we just eventually fell in love with it.

He seemed like a straight ahead kind of dude. You wouldn't know that he was the one that invented the thing. Like Bob Moog, you look at him and say, "He's the guy?" Tom Oberheim… well, Tom kinda looked a little frayed! [Laughs] He had this thing about him [points to hair], but, Harold, you might've thought he worked in a library.

The Rhodes is like Earth. The Clavinet is like Earth. The piano is Earth. You talk in these other kind of terms to get a message across, but, I say the first wireless medium is music. Because there is a conduit to you – to everybody – but, it's not hard-wired. There's something that's inert in what we're doing and to get there, it seems like this instrument tapped into it. I don't know if Harold Rhodes set out to do that. I don't know what he was thinking.

When I first went to his studio and he showed me this thing, I said, "Oh… sounds like bells." I kinda dug it, but, I didn't know what to do with it until I messed around with it and saw the possibilities. He found something and it's still around all these years later. I don't think it's going anywhere. This instrument will be a major instrument just like an acoustic piano. This is one of the major, major steps in musical evolution.

George Duke and Gerald McCauley

Larry Dunn

As the piano player for Earth, Wind & Fire in its '70s heyday, Larry Dunn adopted the persona of a comical keyboard wizard. His talents were too great for the band to hold back as he went on to produce artists such as the Latin Jazz Fusion band Caldera, drummer Lenny White, saxophonist Ronnie Laws, singers Dianne Reeves and Sylvia St. James, saxophonist Stanley Turrentine, percussionist Paulinho Da Costa, U.K. jazz-funk fusion band Level 42 and the legendary Ramsey Lewis. Today he records as a leader, performs EWF classics with his ensemble The Larry Dunn Orchestra, scores television commercials for Japan via he and wife Luisa's Source Productions company, mentors Brian Culbertson and generally leads the good life working from his secluded valley home. Here he waxes with characteristic humor on "The Days of Fire and Rhodes'."

The first time the Rhodes really caught my attention was on the Quincy Jones album, *Walking in Space*. I found out later it was Bob James playing on that. He was one of the first people who could conjure, like, that floating thing… really nice colors. I was a B-3 man… but, I had to have a Rhodes. So I found some of my Mexican brothers who had stolen one… I know, "Bad Larry"… and they wanted $75 bucks for it. I'm like, "I'll give you $25 now and catch ya later." Never saw them again. I tell people if they saw me, it was either, "Yeah, Bato!" or "Where's our money?!"

That was the stage model – the one with the legs. I came out to L.A. and eventually got the '73 [SUITCASE]. When I went to Guitar Center to see Dave Dimartino, his buddy was like, "No, man, Rhodes is pretty consistent." I'm like, "Put me a bottom and give me about five tops!" I went through five different tops and on the fourth, I found the one you have here with that real nice tangy sound. Then I went on and got two of the 88 keys, I had a Dyno and a bunch of them… I actually sold two of them in '85 and my wife was like, "Larry, don't do it!" So thanks to Gerald McCauley, we finally made the trade with my '73 because it was never on the road and he got me an 88.

My main mentor was actually Jimmy Smith, with the organ. Then I got the Rhodes and Herbie was my main influence. Me and (EWF soprano sax man) Andrew (Woolfolk) were roommates and we'd listen to Headhunters every night, then Weather Report.

I was 13 when I met Philip Bailey. Back then you had to be able to play to get in a band. Philip was in a group and they had the 3 best singers. The band I was in had the young cats playing jazz and whatever. So we merged and eventually became Friends and Love. We actually opened the show for the *original Earth Wind & Fire* when they had the two albums on Warner Bros. Maurice White and Verdine White came down to the club to see me and Philip and the band. Eventually, all the guys quit, Philip moved (to L.A.) and I stayed in Denver. Then Philip came back to Denver and I was in a little bar group playing organ opening the show for WAR. So I did, like, a 10-minute B-3 solo and Philip went right to the phone. "Maurice, I think we got the guy! He's a young cat… good dude, just doesn't have a lot of experience."

(I took offense to that. I was playing night clubs when I was 12 years-old.) The rest is history.

I talked to 'Reese, went back to the stolen Rhodes, learned all the tunes off the first two Warner Bros. albums by ear, packed it up and came to L.A. Verdine picked me up and went up the wrong side of Century Blvd. I'm like, "Oh, no, we're gonna die!!" He was funny because he was cursing at on-coming traffic like Mr. Magoo! I'm like, "You're in the wrong lane!" Thank God we made it to Maurice's house. We whipped out the Rhodes and I played a couple of the EWF things, went into a little "Maiden Voyage," played a nice solo and that was it. I was in like Flynn.

I started with the 73, but, as soon as the check came, I got the 88. By the time we were really hittin' – '74/'75 – I had one on stage at all times and one in a dressing room so cats could warm up and stuff.

The night before we recorded "Brazilian Rhyme" (from *All 'N All*), I had the 88 Rhodes and just wanted something different. I had the cats totally replace the rubber tips with harder ones so the lower was a little softer and as you get higher, harder… I wanted a little more twang and percussiveness out of it, but, I still didn't like it. What I did was idiotic, but it worked… I went in that night and ripped off all the tips. So we had just the wood hitting the tines right? I knew I couldn't keep it like that because it would destroy the instrument, so eventually I had him put it back. Then in 85, I did an endorsement with Yamaha. They sent me, like, 20 grand worth of stuff. I pressed the DX-7 and for the Rhodes sound, THAT was that sound. Did I get compensated? No, but, now you know!

For all of us, the spectacle was like, YES! I was about 14 when I saw my first rock concert. It was in Colorado at a stadium – Three Dog Night, Joe Cocker and others… but, when Hendrix walked out, I mean everybody just lost it! I had never heard rock music, so when I heard the guitars and stuff, it was a strange sound to me. I was so excited when Hendrix walked out with his bandanna on, it got quiet… then really loud! There were all these gorillas (security) in front of the speakers that would block it off so you could only get so close. Then I went to a Ten Years After concert. I was way back in the audience. I don't ever get headaches, but, my head was just throbbing.

I forgot the name of the company that did the sound but, man… You could see the big subwoofers pumpin' like, "Boy, everybody's gonna hear this tonight!" I loved it.

Volume is great and all, but, with "The Fire," what we really got into were *dynamics*. It's one thing to turn it all the way up, but if you leave it there, there's nowhere to go.

Charles Stepney was really my mentor. I used to bug the poor man. He's got his glasses pulled down over his nose and he's transcribing a tune – just listening to the cassette and writing down the chords. I was like, "Oh, Mr. Stepney, how do you do that?" He looked at me and said, "Boy, when you've been doin' this as long as me, you're gonna do it too."

I told him I kind of got a little complex because I'm not a great reader, and this made my day – my life, actually. He's like, "Look, man, if that's bothering you, you can always go to school for 6 months and tighten that up, but there's not a lot of cats that can sit at a keyboard and do what you do." I was like, okay, I guess I'll just keep practicing.

Later when I really got into producing Caldera, Ramsey Lewis, Level 42 and all this different stuff, I always remembered him telling about arranging. He said, "Now when you're arranging something, a lot of times it's not as much what to write as what not to write. Space… is a beautiful thing." That was my guy, man.

Three years after *Sun Goddess* (1974), I produced three songs for Ramsey Lewis' album *Tequila Mockingbird* (1977). I was, like, 21 years-old when I wrote that track. 'Reese called me in and said, "Hey man, Ramsey's been calling me, but I just don't have the time. Why don't you help him out." So I did "Tequila Mockingbird," me and Eddie del Barrio from Caldera wrote "That Ole Bach Magic" and I grabbed the Victor Feldman tune "Skippin'." Well, the day that album came out was the same day as *All 'N All*, so 'Reese and I went to the store together and bought them. He calls me two hours later and goes, "Hey man, come to my room. I need to holler atcha." So I walk down to his hotel room and he explodes, "Man, what's all this Sugar Honey Iced Tea?!" I said, "Excuse me? You're the one that told me-" "No, man, I just meant for you to write a song or two… not all this!" Ramsey loved it, though. We did a couple more albums!

One of the biggest concerts we ever did was the first California Jam (a.k.a. "Cal Jam"). It was so big that they had to fly us in with helicopters. They had the stage on train tracks 'cause they had to keep it moving. You'd think you'd be nervous – there are a quarter million people – but, it's so big that you must look like an ant to them. We were doing the old stuff like "Time is On Your Side" and "C'Mon Children" – a great concert!

For sheer levity, I'll tell you about a place we played in D.C. – about a 20,000-seater. It was the "Let's Groove Tour" (for the album, *Raise!*) – Actually, my last tour. We had a stage on, like, a 45 degree angle. It would open up and (drummer) Freddie White would come out. I used to tear him up. I said, "Man, you gonna do your Diana Ross stuff?" He'd stand up and wave his arms like this [motions] "O.K., Diana!" Now me and Freddie are up there, so the rest of the guys come out stepping or whatever. What happened was Maurice or somebody spilled some Coca-Cola on the stage at sound check. Then Maurice had a bright idea because it was sticky, right? He talked to our main stage guy and said, "Frank, we can get more traction if we just cover the whole stage with Coca-Cola!" So the guys came out. First it was just the frontline three: Maurice, Philip and Ralph. Then this laser comes on, we do the soundtrack and as soon as it hits, Maurice was the first one to do a 360 and went *shaboom* right on the ol' bum. Then the other guys started coming up – one at a time – *shabam*, *shaboom*. Louis Satterfield, the trombone player, was a big guy. He's from Mississippi originally and he told me, "Dude, me and (trumpeter) Rahm were back there holding hands tight! If my big ass woulda rolled out, I'd still be going through Philadelphia Street!"

What happened was they forgot that when they turned on the fog machines and the fog met the Coca-Cola, what would happen – Sludge! That was the funniest gig ever. Good thing we didn't have YouTube then. That clip would have been #1.

Monty White, Maurice's brother who was the road manager, called me one day and said, "Hey man, you know you got the biggest keyboard rig in the industry, right?" I'm like, "And?!" However, it was not for show… even though it did look cool! I had my LED light board behind me and all that, but, everything up there was essential.

The kind of shows we did, it's not like Maurice could break out a cigar and be like, "Uh, Larry's gonna do some re-programming. We'll be back atcha!" The show just kept moving, so you had to go from the Rhodes right to the Yamaha piano then to the Minimoog – one for the bass and another for the Vocoder. Then I had the CP-60 for the trombone parts. Before we had the big horn section, me and Andrew had to cover a lot of that stuff. So I had to have all that stuff… 'cuz there was no sequencing or sampling. It was all live.

My favorite "Fire" song is probably "Runnin'" (their Grammy-winning instrumental). I don't even know where that came from. I was just in the studio one night, played it for 'Reese and he was like, "Yeah!" Then we all got together and spruced it up with the horn solos. Then when I did that accelerated synth thing, all I heard was, "Dudes are really spacing out on that!" I said, "Good." Live, I also dug "Magic Mind" because that was just The Funk! The trumpet players would go out front and – I don't know how – but they would spin their trumpets and I was like a groupie. "OOO, look at that!"

The phrase "life-changing" is truly overused, but, the Rhodes absolutely changed my life. When I got the first one – how I acquired it is nobody's business – I was one of the first ones… me and Herbie… to utilize the Echoplex – a delay device made from reel tape. You could speed it up and slow it down. One of the cool things was when Ronnie Laws was still with us, we would do a part where I just played nice chords and he would play over them. Then I would flip the switch on the Echoplex, get up and walk away with the piano still playing. People just lost it! There was an aura about Earth, Wind & Fire – magic and mysticism – that used to just wear people out…

One of the other things that was a mainstay of my sound, was a little square black box… I forgot who even made it… just a little, tiny thing with two knobs. I remember when we were opening for Santana, his keyboard player at the end of the tour was telling me, "Man, when we first heard you play, we couldn't believe it. At first I thought maybe you were doing it with a delay or something."

Then I saw you really playing and I said, "No, it's not that…" but, I did use that box just to a 200 ms… not a lot of intensity… just to widen it a little bit… added some reverb… and always the Boss Chorus. I don't know what happened to all that stuff. I left a lot of it in the EWF locker and it just disappeared. Now with all the different plug-ins, it's not necessary. (Engineer) George Massenburg used to hate it because it was giving me noise in my signal. I used to always ask, "Are you going to remember to put it on there?" He'd be like, "Yeah, I'll put it on" – and he did – but, it's still a different sound than the chorus.

That's what I loved about our live album, *Gratitude*. Nobody could mess with me because it was on the sound. That was my sound and, like I said, it really changed my life… When you first play the Rhodes, you have to approach it as a different instrument. You can play it like a piano, but, if you utilize it for its own personality, it takes on a whole different meaning.

Larry Dunn, Earth Wind & Fire at California Jam

Donald Fagen

There's a mural of the Duke Ellington Orchestra on Donald Fagen's Rhodes which tells you a lot of what you need to know by way of introducing one of the great sophisticates of the rock n' soul landscape. As co-founder of the musically superior and lyrically dubious duo Steely Dan (along with guitarist / bassist / co-writer Walter Becker), Fagen has become synonymous with jazz-inflected blues rock — songs filled with shady characters, heady literary references, sex, drugs, rock-n-roll and a wistful nostalgia for the cool of old. The Fender Rhodes has played a seminal role in bringing these seedy characters and earthy moods to life.

Whether playing Rhodes himself or blowing significant wads of recording budget on hiring the best in the business to sit in and make the magic happen, Mr. Fagen is a crucial contributor on this instrument and one we were fortunate to have for our documentary.

I was doing some studio work in New York and I think there was a Rhodes. Previous to that I was using a Wurlitzer, which is, I guess, the first electric piano I had ever seen. In fact, when I was 17 I think, I got my father to get me a Wurlitzer piano. I brought it up to school so I'd have something to play there. I loved the way they sounded. They had their own character, but they had lots of problems. For one thing, they were kind of fragile.

On the early ones, the keys would just break off! I'm a heavy-handed player. So when I tried the Rhodes – it might have been the Hit Factory in New York – it was great. It had a richer sound than a Wurlitzer. It had better action. It was obviously a next generation instrument. Sometimes I break out the Wurlitzer when something needs a certain kind of retro, mid- '60s sound. The first time I saw a Wurlitzer was Ray Charles using it on stage. He was kind of famous for that… [plays "What'd I Say"] but, the Rhodes was obviously a technically superior instrument so I've been using it ever since.

It was smoother and more adaptable for jazz chords. It was more acoustically accurate so the notes blended better. If you have a lot of dissonance in jazz chords, it has a nicer sound… something sort of between a vibraphone and a piano. It sustained longer than a Wurlitzer. You hit a chord and it died out sooner than a Rhodes – it kind of had a compressed sound although the dynamic range was good. It just had a lot of advantages.

I'm not sure if the Rhodes was primarily responsible for our writing getting "smoother." Because both my partner Walter and I were into jazz when we were pretty young kids, we started moving back towards that. We were very enchanted in the mid-'60s with some west coast bands and blues bands, but as we continued to write, the jazz stuff that we were fans of started creeping back in so the chords got more complicated.

We'd occasionally use the acoustic piano, which was always great, of course, but, with heavy back-beat music, the Rhodes was often the right choice to make for combining jazz harmonies with a heavy beat.

I have more of a guitar style – more of a rhythmic style which evolved over the years. I'm more confident as the years have gone by. I started to play more of a two-handed style.

When I was in blues bands in college, I used to play a lot of roots in my left hand and chords in my right hand which was un-jazz-like. It was more like for playing funky stuff… kind of a primitive '60s type of Boogaloo. As I started depending more on the bass player to play the roots like in jazz, I started playing more jazz-style chords.

Most of the time, I play with some kind of phaser – a MXR phase 90 smoothes it out the best. It's not unlike a device a guitar player might use to improve sustain and make a sustained note or chord more interesting… because it changes as its sustaining. That's why I like this device. I keep it on a slow speed. If you have it on a quick speed it's very obvious, but, when you slow it down – right when you hit that "sweet spot" – it's interesting to the ear, but there's nothing wrong with the straight Rhodes.

The phaser might accentuate "the bark," if it's set right, or sometimes it doesn't… that's the, ambiguity of life, really. It's got a really quick attack. My ear's hearing not an instant attack really, but it's very quick. It's like a filter's opening up and that gives it a little wah-wah sound… like "Bubber" Miley playing trumpet or something… I think that's what people call a "bark."

I don't really have a favorite Steely Dan song that we've used the Rhodes on – we've used it on so many tunes. In the early days, I chose not to play for various reasons. I thought someone else could play the part better. Frankly, I wasn't as confident when I was younger. I liked to be in the booth listening while guys were putting in tracks; a lot of times Michael Omartian – a fantastic player.

Victor Feldman played on "Black Cow." When we moved out to the west coast, we were looking for studio players to add to the regular band. After a while we just replaced the entire band! [laughs] We knew Victor from jazz records. He played with Miles Davis, he had his own group. He was one of the first-rate modernist pianists in the late '50s and early '60s. We were looking for a percussionist and someone said, "Why don't you get Victor Feldman." I said, "Victor Feldman? He's like a jazz piano player." "That's true, but, as a day job he's a percussionist. He plays all the dates – a very popular session player." I said, "Well, great!" He played on one of the first things we did, "Do It Again" – all the percussion you hear is mostly Victor, who overdubbed a lot of percussion. He was a really nice English dude... very proper with a great sense of humor.

We started working on him to play the piano on something. Once he got to know us after a few years and realized we weren't a couple of hippie dirt bags – which we actually were, but, that we also knew a few jazz chords and things like that – he agreed to act as a player aside from his own group and play on some of our sessions. We were lucky enough to get him to play. I think Aja was the first record where he played keyboard. On "Home at Last," he played acoustic piano and on "Black Cow" he played Rhodes and did a live solo, which was a big thrill for us... to actually hear him improvising live.

He played on quite a few other things and started to really like it, you know. He also played vibes on a few things – which he was very good at – and continued to play percussion.

Joe Sample also first played on Aja. We met him through Larry Carlton who, at the time, was the guitarist for the Crusaders.

We had Larry on the date, who was also helping us with some of the lead sheets, copying and arranging. He said, "Why don't I ask Joe if he wants to do it" and I said, "Wow, that would be great." So we did a few of the Aja sessions with Joe playing Rhodes and I'm trying to think, he also played acoustic piano. What can you say? He's the funkiest. His voicings are always beautiful and appropriate and he's funny!

Greg Phillinganes was doing some work for Gary Katz who produced a lot of the Steely Dan albums. Gary suggested he come in and do some stuff. One of the first things we did for my first solo album, The Nightfly, was a cover of an old Leiber & Stoller tune called "Ruby, Baby" – he played acoustic piano on that. At the time he was young, but, everybody started hiring him for everything because he was just so great – like a prodigy, really – and very, very funky... loose, you know. At a very young age, Stevie Wonder hired him as a second keyboard because he knew all of Stevie's stuff cold! We hired him after that gig to play in the studio. He also did a great thing "The Goodbye Look." This company had been hacking me about getting this digital instrument called the Synergy, an early digital keyboard. It had this Island stop on it that sounded like a marimba. He just happened to be in the studio, so I said, "Hey Greg, why don't you try setting up this track with this instrument?" He really got into it and did something spectacular.

David Paich I met because our drummer, Jeff Porcaro, was a friend of Paich. David Paich is the son of Marty Paich, a famous arranger. Jeff and David played in bands together, went to Hollywood High School together and were both prodigies… playing sessions while they were still in high school. When Jeff started playing with us he said, "I'll bring in my pal David Paich." I think that was on *Katy Lied*. He played on "Black Friday" and a lot of other tunes on that album. He's a very clean player and a great Rhodes player. He had a great way of adapting Gospel music to commercial playing.

Paul Griffin was a very special player. The first time I heard his name was when I was in college and noted him as one of the session players on a Bob Dylan record. It might have been Highway 61. When Walter and I started doing sessions in New York, we started learning about who played on what. That was one of our things we were most curious about – who was making the music on our favorite records. We knew this was Dionne Warwick and that was Aretha Franklin, but we wanted to know who the musicians were playing on these records made in New York City. We made it our business to find out who was producing and who was playing. What we found was that on a lot of these small group soul records that we liked, a lot of the times Paul Griffin was the keyboard player – either on organ or acoustic piano. He had this fearsome Gospel style and was very creative. He always had an idea that would make the record – a little melody or a little lick. So when we came East to do some sessions for *The Royal Scam* album, we hired Paul. We also booked Chuck Rainey and Bernard Purdie. They were kind of like a section. Chuck, Bernard and Paul had been playing in studios for years on the famous Chuck Jackson and Aretha Franklin records.

I became pretty good friends with Paul and he taught me some great stuff. I would just watch his fingers. He's really this kind of unsung guy because he had a very eccentric personality that came through in his playing. He was kind of Monk-ish as a player, but, in the Rhythm and Blues field. You can't mistake him for anybody else. There's a tune on my second record, *Kamakiriad*, where he plays the organ on this tune "Snow Bound" and it's just brilliant… fantastic organ player. People who remember hits from the '60s might remember there was that [famous Chuck Jackson record], a Burt Bacharach tune that starts out on the organ. That was Paul's idea. He always had the right idea… a very soulful, great guy.

Both the organ and the Clavinet can be very funky instruments. The organ is a traditional Gospel instrument, usually used with an acoustic piano. Because the Rhodes adapts more to jazz chords, it comes in handy and can kind of glue stuff together because of its sustain properties and its tonal quality. An organ can get irritating with a lot of sustains and the is thin. Essentially, it's for punctuation and percussion. The Rhodes can really glue a rhythm arrangement together, so it can be very valuable. It doesn't have a huge amount of high end. It's a different quality from an acoustic piano.

I think there was a reason why Sonny Rollins liked piano-less groups and why Gerry Mulligan also used to like to not play with a piano. As great as pianos are, some guys like to be free to play. Piano is such a strong, dominant instrument, it kind of leads you. The same goes for a singer. Acoustic piano is hard to ignore, but a Rhodes can sit back. You can mix it low and it's still there, so it's very useful in that way.

If you want to get into why electric pianos instead of digital pianos or synthesizers, the really important thing is simply that you can tune a Rhodes. You can stretch it. A piano tuner normally "stretch-tunes" an acoustic piano. The big secret is that digital instruments and synthesizers – unless there's some new development I don't know about – the top end is flat and the bottom end is sharp... it's just mathematics. With all tempered instruments if you get the fundamentals of each octave in tune, the harmonics are going to go flat on top and sharp on the bottom. The way they adapt for that, when a tuner tunes an acoustic piano, is by cheating a little bit so that it all comes out in a much more musical way. You can do the same thing with a Rhodes, which is what they do. With synthesizers or any kind of digital pianos, you're stuck with pure temperament; where all the fundamentals are in tune, but the harmonics you hear are going to have that quality of flatness on top and sharpness at the bottom... It's even worse because the quality of harmonics on a digital instrument or synthesizer are nasty sounding too. So a Rhodes has a lot of the qualities of an acoustic piano in the sense that it's very musical... the way the harmonics blend with the fundamental.

I'm very sensitive to tuning when I'm singing. In the '80s, when they first started using digital electric piano sounds – those milk bottle through milk bottle "tone-y" ones – singers used to complain about flatness "I can't get my note! Where's my tonal center? Where do you want me to, sing?" You know what? They're used to it now. All the records are out of tune and the audience doesn't care anymore either. So what you have is a state of musical decadence and there's nothing you can do about it.

Here's a synthesizer story to go along with my antipathy towards synthesizers. There was an early commercial synthesizer called the Arp Odyssey which was kind of a useful thing... an early analog synthesizer with a square little board that had a lot of little switches on it. It wasn't very flexible... but, you could do a few things with it. It had a little ring modulator, for example.

The problem with a lot of those early analog synthesizers is that they'd go out of tune. After a 6 or 7 months, thanks to something about the oscillators or the resistors, they'd start to drift.

You'd be doing a take and 5 minutes into the take, you'd be a little flat and have to retune. After you had it for a year, after 5 seconds they'd start to drift. I got so frustrated with this Arp Odyssey... You know when you're doing a take, you're concentrating? This started to happen so often, I just took the thing and smashed it. My rage got the better of me... Then my partner started making suggestions as to what else we might do to the Arp Odyssey and you know, we ended up getting lighter fluid and we set it on fire! We defaced it in any other number of ways, then went out on the balcony of ABC Dunhill Records and just dropped it off the balcony! The guy who ran the studio thought it was so funny that he had it framed. It looked like artwork because it was essentially a destroyed musical instrument. He framed it and put it up in the studio hall for everybody to laugh at.

I also once got very frustrated with a Wurlitzer piano that had some problem with its connection. It kept going off while I was playing it. This was during a gig at some club or something. I started pounding it, it started to slide off the table and I just watched it. It fell over, crashed to the floor and I walked out. I was an arrogant teenager. I don't know if I'd do that now. I'd probably at least apologize or something.

When they first started using electric guitars in the '30s, people were very hostile towards it at first, but, the guitar players loved it because they could finally be heard. Electric instruments got some soul too, you know. I'm not that technically erudite, but, I know enough. With the help of an engineer I can usually get what I want.

Ray Charles was the first guy I ever heard playing an electric piano – a Wurlitzer piano. His huge hit "What'd I Say" had a Wurlitzer piano in it.

Also, Jesse Colin Young had this group called the Youngbloods that was among the first to have an electric piano player. They had that hit tune that went, "Come on people now, smile on your brother." Also, Al Kooper with the original Blues Project played an electric piano. He might have also played it on some Bob Dylan records. He was a good electric piano player.

Me gravitating to the Fender Rhodes was just really a natural thing, you know. As I say, it was very musical. After a while, we just always have one in the studio. I finally bought one and now I own 3 or 4. We give them names like "Our Lady of the Chamaeleos." There's a favorite, then there's Piano B, Piano C… When the favorite blows up or something, we go to Piano B. I have one in my dressing room to practice on when there's no acoustic piano available. It's just a part of my musical life.

Gerald McCauley, Donald Fagen and Benjamin Bove

Ronnie Foster

Ronnie Foster was an organ guy who got hip to the Fender Rhodes and expanded his horizons, including a deal with Blue Note Records during its funky 70's revival. After linking up with George Benson as one of two keyboardists in his world renowned Breezin' band, Ronnie really got noticed. Switching to Columbia Records, he released several albums while also appearing as a guest on great projects such as Stevie Wonder's Songs in the Key of Life, Dee Dee Bridgewater's Just Family, Stanley Turrentine's Wonderland (a tribute to the music of Stevie Wonder), Lee Ritenour's Wes Bound (a tribute to Wes Montgomery), Harvey Mason's Funk in a Mason Jar, Chaka Khan's Whatcha Gonna Do For Me, Lalo Schifrin's No One Home, Earl Klugh's Crazy For You, Flora Purim's Carry On and Will Downing's Love's the Place to Be. Ever soulful, Ronnie shares his evolution with the Rhodes.

The first time I saw a Rhodes and got a chance to play it was around '69 or '70 in Buffalo at a famous place called the Pine Grill. The name of the group was *Revolution Funk* out of Ohio and the keyboard player, who was 16 at the time, was James Ingram. It was fun and very interesting because I was 19 and mainly an organist. When Brother Jack McDuff came to town, he used to let me sit next to him on the organ bench while he played, which was very cool for me. I could see everything going! Joe Dukes, who was the drummer, would take a solo and Jack would hit this F7+9 chord and just hold it while Joe Dukes went crazy on the drums!!

I had been a student of Jimmy Smith's since I was 12. In fact, Jimmy introduced me to George Benson when I was 14. George was a big fan of Jimmy Smith. He was coming in from New York and starting the next week at this club, so he came in a night early to catch Jimmy's last set. Jimmy goes, "Hey George, this here's a young organ player Ronnie I'd like you to meet." So George and I started hanging out, then I started working with George when I was still in school.

The first recording I ever did was with Grant Green and that was one of George's idols. We did this record *Alive* (recorded for Blue Note at the Cliché Lounge in New Jersey) and George let me use his Hammond A-100. He actually took me up from New York in the Bronx to the club and we used it for that recording. That's how I got my first record deal with Blue Note. Francis Wolfe, who was the head of Blue Note at the time, said, "You want a record deal?" After the record with Grant, I did a few albums for Blue Note.

Later, George said, "Hey, I'm putting a group together. You want to come and try and play some piano?" I said, "Sure." Mind you, I was an organist. George went out to Manny's Music in New York and bought an 88 Fender Rhodes. As you know, the keys are not necessarily even throughout the whole thing... Anyway, we rehearsed and it was kind of tedious for me, because of my soft touch with the organ, to get what I wanted. Our first gig was in Toronto at the Colonial House. I'll never forget it – we're playing the gig, my solo comes up and in my head I'm playing the lick right, but, it would come out wrong because I didn't have the strength.

This went on for a few days... I kept waiting for George to call me at the hotel saying, "O.K., well, you tried," but, he hung in there with me. Eventually I got a feel for it.

The making of *Breezin'* was a very unique experience. I had the pleasure of working with the incredible pianist, Jorge Dalto, who is missed a lot. We kind of created a thing. Nobody really in that genre was doing two keyboards. There were times when he was playing acoustic or he was playing Clavinet and there were sometimes when we're both playing Rhodes and I was playing certain rhythmic things and he was doing longer legato type things. That was a great marriage. That experience will stay with me for a long time. Jorge was one of the top players... ever. All you had to do was listen to his solos on "This Masquerade" and "Affirmation." It was a totally creative environment and something that changed all of our careers.

I was with George for close to 15 years. I was the senior member of the group. Now bassist Stanley Banks is the senior. We went through the times before *Breezin'* hit, where we were doing the regular jazz circuit... I remember taking 10 and 15 minute solos each! [Laughs] When *Breezin'* hit, the format became a little different. We'd do this hour show and everything was kind of truncated. I said, "Hey George, I don't feel like I'm earnin' my money here." We were working hard but it was just a different pace than when we were "stretching out." Then we kind of adjusted it and got the energy back. That was a great experience, a lot of history there.

I met Stevie Wonder in Buffalo, my hometown. I was playing another club and you know how word gets around. Stevie was in town doing a concert and Ray Parker Jr., who was playing guitar with him at the time, had worked with me in Detroit. I talked to him and he told me, "Yeah Steve's down at so-and-so playing drums." So I run down there and catch him and his brother coming out of the club. I said, "Hey Steve, I'm Ronnie, dah-dah-dah." He says, "Oh, what sign are you?" I said "Taurus" and he said, "Oh, I am too, brother!" That was that. Then, there was another time I was playing with Grant Green, in Detroit at Mozambique. Watts Mozambique Lounge was a famous jazz club in Detroit. Steve came in and after the set, I heard, "Where's that no-playing organ player at?" I said, "Right over here you no-singing whatever." We joked with each other like that and started talking again.

I was at Blue Note then and they had this kind of convention at the Century Plaza Hotel. This was Steve's first concert after he was in that car accident, you know. We hooked up again, then after that we started really hanging. That's how our relationship built up. He was bi-coastal in New York and L.A. I was in New York at the time, so when I was off with George, I'd fly out to L.A. and we'd hang and vice versa. That's how I got involved with *Songs in the Key of Life*. I played organ on "Summer Soft." We became very, very close, both being Taurus, born a day apart, same year. I always tease him about being his elder because I'm a day older. We had a nice connection. He played drums on a few of my albums.

One time he called me and said, "I want you to help me put a band together to do this tour. You don't have to go out, just help me put the band together." I said, "Alright." Then he says, "Well, you gotta go." So we put the band together and I did that for almost three years, off and on. He's truly one of a kind because anything and everything happens on that stage. He writes tunes right in the middle of a concert. "Hey drums play this! Keyboard, bass – play this!"

One time we were in L.A. and I had Steve drive a car. He was at the top of the driveway headed into this underground parking at an apartment hotel where he was staying. He's behind the wheel and I'm out, 'cuz I was taking a picture. Some people are walking down the sidewalk kind of looking. They do a double-take and I say, "Hey Steve, turn to your left and wave." So he waves and then drives down into the parking lot. They were going, like, "WHOAH!" I actually have a picture of that.

There's another time that we were in his Brownstone on the east side. They have, like, five floors and we're at the top floor. The stairwells were very narrow. Steve says "I'm gonna race you down!" I said, "O.K." and he just takes off! I mean, like, really-really fast. When he gets to the bottom, he beats me. I said, "You know, if you could see where you were going, you wouldn't be going that fast!" Anybody who's played him in air hockey knows you cannot beat him. Everybody's like, "How's he do that?!"

The Rhodes is a very unique sound. When you touch it, you kind of forget if you're not on it all the time… what that connection is from the organic standpoint. It's different if you're playing a controller with a Rhodes sound, but, when you go back and touch it, it's kind of a give-and-take thing. I love the vibrato… the chorus. Even on organ, I don't like the Leslie when it's stopped. I like it slow, so that appeals to me coming from the organ side. It can be funky; it can be out there… It changed music in a big way. To this day, even though they might be using samples of it, it shows you the force of the instrument because it's still being used. Think about how Richard Tee used it, Chick, Herbie, George Duke… so many people have their signature with this instrument.

For a recording I borrowed one of Stevie's Rhodes. You remember when they had what is called the Dyno piano… that was not to be used on everything, but for certain things it worked. You had to be very careful. In those days, we didn't even have it in a case. You'd put the top on and throw it underneath the plane, the bus or whatever… and pray.

One time I was with George Benson at the Bottom Line in New York. I'm always experimenting with sound because I wanted to have this different sound than everybody. So I had a chorus, a couple of phase shifters and a flanger all wired in that I would use for certain things. These guys came up after the show and said, "Hey, we heard what you're doing out there. What do you got going on up here?" They looked and said "Here's our card. Give us a call. We want to bring you out to the factory." You know who that was? It was Mutron! [Laughs]

I think I got three bi-phases and the bi-phase was doing all the things that I was. It was the sound I was hearing and became a staple for my sound because I liked that movement.

DX-7 was the new kid on the block. Everybody started using it for that FM kind of sound. On a side note, within the first week or two, Stevie could program a DX-7 – if you know about how hard it was to program DX-7. Stevie was like, "Oh yeah, this sound" and he would just change it.

I had the pleasure of working on a GS-1, which was the big, FM synth that Yamaha made. It was kind of like the DX-7, but, it had some other stuff going on. I was working at Yamaha's R&D. They had one there and at that time it cost, like, 8 or 10 grand.

There's a lot of sampling going on. A Tribe Called Quest sampled "Mystic Brew" off my first album (1973's *Two Headed Freep*) for their hit "Electric Relaxation" – which I found out by accident. I was talking to a guy in England who said, "We were gonna do a remix on you, but, Tribe…" I said, "Oh, they did?" A few other people had sampled stuff. Earlier on, sampling was very creative. Then they kind of hit a wall. You started hearing, "Oh, that's so-and-so's tune underneath." They had to go back to the real deal to get the foundation to build something because they didn't have a foundation. I'm not saying that in a negative way. It's a fact.

I just think it's important that people realize that this stuff is holding up, showing the validity of music from the past.

Rodney Franklin

Rodney Franklin arrived on the scene as a highly touted young lion with a 1978 Columbia Records debut album titled In The Center. In the liner notes on the back cover, he boldly and somewhat controversially was quoted as saying, "When I was nine years old, I used to listen to Herbie (Hancock) and Chick (Corea) and say, 'I can do that!'" He has since gone on to make lasting contributions to the Quiet Storm and soul-jazz scenes with songs such as "The Groove," "Life Moves On" and the inspirational vocal gem "Song For You" (sung by Howard Smith). He has also worked with Stevie Wonder in concert. Here he details his philosophy on music and his use of the Rhodes.

My first experience with a Rhodes was back in the '60s when it first came out… I heard it on a lot of records. So I had to have one. That was the one thing I wanted when I was a kid. I would tell my dad, "Please… I gotta have that piano!" This was back in the days when everybody's working, so he actually went out and helped me get one. I got my first Rhodes in '72. I was 13 and it was like a dream come true. I thought, "I'm gonna take this thing and really learn to play it." When I was playing in school bands, we used to lug it around in the trunk all the time. You had to make sure you had your extra tines, your little pitchfork and your clippers. That way when you broke one, you'd repair 'em. It's a great instrument though.

Back then you had the Moog and those little Hohner D6 Clavinets – all the funk stuff – but, I played that first Rhodes right and left. I had no idea where it would take me. It had its own way of bringing something different out of you musically that you wouldn't get on an acoustic. That was the beginning… and here we are. Had you told me then I'd be sitting here now talking about this instrument, I never would have believed it.

A lot of the guys in my family were jazz buffs and they'd listen to everything. I came up playing jazz from around 6 years-old because that's what I was exposed to. Let me give you a short history of it. When I was 6, I got a chance to sit down next to a great artist named Oscar Peterson. A gentleman brought me into the room and said, "Why don't you just sit here and watch this guy play." I looked, he started to play and that was it. That led to Herbie, Chick, the CTI days, the Miles stuff, the Coltrane stuff – everything, all day long, that's what I was getting fed. So I was very familiar with Bud Powell, Thelonious Monk, down the list. That's the background that got me to that point.

After watching Oscar and Joe Zawinul, the principal of the elementary school was a [jazz disc jockey], so when guys would come to town, he'd have them come by the school to play. We grew up having these assemblies with God only knows who – just a long list of artists. What a concept! My personal music experience came out of not only the information of how to play the stuff, but, having a chance to look at guys that were professionals at that point in the game. You can learn this, but it can go there. Pioneers are the guys that I got a chance to look at while I was growing up.

Dr. George Butler signed me to Columbia Records back in '78, so I got my first contract when I was like 18 or 19 years-old. It was a dream come true.

You practice all these years and you put your time in and you have this dream that, maybe one day I might be able to become a recording artist and for me it happened. I was just really blessed in that way. On my first record, In the Center, George had Freddie Hubbard and some really incredible artists surround me. It was a really special time. Then we moved to the second album, You'll Never Know that had a song called "The Groove" which went gold and launched my career. It's been quite a journey ever since.

I got a chance to open up for Miles Davis – we were label mates at the time… a fabulous opportunity. I played with the Isley Brothers and Frankie Beverly for a while. I played with Stevie Wonder for several years.

My musical experience had become a fusion of two worlds. It came out the gospel world – playing in churches as a kid and practicing jazz simultaneously. At one point they met. Was that planned? No. They just met and they became friends. That's the bottom line. All of us as artists are a combination of all the experiences and different musical styles that we play coming up.

The Rhodes had a darker, warmer tone that lent itself to different colors in the spectrum that you would play, which would change the way you write. I don't generally sit down and write songs. I just sit down, start playing and soon I have one.

The melding of the classical, jazz and gospel worlds – there's the technical aspect and then there's just the fact that they are. I played all 3 of them. Over the years, they've made a lot of different types of statements and continue to; even to this day. It gets more exciting as I go. Fortunately, I've been blessed enough to make a living at it. I like the fact that there's no end. There's no getting *there*. You just play, you know [laughs].

If I'm playing some of this other stuff, the sounds are great, the samples are perfect, plus, much smaller and a lot easier to carry around than a Rhodes – but, there's something about the original design of anything. The Rhodes is the original sound. Everything that comes behind it may sound like it, but it's not *this*. When they started making samples for acoustics, I've played just about every facsimile, but, there's nothing like sitting down at a "Bosey"

[Bosendorfer] or a 12-foot Steinway. There's nothing like wood and string... how it vibrates and how it makes you play... just because of the components that are there and how it feels under the hands.

There's just something about that. I guess it's what it's got underneath the hood, so to speak, that gives it its uniqueness. I did a lot of stuff with synths. Is it the same? Nah... two different creatures all together.

Gerald McCauley and Rodney Franklin, "The Groove"

Rodney Franklin in his high school band

Robert Glasper

Robert Glasper is the name on most people's lips when it comes to the future of jazz keyboard artistry. Currently signed to Blue Note Records fronting both an acoustic trio (The Robert Glasper Trio) and an electric group (The Robert Glasper Experiment), he just earned a Grammy in 2013 for Best R&B Album for his all-star collaboration project Black Radio. Passionately melding gospel, jazz, rock, pop, R&B, classical and anything else he feels so inclined, he is of a generation that is bullish on obliterating categories, mashing music at will. He speaks of these kindred peers in depth:

The first time I heard Stevie Wonder, I might've been a year old! Ha-ha. My mom was a musician, a singer and a pianist. So, there was all kinds of music in the house. My dad was a Stevie Wonder fanatic also – they'd play Stevie in the house all the time. Obviously, there's a lot of Rhodes in Stevie's music. That's probably the first time I got acquainted with the Fender Rhodes – especially "As" with Herbie [Hancock]. My favorite Rhodes album of all time is Herbie's *Sunlight*, period. That Rhodes sound is like butter. I just want to melt it over some pancakes and just [motions spoon] eat it… or lay on it like a pillow. It's so soft and mixed with Herbie's sound, beautiful! That album was introduced to me by the late-great J-Dilla, a hip-hop producer. I was over to his place in Detroit and he said, "Hey man, have you heard this album?"

I got my first Rhodes in maybe 2001 – bought it pretty cheap off of a dude in college. It was kind of banged up... but, it worked. It's the same one I have to this day. I used to do all my gigs with that Rhodes. I live in New York and I'd take the subway with my Rhodes. It's a Stage model and it didn't have the speaker bottom, but it was still heavy! I had a milk crate cart I used to put the Rhodes on and roll it around; carry it down the stairs in the subway. I paid my dues. So, I'm not taking anything anywhere ever again! "Have it there for me. I got back problems!" [laughs].

I still use a Rhodes in my sound. You can't digitally remake a Rhodes. Something about the way the keys are made that makes you touch it a different way. So a chord just feels different and has different meaning when you play it on the real Rhodes. That same chord can have 3 different meanings with how you play it. You can't get that kind of sensitivity from a digital keyboard. Even if I don't use the Rhodes as a main part of the song, a lot of times I'll pad with it on my left hand – so it's there even though it's not there.

I use the Rhodes as a writing tool. The piano and the Rhodes invoke different emotions. The Rhodes is very lush and dark. When you use the vibrato, the speed of the vibrato is... like a heartbeat. So it will inspire me to do something different versus the piano. Sometimes I'll start a song on the piano, then, finish it on the Rhodes. If I'm stuck on a certain part of a song with piano, I may switch to playing Rhodes and it opens up a whole other world of thought. "AH YEAH" from *Black Radio* is a song all written on the Rhodes.

I'm from Houston, Texas. Once I moved to New York, my musical world got opened up. In Brooklyn, MeShell NdegeOcello lived on my street, Bilal lived 2 blocks away and Common lived, like, 6 blocks away. I was on tour with (trumpeter) Roy Hargrove in 2000 for his record *RH Factor*. My instrument was Rhodes. That whole album was Fender Rhodes. Roy and Erykah went to high school together in Dallas. Roy had MeShell sit in with us at the Monterey Jazz Festival because she was on that album. MeShell and I became good friends. She would call me to play in different things. One was *The World Has Made Me the Man of My Dreams* where I played piano, Rhodes and some keyboards.

When I finally did *Black Radio* which incorporated contemporaries of my time like Erykah, Mos Def and Musiq Soulchild, I definitely had to have MeShell on this record. She's on the sexy song. I emailed it to her because she couldn't come to the studio, so she put lyrics and a melody to it then emailed it back. That song is all Fender Rhodes. It feels live because, instead of the singer singing to music where you miss those little interactions, the whole band is playing to what the singer is doing; which is what you're doing live anyway. That way, everyone is reacting to the vocal. It is a sexy, sensual song.

Some artists I've worked with remind me of the actual Rhodes piano – like, Erykah Badu. Most of her music incorporates Rhodes, so I automatically think of her. I think the whole genre, people call it neo-soul if you will, but that whole genre was kind of evoked by the Rhodes because of the late-great J-Dilla. His beats were the beginning of that genre of music. When he (produced) Common's record

Like Water for Chocolate, there's a lot of Rhodes. It's probably 90% Rhodes. D'Angelo's even on it playing Rhodes. D'Angelo coming out with *Voodoo* and Erykah, Common, Bilal, Jill Scott – all of their albums are very Rhodes-driven. When you think of Neo-Soul or Soul music, you think of Rhodes. Even just thinking of Soul music, like Donny Hathaway, Marvin Gaye, Stevie Wonder, you think of Rhodes. It's definitely a very identifiable sound in that palette of music. It's identifiable in Hip-Hop as well because it was born out of that era of Soul music.

While I'm playing with Lalah Hathaway, she taps into this thing where she sounds exactly like her father. It's like he's singing through her… and it's not like she's trying to sound like him. When I hear that, I go to a place in my mind like his live version of Stevie's "Where Were You When I Needed You."

Gretchen (Parlato) I met maybe around 2004 or 2005 – the most soulful white girl I know because she loves Soul music. She doesn't try to sing like that either. Gretchen just loves it and sounds the way she sounds. We hooked up and started writing together around 2006 on one of her albums. She said, "I want to do SWV's 'Weak'." I was like, "Huh?" I came up with that arrangement on Rhodes at my house. When you come to my house, as soon as you walk in my door, the first thing you hit is the Rhodes. When I had an idea walking around outside, I would walk in and go right to my Rhodes. Anyhow, she has this whispery, really melancholy, beautiful, soft voice and you mix it with the Rhodes… it's a breath of fresh air.

I worked with Carly Simon in 2002/2003. Christian McBride, a good friend and a great bassist, was her Musical Director at the time. She was doing a comeback concert because she hadn't performed in a while, so she did these shows at the Apollo Theatre.

With certain people's music, I'll listen to the recordings and try to get the basics of what they have, but when it's live, you want to give people what they reminisce about as-well-as something fresh. Sometimes I used Rhodes on songs that didn't have Rhodes. I like playing piano and Rhodes together sometimes. So, on "You're So Vain" I was sneaking Rhodes in. It was a great experience! Actually, Carly bought me my first iPod!! [laughs].

I've loved "Smells Like Teen Spirit" since it came out… such a beautiful song. It's really "rocked out" but, the beauty is right under there. The lyrics are so dope and the melody, so pretty. I started playing it in my piano trio a few years ago. Then, when my experiment band started jumping off, Casey does Vocoder, so I was like, "We can do lyrics now!" Songs translate better when you can sing the lyrics. I have an arrangement where I changed the chords. It gives it a real urban twist with the Rhodes; made it accessible to the urban community. That song is one of the most popular songs on *Black Radio*. Even if you don't listen to Rock music, you know "Teen Spirit."

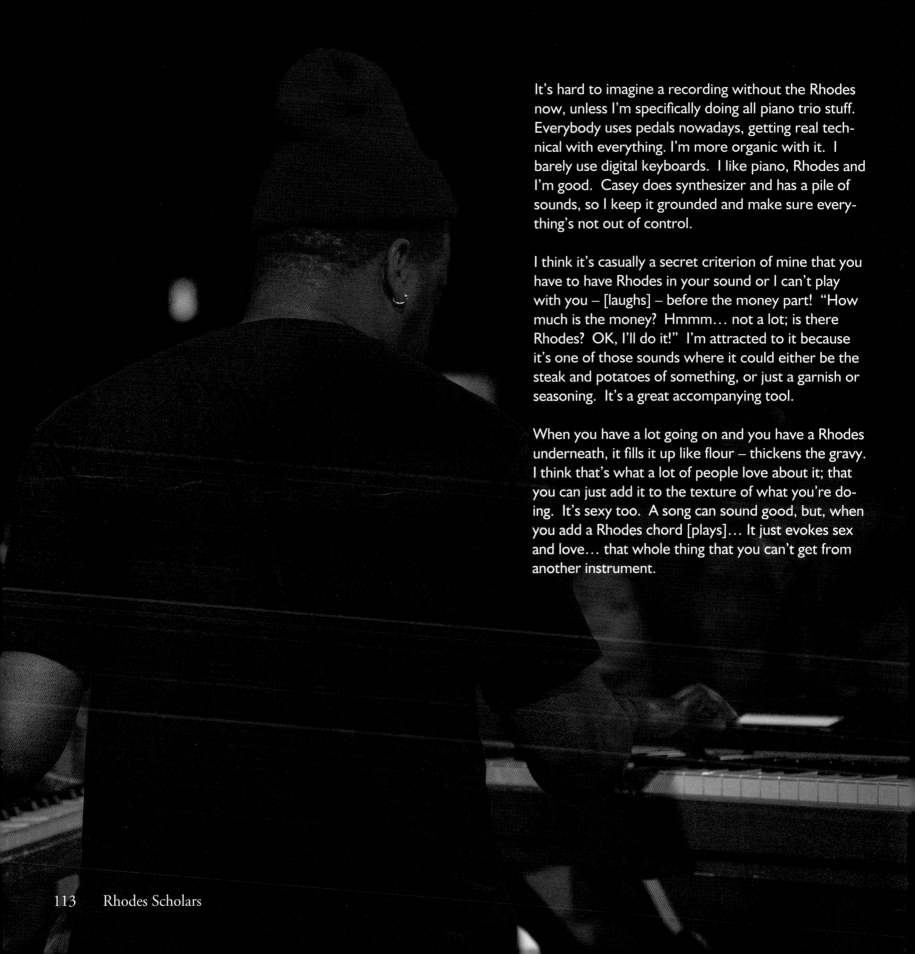

It's hard to imagine a recording without the Rhodes now, unless I'm specifically doing all piano trio stuff. Everybody uses pedals nowadays, getting real technical with everything. I'm more organic with it. I barely use digital keyboards. I like piano, Rhodes and I'm good. Casey does synthesizer and has a pile of sounds, so I keep it grounded and make sure everything's not out of control.

I think it's casually a secret criterion of mine that you have to have Rhodes in your sound or I can't play with you – [laughs] – before the money part! "How much is the money? Hmmm... not a lot; is there Rhodes? OK, I'll do it!" I'm attracted to it because it's one of those sounds where it could either be the steak and potatoes of something, or just a garnish or seasoning. It's a great accompanying tool.

When you have a lot going on and you have a Rhodes underneath, it fills it up like flour – thickens the gravy. I think that's what a lot of people love about it; that you can just add it to the texture of what you're doing. It's sexy too. A song can sound good, but, when you add a Rhodes chord [plays]... It just evokes sex and love... that whole thing that you can't get from another instrument.

Dave Grusin

Be it as a composer, a producer or a player, Dave Grusin has made especially beautiful use of the Fender Rhodes in recordings and in motion pictures. He's recorded a string of albums as a leader under his own name, as a member of the west coast session collective Friendship and in pairings with both his baby brother / fellow keyboardist Don Grusin and guitarist Lee Ritenour. From funky stuff such as television's well known Sammy Davis Jr.-sung "Baretta's Theme (Keep Your Eye On The Sparrow)" and the definitive '70s action film score for "3 Days of The Condor"(the theme of which he himself has recorded three times and was also covered marvelously by the L.A. session collective Rhythm Heritage) to the creamy, dreamy accompaniment he provided for meditative saxophonist John Klemmer on his contemporary jazz classic Touch, laying a sweltering harmonic bed under Quincy Jones' evocative version of "Summer in the City," and scores of beloved Quiet Storm albums he and his business partner Larry Rosen helmed for artists such as Jon Lucien, Noel Pointer, Earl Klugh, Angela Bofill, Patti Austin, Yutaka Yokokura, Dave Valentin, Tom Browne and more (many for their lucrative GRP imprint), the man is truly a mood master when it comes to the Fender Rhodes. Here he recounts his history with the Rhodes in a variety of unforgettable contexts.

I can't remember the first time I played the instrument, but it certainly wasn't on a session. Somebody showed it to me. The thing that was intriguing to me about any electronic keyboard, as opposed to the piano, was the sustain sound that was possible… a covered, tonal quality that made it possible to play a little more like a guitar player, particularly if you voiced chords in a certain way. A guy named George Van Eps had a 6-string guitar, played bass and played a lot of chords with beautiful voicings. This instrument was the first time that I thought the keyboard had a chance of digging into those kind of harmonies and that kind of sensibility. That's what really attracted me in the first place – not as a substitute for a piano – but, a totally different animal.

I graduated from college in the middle '50s and played jazz a long time before that. When I went to New York in '58/'59, I had big band favorites and piano player favorites that knocked me out, but I knew that I would never be able to do that stuff… I'm talking about Art Tatum and Oscar Peterson – just unbelievable kind of playing. Jazz itself was pretty acoustic when I was first starting in terms of pianos and keyboards. Later people like Herbie and Chick are great examples, but, there were older guys, more my age, that were involved in it.

When the Rhodes started to take over, one of the landmarks was when Miles finally OK'd using an electric instrument in his band. That put a stamp of approval on it and the popularity of this thing just exploded. At that time it was a very modern sound and everybody was trying to do the new "new" thing – to be unique with whatever music they were dealing with.

A lot of people impressed me over the years, Bob James for example. Quincy Jones did his fantastic big band album *Walking in Space* (1969) that Bob played on.

Larry and I did an album with Earl Klugh (*Earl Klugh on Blue Note* – 1976) – an acoustic guitar player who was playing rhythm for George Benson at that time. When he became the soloist, the fact that my keyboard behind this acoustic nylon string thing was electric was a fantastic thing. It really sounded like a new kind of music. It evolved over the years. Over the many sessions that I did from the early '70s on, there was never one that didn't have a Rhodes on the set.

Richard Tee was an unbelievable pianist technically… not that he ever showed that off so much. He was probably the best Gospel piano player I ever heard. You know, one of his standing gigs was when some studio bought a brand new piano that was stiff they'd hire Richard to come in for 6 hours and pound it – just pound the hell out of it for 6 hours to make it playable! He had enormous chops and power, but, he really knew how to touch the Rhodes in an incredible way. There's a sensibility about touching a key that reacts a certain way because of the mechanism on a Rhodes that does not exist on any synthesizer. So Richard for me, still, is a big hero in terms of Fender Rhodes.

I got to play on some dates with Richard where he played Rhodes or organ and I played the piano. He was also working with Aretha in those days.

I got to play with Aretha down the road on a live thing where she was playing piano and singing "Somewhere" (from "West Side Story"). I was sitting with a Rhodes and playing right with her… such a thrill. People that used this instrument for those sensibilities were remarkable to me. In fact, the whole sound of this thing had a lot to do with the '60s into the '70s in terms of what we used to call R&B music. In the right hands – it was so locked into part of how that music is supposed to feel.

I bought my brother Don Grusin the first Rhodes he ever had. I loaned him the money and do you know I haven't seen that money yet? [Laughs] I'm seven years older than Don, but he developed his own touch to this thing. When I listen to those old records we did together and others he did on his own, I know exactly who's playing that instrument. The beauty of the Rhodes is that you can fit yourself into its personality because of the variations in touch, how fast it reacts and how it speaks back. If it were a synthesizer it would be called velocity – the V button. That was Don's thing and he still owns it!

To be brothers that are both piano players and to be able to play together is special. We've since done stuff with two acoustic pianos but circumstances are usually that there's only one acoustic piano. If there's a Rhodes you have a chance of doing some interplay and duets that are very nice.

The other monster with this instrument is Chick Corea. He may be the cleanest player of this thing I've ever heard. He was able to translate all those fantastic things he could do on an acoustic piano and make them sound clean as ever on this electronic instrument, which is not the easiest thing.

I used to use the Rhodes a lot in film scores. I haven't for some years. With the rise of the synthesizer, if there's another keyboard player on the date, it's probably what they're going to bring. Instead of hauling a bunch of instruments down, you can find a similar sound to this on Yamaha instruments. For instance, the old DX-7 had 3 or 4 Fender Rhodes sounds.

They weren't exactly right, but they could pass… particularly under a pad in an orchestral situation. I primarily used it as a rhythm instrument. This sound against a harder edged rhythm guitar was fine. They didn't conflict with each other.

Rhodes was the first thing you hear in "3 Days of The Condor" (1975) – a big part of the sound. It was a way to get it started. The line was a Chamberlin and a synthesizer played like a flute patch. The Rhodes was actually the rhythm part underneath – a lifesaver in a lot of ways. The Rhodes was a common denominator for so many keyboardists and people that wrote film scores as well. Not everybody was sure what it was going to sound like, but, they knew enough about it and knew it was going to be the keyboard that did the job. It has a bell quality to it and it's great doubled with other lines as well. If there's a flute section playing a melody line up high, the Rhodes underneath it puts the attack on the edge of the percussive part of the line. It was amazing… amazing!

I just heard a track this afternoon from "The Goonies" (1985), a kid's film I did 25 years ago. We've been playing some of that orchestral kind of music on concerts with symphony orchestras.

Today I heard the end credits – a nice theme that I'd totally forgotten about – and this piano was all over the place... this piano, plus synthesizers and so forth, in an orchestral setting. I can't believe that much time has gone by, but, things do keep changing and on that same end title track, with an orchestra, this sound, kind of a harpsichord, probably a synthesized harpsichord somebody was playing and Steve Schaeffer was playing drums and there were some electric toms in the middle of it. I had this sense that it was symphonic, but, in those years, a lot of us were afraid to leave that element out of straight film scores. John Williams never worries about that stuff. He doesn't have to have a backbeat going on in the middle of these things in order for people to like it. So it's funny how things change.

I met Quincy Jones in the late '50s in Europe. We did a couple of dates in New York. He decided to come out to the West Coast and do film scores about the same time I moved out, so I turned out to be the piano player on a lot of his scores from that era. Then I did a lot of work with small groups at (engineer) Rudy Van Gelder's place in New Jersey with the Rhodes. It got to the point where somebody said, "Does anybody play piano anymore?" It was like a sonic boom for keyboard players. You spend your life learning how to touch an acoustic piano in the right way, but with the Rhodes, you can touch it, then change things with all the effects that were possible... all the stuff that guitar players were able to do with phase shifters and tape delay, you could do on this thing. It was like a miracle for us.

Quincy and me – a lot in the '70s. One night when he called me, we were working on an album for The Brothers Johnson. There were some vocals, but, there was a lot of instrumental stuff. He called me around 8 o'clock – I was just finishing dinner – and he said, "What're you doing tonight? Can you come down to Westlake Studios? We've got a couple of synths here and could use a couple little overdubs." So I came down, he put up all the tracks and they had this unbelievable groove going, but, no melody. I said, "What do you want me to play?" "Well, what kind of tune do you think would go with a thing like this?" So what he really wanted me to do was come down to write and record on this song – which I did! (The song is "Thunder Thumbs and Lightning Licks" from The Brothers Johnson's debut LP, Look Out For #1. Not surprisingly, it was also prominently utilized in a movie score – the Bill Cosby / Raquel Welch / Harvey Keitel comedy "Mother, Jugs & Speed"). It was so much fun working that way with him.

Sergio Mendes was a big proponent of the Rhodes in Brazilian music – a good acoustic piano player too. Deodato really put this on the map in terms of his music too, but, there was another piano player named, Joao Donato who was so inventive in terms of his voicing and it made it sound like a different animal again. You put any melody over it and it'll have that Samba thing – a great utilitarian thing to use for those kinds of patterns.

When I was working with Sergio, I didn't play that much. He would do the tracks then I would write the strings and orchestral sweetener to these things. One time, though, we went to Rio and played 6 nights a week at a theater that this wealthy publisher owned. The shows started about 8 o'clock and we were out by 10:30. That's almost dinner time down there.

His group featured singer Lani Hall and percussionist Paulinho DaCosta who was very visual with his stuff. We had just a wonderful time. It was like having a steady gig. That's the only time I remember playing with Sergio. If he was playing Rhodes, it was probably acoustic piano that I was playing.

Lee Ritenour and I did a bunch of albums together over the years and this was an integral part of the band — more than the acoustic piano in the beginning. There is a club here in Los Angeles called The Baked Potato — still there — and we had a Tuesday night residency. It was Lee, Harvey Mason, Ernie Watts… Anyway, it was like, bowling night! We played these gigs for years, every Tuesday night. Prior to that, it was another club called Dante's that isn't there anymore.

We used to do other people's material — some Jeff Beck and Chick Corea's stuff… our version of these things and this was the piano… the workhorse, for sure.

I met Harold Rhodes briefly at some music event years ago. I didn't get to know Harold that well, but everything I knew about him was intriguing. He had a real different way of looking at science. For instance, towards the end, he was really fascinated by string vibrations. He said, "Vibrations, because of the inharmonic complexity, shouldn't be on a string. It should be on a piece of metal!" [Laughs] He was really locked into not only what it sounded like, but, the theory behind it. It was just fascinating to me.

Gerald McCauley and Dave Grusin

Don Grusin

Beyond his albums as a leader, Don Grusin is the consummate team player. As a member of bands stretching from the Brazilian based Kitchen to the L.A. all-star aggregate Friendship to duo piano projects with the late, great Vince Guaraldi and his own brother Dave Grusin, Don has been the enthusiastic adhesive for a lot of great pan-cultural music. His humble personality beautifully and naturally lends itself to the role of "support" to greats such as Leon Ware (their duo Cd Candlelight), Toots Thielemans, Brenda Russell, Randy Crawford, Lee Ritenour, Dori Caymi and more. Dave's younger brother plays well with others and shares about it all below.

The first time I heard a Fender Rhodes was when Bob James won a national contest with his trio. Then I heard my brother Dave play one. He didn't own one at the time, but, he played one for a film. The first one I owned was in Aspen, Colorado. I got it because I didn't have an acoustic piano when I was living there. Vince Guaraldi (San Francisco based pianist best known for the hit "Cast Your Fate to The Wind" and the classic Charlie Brown / Peanuts TV special scores) was a buddy of mine. He used to come and play and he said, "Why don't you have an instrument? You need to get a Rhodes!" So I did. I had a square-back Volkswagen. Remember the old Beatles had the long sunroof over the top? I could stick the Rhodes out the top – my lil' trick! I went to gigs like that.

Vince had little tiny fingers… an octave spread at the most. When I moved to Northern California in '73 or so, we had a band together. He played piano or I played piano, and he played Rhodes or I played Rhodes. We had a bass player named Seward McCain and Mike Clark might have been the drummer. We were good buddies, knew the standards and had a great time. We played at a place in Menlo Park called Butterfields which was an upscale sort of club… right before the high-tech thing happened. Stanford University was there. Bless his soul, Vince passed away in the mid-'70s… but, the Rhodes and him were interchangeable.

I like to play Rhodes with the piano – left hand on the piano, right hand on the Rhodes. I love that combination… how the two sounds sort of marry each other.

I worked with Quincy Jones on (saxophonist) Ernie Watts' *Chariots of Fire* (Qwest / WB – 1982). He got a Grammy for that album… and that album was all Fender Rhodes! Quincy would say, "Don't worry about it, just play it! You know what to do." He's the reason I got into music, actually. I was teaching on a small campus called Foothill College up in Northern California and working with a (Latin-Jazz-Rock) band called Azteca. I was thinking I could be a teacher, then on the weekends play music and that would be fine. Then Quincy called and said, "Do you want to go to Japan with this super-band I'm putting together?" I said, "Why are you picking me with all the guys down in L.A. you know?" He said, "I think it might be time for you to decide what you're going to do with your life."

He had seen me with Azteca. The band was Pete Escovedo, his daughter Sheila Escovedo… that gang of banditos from the East Bay. Q was also very instrumental in my additional connection to Rhodes because he had an 88 Rhodes at his house… just a beautiful Rhodes. That was a real big turning point for me.

I gave my notice at the school, came down to Los Angeles and started trying to prove it, you know. He opened the door for me to be involved in albums with him like *Mellow Madness* featuring (singer / songwriter) Leon Ware, (drummer) Harvey Mason and all those guys who I've since done lots of stuff with. "Hire Don, he can probably do it," Quincy would say. We became brothers… after all this time.

As Rhodes players, you had to learn how to tune these guys. After they'd been joggling around in the back of a truck from cartage, then the guys would just throw em on the floor, you had to tweak 'em. I could tell you stories…

There were four instruments you had to play growing up. There was the Clavinet, B-3 organ, acoustic piano and the Fender Rhodes. Azteca had three keyboard players at one time. Pete Escovedo and his brother Coke wanted to have this huge sound. George DiQuatro was one of the players and I think he played the Rhodes. Then they ran out of money because it was too expensive to carry three keyboard players. So they said, "Don, can you play organ?" I said, "Yeah. I played organ in Church! I bet I could do it." Actually… I hadn't played much organ.

Joe Zawinul took all of that much, much further. If I had to say so, he's my biggest mentor – not only because of his chops, but, his ideas to invent the strangest Arp 2600 kinds of things, all his crazy sounds and his willingness to use his voice while he's doing it. Herbie, Chick and Keith Jarrett did it too, but, the way Joe would use this instrument was like heaven. His classical chops were so good. Just an amazing guy, rest his soul.

Alex Acuña had been playing with Weather Report on *Black Market* (percussion) and *Heavy Weather* (drums), and ended up working with me in Lee Ritenour's band Friendship (the L.A. all-star band of session greats with Ernie Watts, Steve Foreman and Abraham Laboriel). From listening to two different major stars – Miles when he turned electric and Joe when he progressed to his own direction – we wrote a song based on what Joe likes to do titled, "Let's Not Talk About It."

I also wrote the song "Waterwings" for that *Friendship* album (1979) on the Fender Rhodes. I had a little house in Ocean Park on 6th Street in California. From one of the windows if you looked just right, you could see the ocean it was 6 or 7 blocks up from the beach. (Bassist) Abraham Laboriel and I met in the '70s, when he first came to Los Angeles. He and I invented a language called "Pori di Talla" which went with the melody I wrote for him on "Waterwings." It came really fast. First of all, I wanted to try to get my left hand to do more work because normally it just [comps]. Second, Abraham was hungry for something he could play as a solo, where he could sing and play simultaneously (a la George Benson on guitar).

Friendship got a great one-album deal from Elektra Records – in the days of the advance. We got to travel too. Bands like Tower of Power or Spyro Gyra would open for us. In Europe, we did festivals like Montreux in Switzerland. I just kept thinking, "Wow, this is a nice combination, we're all making a little money and we're doing really well." Then, like a year later, because our music didn't reach a wide enough demographic at radio, WE were opening for Spyro Gyra and Tower of Power. It was funny… Karmic-like.

I went to see Richard Tee at an A&M Records session. He had this sound… He would use the Rhodes that belonged to A&M, but, he would carry the Small Stone and it just had that sexy, groovy-chorusy-phasery kind of thing that none of the other effects had. For the longest time until we started getting interested in other kinds of sounds, that was like THE kit. I also used a Boss Chorus that I had hot-rodded by a guy named Ralph Skelton (of Pacific Innovative Electronics) here in town. I could click on the switch with a foot pedal or a switch up here and I could use the vibrato to make the Rhodes become like a synthesizer.

Before Eddy Reynolds got my piano, I had to use an EQ. After Eddy Reynolds re-EQed it with some kind of 3-stage thing inside, he said, "You want me to make your piano sound good?" I said, "Well, yeah." He goes, "Well, I'm going to have to keep it for awhile because I'm out on the road. I'll do it when I get back!" When he did, BOY did it make it a difference. It was just glorious! It took the possible EQs from here to here [expands hands] – very strong. You could compete with loud guitar players, which was the whole idea.

Brazilian musicians like Milton Nascimiento and Gilberto Gil love the Rhodes. Gilberto came to the US to do his first record and Sergio Mendes was a friend. Sergio said, "I'm not going to have enough time to work with Gilberto. Would you mind?" Would I mind?! So he did the record *Nightingale* (1979). We used the Rhodes – we did not use an acoustic piano that I recall – and it was a huge hit.

At the time, I thought I was interested in Brazilian music, but, what it was is Tropicale – Tropicalismo music from the Caribbean – which Gilberto Gil adopted and melded into Brazilian Music. Then there's Ivan Lins who's got all those great chords that everybody learned. Show him a chord and he'd go, "Oh yeah, new song!" I'm still doing some stuff with those guys… still working on some things in Brazil.

These Rhodes are invincible! They allow you to not think the way you would think with a synthesizer. It allows for concentrated focus… you become comfortable in the sound and then you only play stuff that goes with it.

From the film standpoint, it was really easy to find a pad or undercarriage for certain kinds of scenes that the Rhodes was such a natural for… partly because of the sustainability of the notes that can last forever… You couldn't do that with a piano, so in the original sense of recording for film it was really pretty amazing. I worked on most of Dave's films as the second keyboard player. Mostly it was Rhodes, sometimes a synthesizer or the big refrigerator full of dials and cords. There were a lot of accidents. I remember orchestras not showing up or technical difficulties at the film studio. The great thing about this is if you had electricity, then you always had this – a good back up!

I got to meet Harold Rhodes. I think it was in Fullerton. Some guys with a cartage company were going down there because they dealt with him a lot. I got to sit with him and we chewed the fat for a couple of hours. He was very respectful, very genteel and so proud of what he'd done – how he'd put this thing together. I'm getting choked up thinking about him… but, he was a great guy. I don't remember the exact conversation that we had, but, I remember feeling, like, I'm in the presence of a master guy. He was.

I haven't been playing Rhodes recently. I'm in Boulder teaching, so I didn't take it with me. This conversation is making me feel like I gotta drag that guy out of the garage!

Gerald McCauley, Don Grusin and Benjamin Bove

Onaje Allan Gumbs

The name Onaje is the Nigerian delineation for "The Sensitive One" or "Owner of the Feeling" and Onaje Allan Gumbs has been living up to his name righteously by offering outstanding works as a player, composer, arranger, producer and artist. Among his credits are composing the Quiet Storm staple "Quiet Passion," arranging the song that launched Phyllis Hyman "Betcha By Golly Wow" (for Norman Connors' seminal 1976 album You Are My Starship), Stanley Jordan's chart-topping interpretation of the Michael Jackson classic "The Lady in My Life" and the definitive version of Patrice Rushen's "Sojourn" (from Kevin Eubanks' album The Heat of Heat – 1987).

Still going strong as a leader and sideman with artists ranging from Cassandra Wilson, Will Downing and late-greats Gwen Guthrie and Nat Adderley to Billy Cobham, Avery Sharpe and R&B singer JOE, Onaje reflects on the Rhodes here with exquisite "sensitivity."

In 1971, I'd just gotten out of school and there was a bass player named Teruo Nakamura. I'd heard talk about this instrument you could carry around to different gigs. Teruo was selling his Rhodes for $500, so my father put up the money and I bought Teruo's suitcase model Rhodes. Getting around was incredibly difficult because I didn't have my own car. So a friend who had a Datsun 280-Z would help me take it to the gig – one part at a time.

He'd take the top part, go to the gig, then come back, get the bottom part, take it to the gig and set it up. When the gig was over, he'd break it down, take the speaker part, we'd bring that home, then go back to the club and get the other part... 'cause it was too big to fit in the sports car by itself, but, I loved the instrument even though it was bulky.

I think Herbie kind of started the little electronic doo-dads that were attached to, like the Echoplex and the Phase Shifter. I fell in love with the Echoplex. I used it on a lot of gigs when I replaced Nat Adderley Jr. in a group called Natural Essence back in 1972 which included alto saxophonist / leader Rasheed Ali, tenor sax man Courtney Wynters, singer Yvonne Fletcher, trombonist Earl McIntyre, trumpeter Ron Taylor, Eric Saunders on bass and Buddy Williams on drums. Later Alex Blake and David Williams were also in that band.

Billy Cobham was our producer. I was living in Buffalo then, so they flew me down and of course, my Rhodes was with me. The Echoplex was something that I just loved... hearing the tones coming back at you and you could bend the notes.

Norman Connors was the first one I did a lot of Rhodes work with. He was looking for somebody who could arrange and compose a piece that had Brazilian elements and used strings.

Well, while I was in college I started to get into writing for strings, so when I graduated, I had all this music. He was up there with Pharaoh Sanders and Herbie had just finished his week at this club in Buffalo called the Revilot Lounge. I tapped Norman on the shoulder and said, "I'm the guy to do your work." He agreed.

When I got to New York, he didn't have a budget to rent a Rhodes, so he used my Rhodes on his album, *Dark of Light* (Cobblestone – 1972). He said he was gonna tune it, but when we got to the studio, Herbie Hancock was playing my Rhodes as is, okay. When the record came out, there was a review that said, "...the record sounds great, but, the Rhodes is conspicuously out of tune."

That's one thing about this instrument. It can go out of tune in a minute. As the years progressed, I found myself adjusting my ears so that the Rhodes wouldn't sound out of tune, but, he used the Echoplex on that piece in 1972 and I was very influenced by that usage of the instrument and that device. When I started recording with Norman myself, I did Herbie's "Maiden Voyage" and utilized the Echoplex... I used it on the whole *Saturday Night Special* album. When the vibrato is too fast, it sounds crazy, but, when it's a nice speed back and forth, this warm, lovely sound just penetrates the whole music.

For me, the Rhodes was a separate keyboard unto itself. You had to have a different technique to play the Rhodes. You couldn't just play it like the piano because the notes ring out and just stay there until you let go of the pedal, adding a whole 'nother thing to the music, especially ballads.

When I recorded "Betcha By Golly Wow" with Norman Connors, Jean Carn was supposed to sing that song. No one knew who Phyllis Hyman was, but Norman told her, "I have just the song for you!" With *You Are My Starship* (Buddah – 1976) being an album that had contemporary R&B flavors, Norman saw me as the guy who could balance out the jazz and the R&B.

If you wanted to get that sound at that point in history – the '70s – the Rhodes was the instrument you had to use. If you used the acoustic piano in the context, all of a sudden it was either considered R&B, Gospel or Jazz. The Rhodes aligned the music with a more contemporary R&B flavor. It's a warm instrument and that's one reason I used it for the arrangement.

Whether it's acoustic or any electronic instrument, you have to be mindful that the voice is up front telling the story. As a keyboardist, you want to stay under the artist giving support to the performance. Using certain chords you can attain a kind of fluidity. You can slide into the chords and they kind of creep up on ya… yet, be very unobtrusive to the soloist. Phyllis had to overdub her vocal – she wasn't singing with the track – so we made sure she wasn't overshadowed by the accompaniment.

When I'm constructing an arrangement, the chords that I'm going to use come first – I come with the arrangement then the Rhodes will adjust to the flow of the arrangement. As far as colors and attitude, with an acoustic piano, you can play busier without being obtrusive.

With the Rhodes, you have to be very judicious and discreet about what note you choose. The touch is not as touch sensitive as a piano, so you have to be really careful.

With a piano you can choose almost any note because you have more control in how you depress the key. With the Rhodes, it is very important that you stay in an octave that's not going to intrude on the vocal, because it will cut through very easily.

Staying in the middle register keeps it in a nice place where the chords are close, they can be lush and they can really sustain. When you get too high – unless you're doing a solo – it can become obtrusive.

So the Rhodes has a definite sense of purpose if used right… if you understand where the song's going, where the vocal is going and how you can support. With the Rhodes you have to be totally aware of what notes you're gonna use because you don't want to get in the way. You don't want to draw attention to yourself.

First influential Rhodes records: I think of Freddie Hubbard's *Red Clay* (1970, the inaugural release on CTI Records as an independent entity). There was no acoustic piano on that album. Herbie Hancock played the Rhodes and did a wonderful job. I think of Grover Washington Jr.'s records on Kudu / CTI (which featured Bob James as arranger and player) made a lot of use of the Rhodes. I think of Quincy Jones "Killer Joe" from *Walking in Space* (BJ again).

That had an indelible effect on how people view that instrument because you usually didn't hear anything other than acoustic piano on a straight-ahead song. Quincy using an electronic keyboard on a straight-ahead piece turned the tides of how people saw the instrument and its usage.

D'Angelo is one of the first R&B artists to really bring the Rhodes back to the forefront, Erykah Badu and Jill Scott also made use of it to a good degree on their records.

Herbie Hancock, Bob James, Dave Grusin, Joe Sample and Joe Zawinul are the guys that really saw the Rhodes as an integral part of their musical projection and presentation. Herbie mastered it as a solo instrument, Bob James as more of a color and Grusin especially in film scores, most notably "Three Days of The Condor." That use of the Rhodes was so integral to what he presented in the score because it set up the whole vibe for the musical adaptation. Herbie was at the forefront of the use and did some film scoring work… "Death Wish" was a film that caught my ear. I was a student of film – Henry Mancini was one of the composers that got my ear when I was 8 years-old. Up to that point, you were listening to acoustic piano. When you got to the '70s, people like Dave Grusin and Herbie used the instrument to full effect in dramatic scores.

Patrice Rushen had an indelible effect on me with the Rhodes. I was in L.A. with Nat Adderley and invited Patrice down to see us at the old Concerts by the Sea. I said, "Patrice, I just love how your Rhodes sounds." She said, "Well, I'll take you to where I had my Rhodes worked on." I forget what kind of car she had, but, we put my Rhodes into the car, drove out to the Fender factory and this cat was there.

For $75, he hooked up my Rhodes just like Patrice's Rhodes and I never had to worry about it going out of tune or anything like that. It would just stand up to anything. The touch and the sound were so incredible… so crisp and expressive at the same time.

Then there was Richard Tee with his use of the chorus on a lot of albums for artists like Roberta Flack ("Making Love") and Barbara Streisand ("Guilty"). When he played, you knew it was Richard Tee. He was an incredible keyboardist with such life and vibrancy in his playing. He'd put his shoulder into it, rock back and forth, be smiling and just bring the house down! I did a hit once and Ralph McDonald (who played often with Tee) was on the gig. I played so hard, he and the other guys turned around like, "Wait a minute… who's that playing?!" I said, "Yep, I channeled him… Richard in the house!!"

Donald Blackman and Bernard Wright – who both played with Lenny White – are unsung heroes of the Rhodes. Bernard had a Top 10 dance hit called "Who Do You Love" (1985) – he's one of those cats! Donald Fagen and Steely Dan showed that the Rhodes could be adaptable. George Duke put the funk in the Rhodes and expanded upon it over all adaptability. Lonnie Liston Smith's album *Expansions* made major use of the vibrato creating an ethereality that became his signature.

The artist that I learned a lot from, who didn't use Rhodes a lot, but we did some recordings utilizing the Rhodes because he was a heavy straight-ahead cat, was the late Woody Shaw. On his album *The Moontrane* (Muse – 1975), there was a tune called "Katrina Ballerina" that I felt the Rhodes better than the acoustic piano.

Then when Woody signed to Columbia Records, he asked me to compose an original piece, so I wrote "Every Time I See You" for his album *Rosewood* (1978). The Rhodes was used solely for color, so when I did the acoustic piano solo, the Rhodes was a cushion. So I learned how to coordinate playing both instruments, overdub one over another and on a lot of gigs, sometimes I would actually play them together. (Note: This song was also recorded in 1978 with the title "Everytime I See You" by Roy Ayers as a sexy vocal – with Philip Woo on Rhodes – for his album *You Send Me* on Polydor Records).

When I played with Nat Adderley in the mid-'70s, I would use the piano and the Rhodes simultaneously to create a polytonal effect, which not many other cats were doing. One tune I wish I had done on the Rhodes is "Quiet Passion" (a Quiet Storm classic from his 1990 album *That Special Part of Me* on Zebra Records). The instrument I did use, the DX-7, was an attempt to bring out the color that was started with the Rhodes sound.

The Rhodes came at a time for cats when you come across a gig where there's no piano. When we had our Fender Rhodes, we knew it was going to sound good. It empowered us as keyboard players. For me, it lifted a burden of worry on the gig. I have my own Fender Rhodes just like you have your drum set, you have your bass and you have your trumpet. I was no longer at the mercy of the club or the concert hall. I could get the sound I wanted and customize it to my touch. I think it only kind of fell out of favor because of its size and lack of mobility. Other keyboards like the DX-7 came in, were really portable and cashed in on what people thought they got from the Rhodes, but, after 20 or so years went by, people realized it's the original Rhodes sound that they really want.

Now even new instruments by other companies still go back to the Rhodes. You can punch up, say, "Herbie Rhodes" or this Rhodes or that Rhodes with Echoplex… but, they realize that this is the daddy. The sound will always be here. It's a sound that revolutionized how people look at keyboards. I'm glad I was around when it first started getting its momentum and proud to have played on some recordings that were pivotal in its development.

Brian Jackson, Onaje Allan Gumbs and Gerald McCaulley

Ellis Hall

Savannah, GA-born and Boston-raised singer-pianist Ellis Hall has enjoyed an ironically colorful career for a blind man, as you will soon read. He was featured on Tower of Power's 1987 album Power singing his now-classic and perennial Quiet Storm ballad "Some Days Were Meant for Rain," he was the featured singer on pop instrumentalist Kenny G's multi-platinum breakthrough album, Duotones, singing a cover of the old Junior Walker & The All-Stars hit "What Does it Take (To Win Your Love)." He recorded and co-produced an album for Ray Charles Crossover Records label titled Straight Ahead, that wound up being among Brother Ray's final productions.

The first Rhodes song that comes to my mind is "Riders on the Storm" (by Los Angeles rock quartet The Doors) – that and some of the jazz that Mr. Herbie Hancock played with Miles Davis in the '60s. I thought, "What an amazing sound… " It didn't blossom into what I thought it could be until the '70s with *Music of My Mind*, Stevie Wonder's album with all those different flavors… Stevie had so many songs that featured the Rhodes…

Myself, I had a suitcase Rhodes. Then I got a stage Rhodes because it was too hard to cart. Guys hated to see me coming 'cause I had a B-3 (organ) AND a Rhodes! Needless to say, I didn't have a lot of close friends when it came to handling equipment, but the Rhodes always had a fascinating, incredible sound… very inspiring for writing, you know. Even Ray Charles, in the '70s, got into using the Rhodes very heavily. I also remember Phoebe Snow's recording of "No Regrets" [featuring the late Don Grolnick on Rhodes from her sophomore album, *Second Childhood* in 1976].

I'd also say Mr. Donny Hathaway on his *Extension of a Man* album [featuring the instant anthem "Someday We'll All Be Free," the inebriating instrumental "Valdez in the Country" and the reverent orchestral suite "I Love The Lord, He Heard My Cry"]. Donny also played Rhodes on Aretha's "Until You Come Back to Me (That's What I'm Gonna Do)" – one of the finest Rhodes tracks ever. Of course, you hear the piano, but Donny is doin' some subtle, subtle stuff on Rhodes. I call it the "Ooze Factor."

I loved listening to Les McCann – "whooo" – and Richard Tee! He did so many things with the Rhodes… he would put this… sound on it… not like a Uni-Vibe but some sort of Chorus. He used to call it "Angel ____" … and he would finish that description off with part of a woman's anatomy – 'cause it had a real "juicy" sound! [Laughs]

One of my first recordings with the Rhodes was my solo record, which came out in '82. It was recorded down at the studio where Otis Redding used to cut his records. The guy who produced the record was Jim Stewart – the "ST" of Stax Records. It was a remake of the Motown song "Every Little Bit Hurts" and I played the Rhodes on that. Even without promotion it made quite a stir around the country. I was pleased about that.

I did the *California Raisins Sing The Hit Songs* album, a tune called "Cielito Lindo" for the movie "A Day Without a Mexican" and many more records that I played Rhodes on.

I was the lead vocalist and keyboardist for Tower of Power from '84-'88. In Boston with my band the Ellis Hall Group, we used to open up for groups like Tower of Power, Earth Wind & Fire and the Spinners.

In fact, the bass player for the Spinners was missing after we opened for them, so they came to my bass player and said, "Can you play for us – help us out?" Freddie, my bass player at the time, said, "No, but Ellis knows your tunes." They said, "But he's a keyboardist," and Freddie said, "No, he's a bassist!" I always had a fantasy of playing their song "It's a Shame" – it's one of the all-time great bass tracks. I got to play that for a home crowd.

After Tower of Power saw my group play opening for them, the next night, Chester Thompson [T.O.P.'s long-standing keyboardist] had pretty much the same set up as I did – a Hammond organ, the Rhodes, a Clavinet and an Arp Odyssey. I felt honored that he loved my set and stage set up.

In Boston, I was always complaining about how cold it was. So in '84, I left and moved to L.A. It was February 2nd, 75 degrees and I was standing in front of a Foster's Freeze ice cream shop. They had a phone booth back then, so I called my friends back in Boston and said, "It is 75 degrees, I got an ice cream cone in my hand and I ain't coming back, suckas!!" A few weeks later, I got a call to join Tower of Power, and where in the heck do we go but all the cold places I'd just came from! I'm in Minneapolis sayin', "What happened?!" Needless to say, the funk and the groove will keep you warm… and the truth shall set you free!

I had a great time working with Ray Charles. I lovingly say I carry on the soul legacy… without the "cantankering!" The first time Ray heard something of mine, he called me up and said [impersonating Ray], "Who in the hell are you, where'd you come from, and why didn't some people tell me about 'cha?! I'm gonna have to kick some serious (self-censor).

Get over here – I wanna sign ya!" So I went over and we made some wonderful sounds together. He had some vintage Rhodes in there. Of course, his first hit with (an electric piano), "What'd I Say," was with a Wurlitzer, but (later) he had the Rhodes, too. He had a big 'ol suitcase Rhodes up there and I would just play with it for hours.

Ray, Stevie and I were talking about doing something together. It would have been a serious blind man's convention, but that's all right. I got something for Stevie. I'm gonna do a record called *Ellis in Wonderland*!

've never worked in the studio with Stevie, but we've done a few live things together. One was at the Yamaha booth (at NAMM Show) where he played keyboard and I played electric drums. It was an absolute blast. Stevie always says, "Two or more blind people in a room is illegal, so we're going to jail!"

Michael McDonald and I did a couple things – most memorable was working on "The Bob James Showboat Cruise to Mexico" with Tom Scott & The L.A. Jazz All-Stars. We were Michael's back-up band for his set. I was imitating Michael as he was coming in. He comes up and taps me on the shoulder. Everybody's tryin' to tell me, "Michael's here!" He starts laughing and I say, "You know, Michael, it's such an honor… "

had known Michael since 1979 'cause he used to come into my sessions when I had the Ellis Hall Group. had Earth Wind and Fire's horn section (The Phenix Horns) and stuff… Unfortunately, the record never came out. Michael used to come in and hang out with this girl from Kendun Studios where we recorded. So when he found out I was on the cruise, he said 'Oh, no! You're not getting away! We're going to sing some duets together!"

So we sang "Takin it to the Streets" and "What's Goin' On"- a great time. Michael is an amazing writer. On the Rhodes, he has what I would call a delicate, loving sound. The Rhodes has a tendency to become a "sonic pillow"… Of course, they always say, "It ain't the gear, it's the engineer." If you massage the notes right, you'll get that sound… and it will be inspirational for ya – Boom Shock-a-Locka, Aww Yeah!

George Duke is another piano / Rhodes master. He called me in for a project he produced called *101 North*. I had met George in 1977 when he came through Boston, so we were swappin' road stories… George is crazy! He loves to talk about Bootsy, you know. He had the "Dukey Stick" – a little keyboard that was attached to a synthesizer – and he'd be struttin' around on stage with it. Then he'd go over to his Rhodes and just break your heart with some of those things he'd be playin'.

I used to open up for Herbie around the time of *Headhunters*. We did four dates together and he was just the kindest gentleman – talking to me about the set up. Also, when I was doing some work with Earth Wind & Fire, one of my things broke. Larry Dunn – a monster keyboardist and Rhodes player, one of the unsung masters of music as a member of EWF – let me use some of his set up. I never forgot that. Today, Jill Scott, Erykah Badu, JOE and the band Mint Condition make lovely use of the Rhodes.

It's excellent to write on a Rhodes. When you get gifts from God, don't hold back! I'm honored to have a big ol' box of crayons… and proud to open 'em up and share them.

Herbie Hancock

Herbie Hancock is arguably the most influential keyboard player to spring from the realm of jazz. He has left the biggest footprint where the Fender Rhodes is concerned. His touch on the instrument is the gold standard and most emulated of all. Like the title of his funk-jazz fusion master-piece "Chameleon" from 1973, Hancock has consistently been ahead of the curve, able to achieve unprecedented commercial success with hit recordings that span generations and musical genres – "Watermelon Man," "Maiden Voyage," "Tell Me a Bedtime Story," "Getting to the Good Part," "Rockit" – then ducking into headier, avant garde experiments that are just as definitive such as his early film scores for "Blow Up," "The Spook Who Sat By The Door" and "Death Wish," his Afro-centric jazz ensemble Mwandishi. Like his mid-'60s employer, the ever forward thinking Miles Davis, Mr. Hancock is a restless spirit always challenging himself with new forms of expression. Unlike Davis, however, he does look back with fondness and continues to embrace all of the great collaborations and creation he has amassed across one of the most enviable lives in music. Recent works include the Possibilities project (collaborations with new and veteran artists in world pop music),

The New Standard (highly conceptualized reinterpretations of contemporary pop songs in straight ahead jazz forms) and The Joni Letters (jazz interpretations of singer-songwriter Joni Mitchell's works that earned Hancock an "Album of the Year" Grammy Award – a major coup for an artist first and foremost recognized as a jazz musician).

Herbie Hancock touches on highlights of his career as they pertain to his revolutionary uses of the Fender Rhodes, starting with the legendary story of how Miles Davis first forced him to play one.

Miles Davis called a recording session so I showed up to the recording studio. (Drummer) Tony Williams was there tuning up his drums, but I didn't see a piano, so I figured maybe it was coming in later. When I finally saw that nothing was coming, I said, "Miles, what do you want me to play?" He said, "Play that." He pointed to the corner of the room and there was this electric piano. I recognized it as a Fender Rhodes because I'd seen pictures of it. I said, "Oh, really, okay," but, I was thinking in my head, "Wait a minute. Miles wants me to record with this… toy?" Even though I'd never seen one and I hadn't really heard one, I heard about it from other people and they told me, "Naaah, that's not a real piano that's just some toy." I thought, well, "The master wants me to play it, so o.k… " So they moved it in place. I turned it on, played a chord… and I liked it. It had this bell-like sound. Suddenly, I was thinking of every kind of a combination in my head.

It was guitar-like in a way, but not really. It didn't have the hard edge of a piano. "It has a warm sound," I thought. "Not only that, I can turn up the volume and be just as loud as Tony!" That's what I was thinking too. Tony wouldn't have to lighten up on the sticks when I played a solo. I was *really* intrigued by that idea!

I also learned another thing – and this is very important: to never take someone else's opinion as your own unless you've checked it out yourself. That changed my life forever… and that was because of the Fender Rhodes piano.

When I left Miles in '69, I formed a band based off of the sound of my Blue Note album, *Speak Like a Child*. I had three horns – Flugelhorn, trombone (I actually had bass trombone on *Speak Like a Child*, but most of the guys I knew didn't a have bass trombones), and a reed player – someone that played primarily saxophone, but could also play flute or alto flute. I had that sound for a couple of years after I left Miles. More and more, the avant-garde was prodding me. So that nice, gentle sound kept getting further and further out. Eventually, I got this band that we called the Mwandishi band, based off the second album I recorded for Warner Bros., *Mwandishi* – a more avant-garde kind of band. I played acoustic piano in that band… and I played the Rhodes.

I played it because I thought it was an interesting sound. The reason that a piano is not in an orchestra, is because the piano doesn't blend. It's a soloist instrument. You'd see piano concertos, but, it's not an instrument in the orchestra… because it doesn't have a character that mixes with anything. The Rhodes mixes with almost everything. It can hide in between the character of the acoustic instruments or be on top. It's very flexible.

I also played it for the characteristics of its own sound. It's got that kind of distorted sound if you hit it hard, then it's more bell-like if you play it soft, then it's got this bottom that has a lot of different colors... you can hear different overtones depending on how hard you hit it. The acoustic piano has always been the instrument for me, but the Rhodes was an extension of what I might be able to do on the acoustic piano. It's much more than an accessory. It has its own voice. However, it's not a replacement for the acoustic piano and an acoustic piano isn't a replacement for the Fender Rhodes, either.

As much as I enjoyed playing with the Mwandishi band, over time it began to lose its luster. Something in me was not being satisfied and I didn't know exactly what it was. I got tired of playing music that required an individual's undivided attention and I wanted to explore some other territory. I had already been listening to people like Sly Stone, James Brown and some others, which got back to my roots from when I was a kid – when I listened to rhythm and blues and also listened to classical music. I wanted to explore that territory because I hadn't really explored that since I had been playing jazz. I got into a little of it in the Mwandishi band, but it had a spacey flavor.

What I was originally trying to do with Headhunters was create a funk album, but it wound up being funk-jazz anyway! (Laughs) What I learned over the years – and since then, it's been proven to me many times – is that you can start with a certain idea, but, at a certain point the music begins to tell you what it wants to be. It's better to go with that, "the true flow", instead of being stuck on one idea.

So I put together a band of musicians that I thought could cover this funky territory and still have an empathy for and understanding of jazz. I got all the right people – Paul Jackson on electric bass, Bennie Maupin on saxophone and bass clarinet. Drummer Harvey Mason was suggested to me by Billy Hart who had been playing with the Mwandishi band.
He told me, "No matter what genre of music, Harvey's got it covered!"

I had met percussionist Bill Summers when he was a student at the University of California at Berkeley. There was a gallery showing and he was performing and I played after that. He was an interesting player because he was studying ethnomusicology and African traditions.

I had a Clavinet – which I used as a substitute for a guitar – and I had the Rhodes. So I had a lot of different colors to work with.

In the very early days of my playing the Rhodes with the Mwandishi band, we were performing at the jazz club The Lighthouse in Hermosa Beach. Harold Rhodes came by to see the band and to see how his instrument was being used. He comes in, looked on the stage and saw that I had the top off of the keyboard with wires coming out of it plugged into an Echoplex, cry-baby wah-wah pedal and wires outta these going into the Rhodes. So the sound went from here, through these devices, then out into the speakers. Harold was appalled!

After we finished the set and people were going crazy, Harold said, "What are you doing to my instrument? Why did you take the top off of it?" I explained what I had done and said, "A lot of musicians are going to want to use devices plugged into your instrument. You should put some jacks where they can plug-in in the front without having to take the top off and destroy the look of your beautiful instrument." He thought that was a good idea, so they started putting jacks out front.

Because I was thinking about recording, I also suggested that he put some jacks on the side of the instrument by the amp – what they call quarter-inch jacks and XLR high impedance... well, it's even more technical, but another way of plugging something in so that it can go into the recording board. There may have been other people that suggested that to him, but he started adding those elements to the instrument. I was pleased to see that happen – that maybe I had some part in him deciding to do it.

I don't remember the first time I met Joe Zawinul, I've known him for so long. One of the first things that Joe and I did when we struck up this friendship was to go down to the old Half Note club in New York – on Hudson and Spring – to see the John Coltrane Quartet with McCoy Tyner [piano], Jimmy Garrison [bass] and Elvin Jones [drums]. We'd get knocked out by their playing! Since we are both keyboard players having played classical music, both our eyes were wide open looking forward to finding new ways to do things. He was very open to electronic elements and also to adding funky elements. He wrote "Mercy, Mercy, Mercy," which is an amazing hit, for jazz... I mean a real hit! There weren't that many real hits in jazz during that

period of time... but, "Mercy, Mercy, Mercy" certainly was one, and my tune, "Watermelon Man" was too.

I was just thinking about how Joe, Chick Corea and I all really made the Rhodes a cornerstone instrument for ourselves and how we interacted on some of Miles' records. I remember going into the studio and there were three keyboard players. There was Chick, myself and Joe Zawinul – sometimes it might be Keith Jarrett. We might all be playing different instruments... someone would be playing a Farfisa or a Clavinet, usually there were two guys on Rhodes. Evidently, Miles really liked the sound of the Rhodes.

When I think of one of my favorites of the songs I've done on the Rhodes, what crosses my mind is "Butterfly" (from his classic fusion album, *Thrust*, on Columbia – 1974, as well as an amazing live version on the Japanese import double CD, *Flood* – Sony Japan – 1976)... It's one of the most memorable songs that I had a chance to write along with [reed master] Bennie Maupin.

One thing that I really liked on the original ones was the vibrato. The sound would sweep from one speaker to the other. They used little light bulbs in the preamp that would dim then brighten... I guess it affected the voltage to each of the amps for each of the speakers, so they smoothly went from one to the other and it sounded great. Then they started using a chip, one thing would be on and the other would be off. I hated it... hated it! [Laughs] After that, they tried to simulate the original thing, but it never got back to the smoothness of the original vibrato sound. The reason they changed it was because the light bulbs would break, so they made the instrument sturdier.

I understand the reasoning, but, it's too bad they couldn't have invented or found a chip at that time that would make that gradual transition the way the light bulbs did.

The Rhodes did go through some growing pains. It used to go out of tune so easily. Each time that I went back to the factory with a complaint about something, they would seriously try to make modifications to improve it. When the next iteration of the instrument came out, certain things would be better because they'd worked on it. I tried to give as much input as I could because I really loved the Rhodes. Harold Rhodes was such a great guy. The technicians at the factory were also very helpful.

I remember the tines – the little thin bars in the back that would get struck – would break a lot. In the beginning if something broke, I had to take it back to the factory. After awhile I realized I better learn how to fix this thing myself because they used to break over and over again. Eventually I got a kit that had a certain kind of glue that they used, some extra tines… extra everything! Then I had to make certain adjustments which would take awhile… but, when you were working on the instrument yourself, it was like a guy who is a car fanatic working on his car – fine tuning it in a way. I was able to do that and get a real understanding and love for the instrument because I had to nurse it back to health so much. Talk about it being human, it was in many ways.

Rami Jaffee

As a member of the Wallflowers and the Foo Fighters bands, Rami Jaffee has kept the spirit of the Rhodes alive in contemporary rock music. He is an avid collector of vintage keyboard instruments and owns several Rhodes pianos spanning makes, models and years. He discusses his acquisitions and the unique ways in which he uses them.

The first time I really heard a Rhodes on the radio or on an album was Billy Preston playing it on the Beatles' "Get Back." I didn't know what that instrument was. I knew it was something like a piano but... I just remember it made the track sound so cool. Billy was just ripping a solo on it! It was a little different than Ray Charles' Wurlitzer.

When I got to 7th grade and walked into band class, there sat three Rhodes side by side. For me it was like instant classic rock – between Billy Preston on the Beatles and Ray Manzarek on the Doors' "Riders on the Storm." I really identified with it and those hipster rockers. I remember we had some kind of spring program or something and the band played "Fame" (the Irene Cara movie theme). There I was, sitting and banging on a Rhodes.

What really introduced me to the instrument just a few years later was when I started shopping for keyboards during the early '80s. At the time, to be honest, I was always trying to find this digital keyboard... because I was into classic rock and a little bit of prog rock. The Rhodes was pretty basic – not too many knobs – so it wasn't flashing in my mind to purchase one.

Instead I was purchasing DX-7s and things I barely use now. When I started collecting and buying Rhodes, a lot of the regular stage models had different effects units, almost like a post-Fender Rhodes upgrade – like some bizarre phaser with a flashy '60s logo. I couldn't even remember these names. That gave me the mindset to start plugging in different pedals, but when I came across the speaker version with the left-and-right, it gave me a whole different look at the Rhodes as a keyboard sound that's not a piano. When I use it in songs I really pedal-to-the-metal, sustain, letting the sound and vibrato do the trick. It's almost "the after-sound" of what you're playing and it really has nice, strange quality to it.

Towards the end of the '80s, even in David Bowie's music in the '70s, there was this great use of the Rhodes. Being from L.A., where everyone was into Glam Rock and borderline Heavy Metal bands, I was searching for a sound… to be included in a band and have elements of modern music. There was this keyboard player named Joe Simon who played in local bands, *The Broken Homes* and *Burning Tree*. These bands evolved into members of them playing with Lenny Kravitz and The Black Crowes. He had a Rhodes and it was an odd model… it was just so torn up in the front. It was a stage one and he didn't have the proper legs of the Rhodes. After the show I went up and asked him, "What is that thing?" I turned it around and it was a Rhodes. "Whoa!"

Before "eBay" and "Craigslist" we had something called The Recycler, a little LA newspaper that you pick up at the store. I'd get The Recycler, call "Fender Rhodes $50" I mean you know, that was a lot of money to me, but it was worth it.

Even at that time, a decent keyboard at Guitar Center would be $400, $500 bucks. So, I really got into it… and each one sounded different.

Sometimes I'd buy a Rhodes for $20, but certain keys would be broken. Of course, I didn't have the mindset of "lets get that fixed." I would either tape it up or not play those keys and just use the quirks of the machine to my advantage. You end up buying a second one and it has a different effect unit in it. They really started getting popular, out of nowhere. Ben Montench of Tom Petty and the Heartbreakers has a B-3, Rhodes and piano on a lot of songs and it sounded like modern rock at the time. When the Wallflowers' record came out with "One Headlight" on it, I remember buying Hammonds for almost nothing… like, "Please, you pick up from church, it's yours!" That would be the ad in the paper. Now it's gone to $2000, 5 10, $20,000 for the thing. I wish I could go back and shop at those prices.

There was a time, I think in 1997, Wallflowers were on top of our game out there on the road. My thing was, in every town in the world, I would look and try to find a Rhodes. They were still almost giving them away. What I'd do is buy them, put them on the truck at sound check, the next day I would ship them out to all my keyboard player friends in L.A. Every one of them was getting a Rhodes, whatever model. I was buying them between $100 and $200 bucks… sometimes $50, sometimes $300. Now to find a clean Rhodes, it could be up there in $2,000 and $3,000. It really pisses me off that I didn't do a little more shopping back then.

When the Counting Crows and the Wallflowers hit the scene – kind of Americana Rock and Roll, but, Pop – a lot of those bands brought it back… it was really encouraging. Friends would call and say, "Man, see what they're trying to do?!" I'm like, "The more the better!" If I'm listening to the radio and I hear a Rhodes or a Hammond B-3 and it's not me, I'm still happy… it still makes me feel fuzzy, but, yes, D'Angelo, The Fugees and the Wallflowers had some private show for Giorgio Armani and other VIPs. I'd never heard of D'Angelo. The guy made it sound so cool. Jamiroquai is another one that was around in the '90s. Those bands are still using them and that's really what's raking up the price on even the vintage ones. That's why I have to take care of the ones I have here in the studio [hugs Rhodes].

In the '70s, I was so young… my older brother and older sister had tons of records. Most of them were classic rock. My brother turned me onto Steely Dan… what was it… "Hey Nineteen?" It just pokes out at you and says, "This is the coolest sound ever!" I remember really digging that. To be honest, Steely Dan and Michael McDonald were always too smooth for me. I mean, I love their use of the Rhodes, but I swear, the first time I got a Rhodes they had the different effects and stuff. I started getting distortion in there… It was the '80s so, keyboard players had to get on that stage and make as much noise as the guitar player guys. I would kick in distortion, run it through Marshalls and people would be like, "What the heck was that thing on there?!" It was a controller. People seem to think a Rhodes doesn't have much on here. "Are you gonna carry this thing around for one thing?"

I'm like, "No, I'm carrying this around as my MIDI controller for pedals and sounds and different amps." It's a very useful keyboard that crosses genres and tones.

As a keyboard player, the Rhodes is the number one sound. You go out to the shop today, 10 years ago – 20 years ago – 30 years ago, any modular digital keyboard right after piano is Rhodes electric piano. It is so central and so undeniable. Sometimes you have to play a TV show and get, "There's no Rhodes here, sorry." You'll be somewhere half across the pond in Italy doing some funky TV show and you gotta use what they got… but, you look in there and even in a different language there's a Rhodes sound. Yes! Luckily, being a staple and sought after, every keyboard player has kept it in the presets of a synthesizer or electric keyboard.

The beauty of this thing is that as basic as it is, it really has so much character. At the end of the day, character on a keyboard is what I search for. That's what I want to bring to a record and bring to the world. The problem when you get a sample is you're getting one note – you're getting one piece of an 88 Rhodes or even a [73]. It's almost like a prepared piano, one of those avant-garde things. Sometimes I'll have one note be my "CLICK" at the beginning of a song, so then it becomes percussion! You're NEVER going to get that on a copied sound, a synth or an electric keyboard you buy in the store.

In the last 20 years, I've learned that a vintage instrument can have such character that sometimes it can challenge you. It can be notes that are dead or notes that are ringing.

There you are with the red light playing this famous pop record and you gotta somehow turn your "Sanford & Son" shop into, you know, "American Idol!" It challenges you at times, but, I know in my heart that the connection I have with it just brings so much more. It's almost become a crutch to me. Sure, I've got personality as a player, but what's better than my personality is my personality with another personality. It's like people are getting 2 for 1 over here, you know. It helps me because people will go, "God, Rami's so weird!" No I'm not. My keyboard was weird… maybe I was too. The weirder the better with some people, you know what I'm sayin'?

The difference between a digital keyboard and having a real Rhodes, obviously, is the convenience. On the last Foo Fighters tour, we had a little problem because Dave had a great idea of having a stage come out of the ceiling in the middle of the arena. So management gave me that call: "About the Rhodes and the Hammond… ya knooooow, it's just not gonna work out… they're a bit of a hazard because of the weight." I'm like, "Oh, no, you've got to be kidding?" Of course, when that stage comes down, that's where I really shine. There's a lot of keyboard-heavy songs in that little section of the set and for the first time I want to be a diva and say, "No, can't do it!!" Unfortunately, I had to. I actually had a gutted-out Rhodes with a digital thing in there. Let's face it, I'm in the entertainment business where the truth comes down to, "Is it going to affect album sales if I don't have a Fender Rhodes?" I've gotta channel all the times I've had with the Rhodes and bring them to this convenient digital keyboard… but, it never compares.

My favorite Wallflowers song with Rhodes is "Here in Pleasantville" (from *Red Letter Days* – 2002). It had the sweetest little Rhodes part. I was already a few Wallflower records in, where I had a Rhodes part that was prominent in the song, but, it's always in my arsenal. To me, it's a piano on steroids.

It could be very basic to work out a song with somebody, but within two seconds you start adding a couple little effects and playing that weird key that's out of tune there. Suddenly you hear, "Something sparkled there!" I'm like, "Yeah, this broken key here."

With the Foo Fighters, my Rhodes is buried somewhere under "The Pretender" (from the album *Echoes, Silence, Patience & Grace*). There's some mini string thing covering it up. When I first met Dave Grohl, he was making the record *In Your Honor* (2005) and that's when I got in there. There was what he called "The Acoustic Record" and there was a double CD. "Yes, we know it's an electric piano, but… " Even incorporating keyboards into the Foo Fighters was like… the different dimension I used the Rhodes and Hammond B-3, even Mellotron and Chamberlin sounds. We explored all of that. Now we're three records down and there's keyboards floating around on the records.

The biggest problem that happened to me is when I got successful, I had all this money, so I thought, "Oh I better take all these vintage things and shine them up a little bit." So I'd take them to these great specialists and they fix it so well, I swear it comes back and you might as well get the convenient sampled digital keyboard.

They're all proud like, "We took out all the tubes and got you all squared away – took out all the tines and we have this little digital router…" I'm like, "No, are you serious?!" You have to pay close attention to what to fix and what not to fix.

Sometimes drummers don't change their drum heads. In my experience, I thought you changed your head before every show… or ALL the heads… I've seen that go down. Same with guitar strings. The newer something is – the more polished it is – you're taking away personality that was free!

There's a few Rhodes kings. Herbie Hancock has really taken it to a level. The Doors' Ray Manzarek… he really "Rhodes'd out!" He even had the Fender Rhodes Keyboard Bass to do bass parts. That's like getting two guys out of one.

Then there's John Paul Jones of Led Zeppelin on "No Quarter." He made it dreamy. Those are the guys I grew up on that inspired me to use a Rhodes in my arsenal.

Digital keyboards always have Rhodes sounds which are convenient when you really need it, but ummm, next to a Rhodes, it's like night and day. What you're getting on a digital piano is one clean note from a Rhodes that they reproduce up and down the keyboard. You get the heart and soul of every note on a real Rhodes.

On records I love to play simple things. I'm not there to riff out too much. When you have a digital keyboard, you're presenting a plastic soulless being. When you play a Rhodes… it just makes people feel better and that's what it's all about.

Gerald McCauley, Rami Jaffe and Benjamin Bove

Bob James

After receiving his B.A. in composition from the University of Michigan, Marshall, Missouri-native Bob James recorded the jazz trio album Bold Conceptions for Mercury in 1962, followed three years later by the more avant-garde Explosions (on ESP Records). He spent four years as Sarah Vaughan's Musical Director before becoming a staple of Creed Taylor's CTI productions, contributing to records that included Quincy Jones' Walking in Space. On that 1969 milestone, Bob on Fender Rhodes is the first sound you hear on the intro of "Dead End" and remains prominent throughout – from a brief solo on the title track to the album-closing "Oh Happy Day."

He became an in-house arranger for CTI, working with players ranging from Paul Desmond to Stanley Turrentine. He was heavily involved in the first five albums that saxophonist Grover Washington, Jr. recorded for CTI's soul-jazz imprint, Kudu Records, including the gold-seller Mr. Magic. Other Kudu classics that Bob helmed include drummer Idris Muhammad's seminal debut Power of Soul and guitarist Gabor Szabo's Macho. Bob James went on to record as an artist in his own right for CTI. The first album, 1974's One, contained his version of the Roberta Flack hit "Feel Like Makin' Love" which became a seminal recording of the Quiet Storm and later, smooth jazz radio formats.

Taking full advantage of the opportunity to arrange for a full orchestra, Bob also recorded several jazz adaptations of well-known classical music pieces. After four albums for CTI, Bob joined industry giant CBS Records as Director of Progressive A&R, which led to his handling some production, arranging and orchestration for pop stars such as Kenny Loggins (Nightwatch), Paul Simon (Still Crazy After All These Years), Phoebe Snow (Never Letting Go) and The Fania All-Stars (Rhythm Machine). Also in cooperation with CBS in 1976, he started Tappan Zee Records. The label housed his own subsequent recordings (including a phenomenal Grammy-winning duo project with acoustic guitarist Earl Klugh titled One on One) as well as those of fellow keyboardists Richard Tee and Joanne Brackeen, Cuban conguero Mongo Santamaria and guitarist Steve Khan, while also introducing guitarist Wilbert Longmire and saxophonist Mark Colby. Most lasting of his artist launches has been tenor saxophonist Kirk Whalum, who bowed on Bob's 1984 album, 12. After a switch to Warner Bros. Records in 1986, Bob recorded a Grammy-winning duo project with longtime friend David Sanborn titled Double Vision.

1991 found him co-founding the contemporary jazz super group Fourplay with drummer Harvey Mason, bassist Nathan East and guitarist Lee Ritenour (later replaced by Larry Carlton). Bob also introduced his daughter, Hilary James, on the label. Of recent note is the project Angels of Shanghai, a melding of Asian folk music with modern jazz and a 2008 team-up with Hilary titled Christmas Eyes (Mr. James was born on Christmas Day, 1939).

I really couldn't pinpoint it to any one session. At the time I became familiar with it, I was doing a lot of studio work. When I was hired, I wasn't even sure what kind of piano I was going to be playing when I got there. Gradually, most of the sessions that I did had an acoustic piano and some kind of electric piano. Maybe it was somewhere in the early '70s that the Fender Rhodes became the standard second piano that would be there in the studio. One way or the other, I'd end up playing it.

I can't say that it was a conscious step on my part – that I wanted (the Rhodes) to be part of my sound – because I didn't even have a sound, at that time... or I didn't *think* that I did. I was just a piano player doing whatever was required in a recording session.

The first time I remember (the Rhodes) specifically as it related to me was my first solo project for CTI Records in 1974. The record was called *One*. I had just come from a recording session with Roberta Flack. The producer was Eugene McDaniels and he had written a song called "Feel Like Makin' Love" for Roberta. They asked me to play Fender Rhodes on that session.

As soon as I heard it – actually as soon as any of us in the studio heard it – we ALL knew that this was going to be a hit. It was sooo good. The session went well… and that piano sound was an important part of the record.

No more than a week or two after that, I was talking creatively with Creed Taylor about what songs to use on my project (*One*). I told him, "You know there's this great song that Roberta Flack just recorded. I would love to have the first instrumental cover of this song." So we recorded it. We actually used the same rhythm section that had played on Roberta's record – Richie Resnicoff on guitar, Gary King on bass, Ralph McDonald on percussion, and Idris Muhammad on drums. As things turned out, it took longer for Roberta to finish her project than it did for me to finish mine, so my record actually came out first. She and her people were quite angry about it because, of course, she wanted the exclusive for the record. It was not intentional. It just happened that way… and I got a lot of mileage out of it. DJs started to play both versions, back-to-back. I had done mine in the same key that she recorded her version in. Hers took off, I piggy-backed and it changed my whole life. It was a very big deal to me and the Fender Rhodes was definitely a major part of that sound. I suppose that's when it really sunk in that, whether I liked it or not, (the Rhodes) was going to be part of my sound during that time.

I certainly can't claim to have any monopoly on it, although I would say that the more straight-ahead players were more resistant to doing it than I was. I didn't have any qualms about it. I didn't have any reluctance to play the instrument, especially if they wanted Fender Rhodes and I got a gig out of it! [Laughs]

"Yes sir! I'll play the toy piano! I'll play the celeste! I'll play whatever you want!!" Whatever is required was my attitude. I was really enjoying doing studio work.

At first, I didn't have any feeling that it was going to be a sound that would be identified with me, my style or anything like that. It was just a gig. The guy that I remember who was most identified with (the Rhodes), and played it a lot was Richard Tee. I became friends with Richard – a great player – and he was kind of going back and forth between playing organ and Fender Rhodes. I knew that he was playing it a lot because I had found a Rhodes at Carroll Rental Studio, which was the studio that most of us used to get our instruments to do sessions. There was this one particular piano that I loved. "9" or "9a" is how Carroll used to identify it (NOT a model number). There was a pretty wide variety and if you didn't get one that you liked, it would really change the sound. If Richard had a gig and got to it first, then I wouldn't be able to get it! [Smiles] So I was always telling the people who hired me to make sure that they got that #9 quickly… otherwise Richard Tee would get it.

It was very sad. He is missed. He was such a unique musician in so many ways. So much spirit… I had a lot of opportunities to play alongside him.

Sometimes they would hire two keyboard players and if it was me and Richard, he'd be playing organ and I'd be playing piano, or sometimes vice-versa. I learned a tremendous amount from him.

Earlier today I was thinking that if we were going to talk about any of that stuff, one of the things about the Rhodes that was always problematic to me, is that it didn't sustain the same way that an acoustic piano did.

If you had habits of holding notes down in a certain way, it wouldn't come out the same way that it does if you played them on the piano. To my ear, the sound was closer to an organ than a piano. It sustained too long… That would be a problem. I kept wanting to pick my fingers up off the keys because I didn't like the sound of it when it was just this flat… aaaghh… sustain thing! Maybe that was an influence on Richard and other guys that played it (such as Leon Pendarvis)… always wanting to have some kind of chorus, or use the vibrato, or something to make that sustain not be so cold and sterile sounding.

Richard used a lot of Chorus (effect). I almost avoided playing with those "Chorus" or "Phaser" devices because as soon as I would, I started sounding like Richard! [Smiles] I wanted to have my own sound.

My first CTI album, *One*, had three songs on it that later became identified with me.

"Feel Like Makin Love" was the first that got me airplay. "Night on Bald Mountain" was another piece that got played a lot. I was identified with it, but it was also very much identified with drummer Steve Gadd. It was early in his career and my arrangement of Moussorgsky's "Night on Bald Mountain" totally featured him. He played this amazingly great drum part. Steve was just establishing his reputation and this piece really showcased him. That was a really cool thing for me too.

The story is totally crazy about what happened with "Nautilus" though. I liked it when we did it, but, it was just a tune… just a tune on a record date and it didn't get any attention at all. It didn't get any airplay (then). Those were the days of the Lp and "Nautilus" was not only on side B, it was the LAST CUT on side B.

So, most people never even found it. Lo and behold, 25 years or more go by and I gradually began to be aware that this recording was being sampled. It really caught me off-guard. First I thought, "Well, if they were going to sample something from my repertoire, why pick that?" I admit that I didn't get it at all at first. Now I've had more than 10 years of hearing over and over and over again from different hip hop producers and artists, THAT's the cut of mine they recognize the most and gets most used. Hey, I'm happy as a clam! Who am I to argue about that?

I've even started to understand more what it was (about the piece that hooked them) – this magical groove that Idris Muhammad played… a simple beat based on repetition. What's interesting is I don't think that "Nautilus" is all that easy to sample because it wasn't done to a click (track). With samples based on the whole idea of loops and something that is "predictable" in the way it falls in time, (a producer really has to) play around with ("Nautilus" to make it function as a sample) because it's very loose. If you listen to it closely or if anybody put it up against a click track, you'd see how much flexibility there is in Idris' time and in the way we approached playing that tune.

We've gotten used to rhythm in recent years. We think it grooves because it's solid from beginning to end. But in some ways that's like a strait jacket and great rhythm players would not feel comfortable. I doubt whether Idris ever felt comfortable having to play with a click in his head or to play with something that didn't have any flexibility in it. So it's ironic to me that "Nautilus" got picked to be a loop.

Hip Hop artists have taken four bars from "Nautilus" and looped them from the beginning to the end on a tune, but I'm sure that they had to cheat a little bit to make it fall completely into something predictable, because it doesn't and it isn't. We didn't want it to at that time!

So, it's definitely fun that "Nautilus" had a life of its own. In my memory it was almost a throwaway. It wasn't a tune that I focused on during that project or spent any time on. It was just a little bass thing… a riff… something to get us started. The fact that it has this new life is just an amazing aspect of the music business. You can't predict it.

Well, because "Feel Like Makin' Love" received so much attention and my CTI debut *One* sold very well – I'd love to have those sales right now, as a matter of fact, it kick-started me into a solo career that I wasn't really expecting. When I recorded that album, I thought it would end up being my only album and that I would just go back to doing studio work as an arranger and sideman… but, as soon as this record started to become successful, Creed Taylor invited me to make more.

My second album, *Two*, had several tracks that featured the Fender Rhodes. There was another cover of a classical piece, Bizet's "Farandole," that got a lot of airplay. [Note: The intended sequel to "Feel Like Makin' Love" was a cover of Thom Bell and Linda Creed's "You're As Right As Rain," first recorded by The Stylistics and later by Nancy Wilson, as arranged by Gene Page.] I played very little acoustic piano. Creed wanted me to play the Fender Rhodes because it was associated with "Feel Like Makin' Love."

He thought my fans were thinking of me in that way and life just dealt me that history of this sound becoming identified with me in a way that I just had to keep following up on it.

My third album, *Three*, had a song called "Westchester Lady" that was commercially successful in a way that also caught me by surprise. It was another one of those pretty simple riff-type tunes that we were doing just to get a groove happening so we could improvise. I remember being very interested in shifting away from the swing type of rhythm that I had played in the 1960's and in which the bass was, generally, walking. We wanted to pull away from the straight up 1/4 note fours and the chord changes that came out of standard tunes.

There was a strong movement toward modal one-chord or two-chord tunes – where the chord stayed the same for 8 measures or 16 measures. Instead of a walking bass, the bass was taking on more of a melodic role. The same way I was shifting over from acoustic piano to the Fender Rhodes, bass players were shifting over from upright to electric. There were a lot of guys that were doing both. Even Ron Carter, who is known mostly for his acoustic bass playing, was kind of pressured into playing some electric bass too, because on the gigs he was getting, that's the sound that they wanted – the sound of the electric bass, which was so different and the approach to playing it, which was more guitar-like.

So I started writing my tunes that way. Even "Nautilus" was based around a bass line instead of a walking thing. With "Westchester Lady," the bass line is as much a part of the signature of that tune as the melody. It's easy to look back and see things with the benefits of hindsight, but during that era we were just doing it!

A session was called for Monday morning and you had to show up with some music so that there would be something to play. With "Westchester Lady," I definitely remember the day before going to the studio and I had to have something done. "This is the best I can come up with for today." You put it out there and hope for the best... I wouldn't even want to pull out some of the things that were done during that time that did NOT make the cut – the ones that have found, you know, a little peaceful death somewhere in the bottom of the trunk!

I had the great fortune to be intimately involved in all of Grover Washington, Jr.'s early records (*Inner City Blues*, *All the King's Horses*, *Soul Box*, *Mister Magic* and *Feels So Good*). His first one, *Inner City Blues*, came out in 1971. By the time we got to *Mr. Magic* in 1974, he already had a very strong reputation and was a big star in the contemporary jazz world. Creed Taylor was pushing him really hard.

I was involved in choosing the tunes. One day Creed gave me this cassette and asked me to take it home and listen. It was a demo reel from Ralph McDonald's publishing company – he, his parner Bill Eaton, and maybe one other guy that was involved with them in writing songs. I'm looking at it and I was going to listen through to all of them, when I saw down toward the bottom of the list of these songs there was a song called "Mr. Magic." I hadn't even listened to the song yet and I thought, "What a great song title for Grover... *Mr. Magic*." I was really excited about listening to the tune, but when I got to it on the tape I almost decided to drop it. First of all, it was a ballad. Second of all, it was a vocal. Creed Taylor was not looking for a vocal, particularly for Grover. [Note: Roberta Flack recorded the vocal version in 1975 on her *Feel Like Makin' Love* Lp.] He wanted something funky! So when I heard the tune for the first time I thought, "This is just not going to work for Grover... "

Then I decided to see if I could shift it over into a completely different groove than they had on Ralph's demo. So I came in with this simple little piano riff and I had a little bass line thing. Eric Gale was playing guitar on this session. He took one listen to this little thing, which was not very much, and came up with this amazing guitar answer that just fit right between the cracks. It's just funny the way it laid... the guitar and everything else. The two things just gelled. Coincidentally, we had Harvey Mason playing drums, who's remained my very close friend and collaborator. That was a pretty powerful rhythm section there that day! Obviously the tune worked great. Grover played soulfully like he was doing in that era, full of magic and it became a big hit for him.

How fortunate it is to become associated with a particular piece that has some commercial success... Mine turned out to be the theme from "Taxi." I was so lucky because it was the only TV music I ever did. I wasn't particularly interested in going into that field – at all. In fact, I was resisting it! But I was approached by two of the producers of that series. When they were working on the first episodes, they were just going through their record collection and trying different things to see what sounds seemed to relate to the series. One of the records that they had was my fourth CTI record, *BJ4*.

They liked the sound of it – thought it fit the mood of what they wanted to do for the series – so they contacted me. They asked me, "Would you be interested in writing some new music in that style?" I perked up in a big way because I wasn't being asked to write music like somebody else or to do some standard TV thing. They were asking me to do my own thing. I thought, "This is fantastic!"

However, I was very candid with them. I remember saying, "If we're just going to go into the studio and record 10 or 15 seconds worth of music (the way a normal sitcom score would be put together), I'm not going to be able to get the jazz players that I work with to be comfortable doing that. Part of the thing I think you like about what I do is that it's loose and the musicians stretch out. They're used to playing 6 or 7-minute songs and sometimes the grooves take awhile to develop. So I would like to approach this more like I was doing another record."

For the first session, I didn't even look at any (video). I hadn't seen any of the show. I said, "Let me just give you a variety of music – fast, slow and medium – see if there's something you can take from it... treat it like a music library type of approach." I had one song in my head, though, that I was aiming to be the main theme. At another meeting, I brought it in and played it for them, and I think they liked it... but one of the other pieces I had just done – thinking that it would be background music for the show – they said, "Well, we like *this*!"

I'd titled it "Angela" because the pilot featured a telephone operator that Judd Hirsch (the show's star) was about to have a blind date with because he liked her voice over the phone – a very sentimental episode. They wanted some music that would play under when he walked down the hallway of her apartment building to meet her for the first time. So I had this sort of melancholy little piece and they said, "Would you mind if we used that instead of the piece that you submitted?" Who was I to argue with them? It was their show, so I agreed.

It surprised me, though, because "Angela" was such a mellow piece and the other piece I'd written was a higher energy piece. When I wrote it, I was thinking New York City cabdrivers... the hustle and the bustle and the car horns... That was the mood I'd assumed would be more appropriate. They did end up using that other piece on several of the episodes. I got to use it too: as the title track of my sixth album, *Touchdown*. That piece and "Angela" became the first two songs on Side 1 of *Touchdown*, which came out shortly after the series started.

"Taxi" is just a different version of the "Nautilus" story in that some things come along that you could never expect or predict. In this field, it is very difficult to try to do things in a predictable way. Magic is what you're looking for. Sometimes that makes for sleepless nights because you do have deadlines and are expected to meet them while you deliver this magic! I guess we have to be patient and just trust that it is going to keep coming along. We just don't know when.

Actually, in the early days there were some pianists that I did not like hearing play the Rhodes. One of them was my very favorite pianist at that time – still is – Bill Evans, who has maybe influenced more jazz pianists than anybody else. Occasionally he was called upon to play the Fender Rhodes. I just never felt – on any of the recordings that I ever heard – that he was comfortable with it. [Note: Those Lps include 1970's *Left to Right* on Columbia and a collaboration with orchestrator Claus Ogerman titled *Symbiosis* for Verve in 1974.] It just didn't seem to fit his touch or his ear.

There were even some recordings where he goes back and forth – playing the acoustic piano then switches over to play a chorus on the Rhodes… Every time I hear it, I think, "Oh, no-no –no! Go back to the acoustic!!" I didn't like the sound. It was as if he was trying to make the piano come to him… and it wouldn't. The Fender Rhodes just has its own personality and you're either gonna go there or not.

In the way my ears were telling me that I had to change my style, I had to change my touch. We talked earlier about how on certain things if you "sustain" even just a little bit too long, it's not going to sound good. If you play it a little too hard, unless you're doing it for percussive effect, the Rhodes just doesn't have the dynamic range of a great concert grand. So you're going to get a distorted sound. Maybe that's cool if you're answering some drum or percussive thing, but as a conventional piano, it starts to sound funky – in the wrong way – to my ears.

On the other hand, Richard Tee and certainly Joe Sample really understood it. His ears completely got it. Joe plays Fender Rhodes on many of his recordings with The Crusaders [including their smash hit "Put It Where You Want It" to the more sublime "Rainbow Visions"]. He could play any kind of a piano and sound great on it. His instincts are just awesome. He's definitely one of my big favorites. Of course, Herbie (Hancock), who again, could play on anything and it would be great. He certainly was very associated with the Rhodes on some of his very famous recordings ("Tell Me a Bedtime Story," "Butterfly" and the middle passage of "Chameleon," to name three).

I often regret that I didn't get to know most of those pianists. Normally, there's only one piano player in a band. If they get the gig, I don't get it, so I'm not there. I did have the opportunity to work directly with Joe Sample, but I had to initiate it. I invited him to play a duet with me on one of my projects. We actually played back and forth together in the studio and that was fantastic! I could feel his unique rhythm, style and pulse, and react to it. Joe and I had a chance to vibe, but Chick Corea or Joe Zawinul – sadly, no.

I guess that piano sort of made my solo career happen. Whether it would have happened without that phenomenon, I don't know… but, as an acoustic pianist, I was on the periphery of the jazz field. I was working fairly steadily, so I had a decent career going in New York. I was getting a lot of dates, but not really thinking about having a solo career. I was thinking about being an accompanist and a sideman. The fact that the Rhodes was starting to become more and more popular – and I was on the right session at the right time with the right producer where I suddenly found myself being visible playing this instrument which became identified with me – was a very big deal. It changed my life, so I have sentimental positive thoughts about that. I have deep gratitude that the phenomenon happened… gratitude that this instrument came along and allowed me to demonstrate that I had a particular kind of touch.

I'm pretty confident in saying that I made the piano sound good. I think I understood why it's a unique instrument and why it was a long way from some of the more primitive electric pianos that preceded it. Sitting here now next to one of them and talking about it brings back some very nice, warm memories.

Ramsey Lewis

Though he became an international million-selling artist playing acoustic piano as the leader of his Ramsey Lewis Trio in the '60s on Chess' Argo and Cadet labels, the man also made some of his most lasting musical statements on the Fender Rhodes beginning with selections such as "Wanderin' Rose" (pretty) and "Bold and Black" (earthy) on 1969's Another Voyage, then more consistently upon his association with Columbia Records on albums such as Funky Serenity (1973) and the criminally underappreciated Solar Wind (early 1974) From his priceless renditions of Seals & Crofts' "Summer Breeze" and "Hummingbird" to the pristine beauty of "Nicole" from Salongo

(1975) and "Juaacklyn" from Don't it Feel Good (1976) to his signature smash "Sun Goddess" (Summer 1974), Ramsey Lewis graced the world with an exquisite touch on this instrument. Here he warm-naturedly shares his memories of the instrument and ever keeping his approach to it tastefully musical.

When I first started playing the electric piano, our bass player L. D. Young said, "Try the Wurlitzer." I said, "It's electric – I don't want to do electric piano!" We tried it, anyway. I went from the Wurlitzer to a few other things. I don't know if it was a rock group or whatever… but, when the Fender Rhodes came along, that was like, the 747 of keyboards – VERY inspiring. I wanted one!

They put me in touch with Harold Rhodes who was not only a technician and knew all about how to put these things together, he had a great relationship with musicians. He'd say, "I'll send you one, then you tell me what you think about it – how it feels or if you have any suggestions" and I'll be darned if he wasn't really concerned with how it felt to me. We must have gone back and forth shipping these things three-four-five times! What made it such a pleasure was I felt like he was trying to custom make it for me. At first it was just the top, then we had the suitcase model and he said, "If you want to try putting other speakers in there… " So we put some JB Lansings and did all sorts of fun things. I fell in love with the Fender Rhodes.

I did some trio records, so I started playing the Stein-way… again. Shortly after that, Maurice White was talking to me in the studio and said, "I got this song that you should record. It's going to be bigger than any record you ever had." I said, "Bigger than 'The In Crowd?'" He said, "Yeah! But, I want you to use the Fender Rhodes." I said, "Sure. I still love that sound anyway." So the song he had was called "Hot Dawgit." It took us 3 days on that song because he says I'm destined to make this the biggest hit I ever had. We finished it and it sounded really good. So everybody's packing up and he says, "Oh, we have this melody – really simple… we're never gonna use it. The solo part is just over two changes and it's mainly a solo song… but, it has a nice melody. Why don't we just put it down?" Where it took 3 days to do the so called hit, it took us about 3 hours to do the one that he almost forgot to give me. He brought over the guitar player, Johnny Graham, his brother Verdine and the guys, and we recorded that. He didn't even have a name for the second song. I said, "What are you gonna name it?"

He says, "Oh, uh, call it 'Sun Goddess.' You got your hit… don't worry about what the name is!" Of course, "Sun Goddess" became a very big hit and the Fender Rhodes electric piano, as far as Ramsey Lewis performing on it, became popular again. So I start carrying it on the road again which was fun.

With most electronic instruments it's very difficult to get your own sound, but with the Rhodes, Bill Evans, Chick Corea, Herbie Hancock, George Duke – all the Rhodes guys – you could tell them all apart. I felt that I had my own sound and I'm sure that's due to Harold Rhodes working personally with these guys.

I'm not a volume guy. Even when I had the Rhodes sitting next to the Steinway, I would switch over mainly for the difference in sound. I did not like to compete with the guys who had the knobs just because now I have a knob. We didn't get into that! For guys that didn't stay sensitive to what acoustic instruments are about, raising the volume did not make the music better.

The Fender Rhodes did have its place in music, especially in the '70s. Groups did pump up the volume for energy because they were playing 20,000 seat stadiums. I had the pleasure of doing 25 dates with Earth Wind and Fire after we put out Sun Goddess. I know Larry Dunn was just elated that he had the Fender Rhodes because he could pump up the volume and be a part of the landscape. I took a bigger band with me when I did that – had a keyboard player besides the Fender Rhodes because that's the way things were in the '70s. Fusion music was predominantly electronic and the Fender Rhodes definitely was a major part of that sound.

There were those critics who thought that jazz should always be acoustic. There were as many not-liking what Miles Davis did with Bitches Brew... it's a funny thing. Eddie Harris and others were using electronic instruments and the critics were thumbing their nose at them. Miles Davis did Bitches Brew and they're like, (clears throat)... "Well, I guess it's okay." It was the late '60s when Miles did In a Silent Way and all that Fender Rhodes music. Going into the '70s, that instrument was at the forefront.

Charles Stepney was producing some stuff for me in the late '60s and well into the '70s. He was a Fender Rhodes guy. We did Herbie Hancock's "Maiden Voyage" and he had a song called "Le Fleur"... oh, yeah... That was a good song. I might play that again! [Smiles]

Charles Stepney was a genius. I did an album called Mother Nature's Son that had all Beatles' songs from the White Album. He played that for me and the Beatles were doing a good job, but, I didn't hear them in a jazz way. He said, "Can I just arrange a couple of them to show you what can happen?" He did, and it was one of my biggest albums. Stepney had a lot to do with Minnie Riperton's career and others. So when you talk about that era, Charles Stepney's name should be remembered. Unfortunately, he passed away at a very young age... but, he was a genius.

The first time that I ran into Stevie Wonder in New York City, he said, "Ramsey, I might have some music for you. Come over to my hotel." So the next day I did, he had stuff all connected in his room and he wrote a tune for me called "The Distant Dreamer" (from The Piano Player – 1969).

We struck up a friendship and it lasted a long time – well into the '70s. Stevie wrote several songs recorded on the Fender Rhodes.

In fact, they would not have sounded as good as they did had they not been recorded on the Fender Rhodes. The Fender Rhodes became one of his children. He still uses it.

Well into the '80s, the Fender Rhodes was part of my arsenal – a definite part of my sound – especially when I would move from the Steinway to the Fender Rhodes. It would add to the color of what I was doing.

I think Bill Evans is one of the best examples of being able to transfer your keyboard sound from an acoustic piano to the Fender Rhodes. I don't know if any other keyboard would allow you to do that, but when Bill Evans was playing the Fender Rhodes, you still knew it was Bill Evans – like most of the masters. It allowed you to maintain who you are. With other electric pianos you'd have to make adjustments and the keyboard would tell you, "If you really want to sound better, you better play it this way." Not the Fender Rhodes. In fact, the Fender Rhodes encouraged you to try different things... because the sound sort of tickled your inner being. It would say, "Well, that sounded good. How would this sound?" You found yourself searching and being curious.

If somebody put a record out, especially jazz, that didn't have the Fender Rhodes sound, you missed it. You'd think, "Something's missing here... " It became part of the very fabric for a good 30, 40 years... It's interesting how things evolve. I don't know... maybe it's time to go back to it.

Jeff Lorber

Philly-born Jeff Lorber represents the second wave of funk-fortified jazz musicians that arrived in the late '70s. He has had a long and varied career as a player, band leader, composer, producer, talent scout and more. It says a lot that both pied piper Kenny G and "Superwoman" singer Karyn White sprang from his touring and recording groups. He's a man who wears many hats well which has kept him busy to this day in front of and behind the scenes. He discusses the long, winding often strange twists his career has taken down his personal stretch of musical / metaphorical "Pacific Coast Highway" – and how the Rhodes stayed with him at every turn… bringing new meaning to the phrase The Jeff Lorber Fusion.

The first vivid memory I have about a Rhodes was when I bought my first Rhodes. I was about 16 or 17, living in Philly, and had a friend who was a really good drummer named Ronny Margolis. He used to go to Manhattan every Saturday and take a drum lesson with some real hot drum teacher on 46th street – and I used to tag along. There were all these great music stores. Manny's Music was right there in Midtown Manhattan. Somehow the people that owned Manny's were distant relatives of mine. They weren't close relatives, but, there was some kind of connection.

I actually played guitar and sang for the first band I was ever in, only because I didn't have anything portable. Keyboards were my main instrument, but an electric keyboard was an expensive proposition compared to a guitar. Finally a few years later, I was able to put enough money together to get a Rhodes.

It was about $495 for a 73 silver top suitcase model Rhodes from Manny's Music in '67 or '68. At that time, this was the most crazy, extravagant expenditure you could imagine – equivalent to like 4 or 5 grand now… but, buying that first Rhodes piano, bringing it home and starting to play it was an amazing, wonderful experience – definitely a highlight of my life at that time.

I played in a couple bands when I was in high school and one was a blues band. The kids that lived in my area weren't into blues at all, but through some fluke I met these guys that lived in a suburb of Philadelphia called Cheltenham. Another 30 or 40 minutes north of Philadelphia was this town called Ambler, which was much more rural. I hooked up with these guys that were really into Eric Clapton, the Blues Breakers, John Mayal and the Paul Butterfield Blues Band. I really dug that stuff too, so that was the first band where I really played the Rhodes. We used to jam a lot. We'd go into my friend's basement, turn the lights off and the only thing you could see was the little L.E.D.s on the amplifiers and stuff, and we'd play these blues songs. I really enjoyed that experience of kind of getting turned onto the blues at an early age and playing with guys that knew a lot more about it than I did. Blues is a huge part of my musical personality. Everything comes back to the blues one way or another.

After that I played with some guys that lived closer to my neighborhood and we basically did sort of R&B and what was on the Top 40 at that point. We played people's parties, in barns and little country club gigs – all that stuff is really valuable. When people ask me about how to make it in the music business, I always tell people, those little gigs like playing weddings, bar mitzvahs and whatever, it's really valuable to learn cover songs, standards, polkas and the blues. It all helps to teach you things.

A long time ago I found some old tapes in my garage and had them transferred to digital, but there was this one tape that would never play back. I have a little oven that I can bake tapes in – because that's what you literally have to do to make old tapes play. I figured I'd bake this tape an extra long time before I threw it away to see if I could get it to play back. Sure enough it did and it was some of the earliest demos I ever made – all 16-track stuff. The thing that was funny is at the time, 16 tracks seemed like tons of tracks. Like, "How am I ever going to use up 16 tracks?" It was 4 tracks for drums, 1 track for the bass, 1 track for the Rhodes, maybe a piano, a couple of synthesizer tracks and a couple of horn tracks. This tape included a bunch of things from my first album, The Jeff Lorber Fusion (Inner City – 1977) and all were, at most, 13 tracks.

I was listening to the Rhodes sound of those early Jeff Lorber Fusion records and that was definitely a big part of the sound of that band when we got signed and our demos. I think one time we borrowed some kind of digital delay. The only effect they had in the studio in the mid '70s when we were recording was a plate… a reverb device that vibrates when electrical signal goes into it… sounds very good actually.

Herbie Hancock and Chick Corea were my heroes and my models on the Fender Rhodes – also George Duke and to some extent, Patrice Rushen and Joe Zawinul. The first Herbie record that made me go, "Wow, that's what I want to do," is the *Fat Albert Rotunda* album (1969).

He was playing the blues with the Fender Rhodes. Even though that record was made with jazz musicians like Joe Henderson and Albert "Tootie" Heath, these straight ahead cats were playing Boogaloo-style jazz.

A few years later he did the *Headhunters* album (1973) that took this idea of funky Rhodes playing and propelled it 100 times more powerful. He wasn't working with the straight-ahead musicians playing boogaloo anymore. All of a sudden he's working with Harvey Mason, playing a really sophisticated kind of funk. Later on, Wah-Wah Watson on guitar became a huge part of his sound.

Chick showed how the Rhodes could be used in a Latin context. His album *Friends* was just an amazing record with Steve Gadd, Eddie Gomez and Joe Farrell. They got such an intimate, warm ensemble approach that blended those simple elements of the Rhodes, drums, flute and bass. The first Return to Forever album was like that too, with vocalist Flora Purim. It had a very intimate beauty to it also that was really different than the stuff that Herbie was doing.

We could get into a whole other thing with the kind of sounds that Joe Zawinul got into using heavily cho-rused Rhodes sounds with wah-wah pedals. It just gave it a whole other character that no one had ever heard. From a sonic standpoint, the stuff that he was doing was even more creative.

There is a very funny story about my first album. I only had $1,000 budget for the album. Even during that time that wasn't enough money to make a record. So I had to trade the guy that owned the recording studio my Clavinet AND my car. I didn't drive for about a year after I made that record!

I was riding a bike and public transportation. I also had to transcribe all these country songs for him. The tough part was I could never understand what the guys were saying because they had this heavy accent.

Anyway, that record actually did reasonably well for $1,000 budget. It only did well in the Pacific NW where my band was playing, but it was enough so that my second album, *Soft Space* (Inner City – 1978), got an $8,000 budget. We were like, "Wow, what are we gonna do with all this money?" The sax player I had at the time wasn't quite the right guy for a couple of the songs I was writing, so I was thinking about getting Joe Farrell to play on the record. I had written to Chick and Chick was really nice, wrote back, and we kind of had a little bit of a communica-tion going. He's the kind of guy that likes to help out young aspiring keyboard players. I kind of knew his manager, Ron Moss, who many years later be-came my manager for a few years too. So I hooked up hiring Joe Farrell to play on a couple of songs on this second album. When I told the sax player in my band, he got mad and said, "Well… why don't you get Chick Corea to play your parts!" I thought, "That's a fantastic idea! I should invite Chick to play on the record, Sweet!!"

Both of those guys were so gracious to come in and play on that album. It was quite an event for me because at the time I was living in Portland and had never really been in a real recording studio in a big city. I flew down to L.A. and went to the old ABC Studios – a legendary studio in Hollywood where Steely Dan did all their records. I think it was later bought by Kenny Rogers, but it was a recording studio where tons of great albums had been recorded. I was friends with guys in Pleasure, an R&B band from Portland that was recording down there with Wayne Henderson, so that's how I sort of hooked it up.

It was a thrill to go into that studio and work with Joe. He came in, played the song down one time and thought that was going to be it. I had to say, "Joe, let's do a couple more takes, man! C'mon!" I had to convince him to give it a couple more shots, which is funny because the song that he played on was a song of mine called "Katherine," which became a pretty big radio hit. Joe ended up recording it himself on his very next album (*Night Dancing* in 1978 on Warner Bros.).

Having Chick come in and play this incredible Minimoog solo was pretty terrific also.

When rappers started sampling "Rain Dance," I think it was because of the sound of the Rhodes with an Oberheim 4-voice at the time. It had a terrific sort of brass sound that I doubled it with. It had an interesting quality – unusually colorful voicings for those chord progressions. The drummer Dennis Bradford put a real cool swing on the thing. There are a lot of songs from that era that have those ingredients, but, obviously there's something special about "Rain Dance" that attracted producers in hip hop.

It's been sampled, a few times... The very first time was on an album hardly anybody ever heard called *A Death Row Christmas*. [Laughs] Even though that was very obscure, I think it gave my song some sort of hip hop credibility. My stuff started getting sampled more and more by other artists like Jay-Z, who used a similar syncopated groove from my song "Night Love" (from *Galaxian* – 1981) for his track "Who You Wit" (from the soundtrack of "Sprung" – 1997).

It's great to have this music that I made so many years ago get another shot at life and a new generation gets exposed to it. When I first heard Lil' Kim's song "Crush on You" (featuring The Notorious B.I.G. from her album *Hardcore* – 1996), nobody told me it had been sampled. I was driving in my car, turned on the radio and just heard the song. I had to pull over to the side of the road, like, "What's this?!" Sometimes samples are used in ways that you can't really tell where they came from or how they're being used... but, this one was very exposed – you hear the entire original "Rain Dance" track in the intro – all the little drum fills and all the detail of the original production. There's not much to it except this guy Fanatic who produced the track added a SP-12 kick and snare, that's basically it. He just put some more drums on it, chopped it up in interesting ways then played back different little pieces of it along with the vocals.

I didn't own the publishing on "Rain Dance" because I had sold my publishing years earlier, although I still get a little piece of it. They had cleared it and everything was cool, just nobody told me about it, so it was sort of a shock.

I got into sequencing really early. I went to a rehearsal with my band one day and they informed me that they wanted to get writers credit on all the music that I had been writing because they had been putting their little two cents into the songs. So, the next rehearsal I had every note written out for everybody, including the drummer. At some point I thought, "Well, as long as I'm doing all that, I might as well just play the stuff." I had a little 8-track and a Roland Rhythm box. I'd start making all the demos myself, playing bass and getting some drum stuff going.

When the first sequencer came out, which was made by Oberheim, they made an OB-8 and the DMX-DSX. That turned out to be a great thing for me because when I moved to L.A. I started working a lot. (Record Producer) Richard Perry was the first guy that gave me a lot of work. I was working with a lot artists that he was producing like the Pointer Sisters, Barbara Streisand and Jeffrey Osborne. He had a great little group of people he discovered before anybody had ever heard of them like, Diane Warren, Robbie Nevill and Greg Phillinganes. It was really fun to work at Studio 55 and do that whole sequencer thing. I was, way into that! I was making all these records – big pop records that I was sequencing, bass lines and all this busy drum machine stuff.

Then my friend David Frank, the keyboard player for a duo called The System who sort of invented the whole idea of 32nd note synthesizer bass parts and drum parts, was the first guy that really used a sequencer and drum machine to make it do stuff that no human being could or would ever play. He lived right around here in the Pacific Palisades. I went over to his house one day and he had a Wurlitzer. I sat down, played it and was like, "Whoa, this is great!" I was missing out because I had already migrated into DX-7 and all this other stuff and wasn't playing Rhodes anymore.

It was a big revelation to me that this is where it's at and I gotta go back to the real instruments – to the real Rhodes, the real Wurlitzer, the real Minimoog.

To this day, even though I use a lot of synthesized elements, I really love the Rhodes. I love the sound of the authentic older instruments.

They have a depth of dimension and expressivity you don't get (elsewhere). I love the Yamaha Motif and S90 ES keyboards, which I use all the time when I'm on the road, because one of the big problems about the Rhodes is that it's heavy. So that means when people carry it, when they put it down it goes BANG. When that happens, a lot of things can go wrong inside. When you're on the road and you try to rent a Rhodes, they're usually going to be wrecked. So, I have to use something else, but when I'm in the studio and play this thing (the Fender Rhodes), that's what I like to do.

I was just in a piano store the other day and we were talking about these Yamaha pianos. They make fantastic pianos, but they're coming out with all this electronic stuff that just becomes obsolete so fast. That's what happened with the Rhodes EK-10. If you look at the electronics that were in that thing now, they're crazy obsolete. What they were trying to do was combine sort of an oscillator-driven organ with the Rhodes. I can understand why they were doing that because, at the time, there were tons of synthesizers coming out. They figured if they jazzed up the Rhodes with some of that, people would dig it. From a modern perspective, that stuff is just so obsolete, but the Rhodes itself is such an incredible sound… somewhere between a celeste, vibes and a piano. It's just unique.

The Rhodes has such an interesting spectrum of frequencies. If you listen to the high edge of the sound, it's kind of unpleasant if you really analyze it… sort of noisy. There's something about the harmonics that come off of it that aren't like string harmonics. It's like a gamelan with some kind of odd harmonic spectrum. Depending on how loud you hit it, it has a totally different character. Obviously, it made its presence felt in popular music. All over the place it's almost become more common to hear the sound of a Rhodes in a typical pop arrangement than even a piano. It creates such a warm bed to build a song upon… I'm really lucky that I got a great one here. I play it almost every day on everything I'm doing. I just really dig it.

I was working with Herb Alpert on one of his albums. He had a bunch of gear in his basement. At one point, he took some of the stuff back and I got to keep some of it, including this Rhodes.

I'm not sure how it all worked out, but basically I worked with Herb, I ended up with this thing and I'm very grateful! [Laughs] I've never had it worked on or looked at. I just record it through an API preamp straight into Pro Tools and it sounds really good. Herb had this box built around it. I guess it keeps it from moving. I never really thought about it because I'm not really moving it around, though it does have wheels.

Over the years, I just kept trading them… When they came out with the 73 model it seemed like a good idea. The stage model was so much lighter – less stuff to schlep around – so I got into that. I kept trading up to get the latest and greatest versions.

It's nice to see that his little invention has stood the test of time and that people still love it as much now as they ever did.

Robin Lumley

British keyboardist Robin Lumley is best remembered as a member of the inventive progressive rock band Brand X whose members included bassist Percy Jones, percussionist Morris Pert, guitarist John Goodsall, drummer Phil Collins (with Kenwood Dennard filling in when Phil was off with Genesis) and second keyboardist Peter Robinson. He also produced former Yes and King Crimson drummer Bill Bruford's amazing debut album, Feels Good To Me (featuring guitarist Allan Holdsworth, bassist Jeff Berlin, keyboardist Dave Stewart – not the Eurythmics one – singer Annette Peacock and Flugelhornist Kenny Wheeler), and briefly toured with David Bowie on his "Spiders From Mars" tour.

Also a magazine columnist and instructional video maker, Lumley remains passionate about how the Fender Rhodes was such an ironic lynchpin in the dizzying pan-cultural pastiche that was the Brand X sound.

The Fender Rhodes was the actual heart and soul of the set of instruments I used. Any of the others were dispensable at a pinch, but the Rhodes was the centerpiece. Of course, I had things like a Minimoog (who didn't?) which was marvelous for solos and basic string synths for layering and painting audio canvasses behind the main lead / solo lines… but, everything evolved around the Rhodes. I've actually still got my original Rhodes, which I bought in 1972. Unfortunately, it's in the UK in storage.

I will one day have it shipped to Oz (Australia). It's been around the world a few times on tours and has been on some 30 albums, I believe. It even survived intact (admittedly in a good flight case) after being dropped down a backstage lift shaft in Toronto! After seeing a special dry powdered lubricant in use as a liner for fiberglass boat moulds, I decided to treat all the wooden articulating surfaces for each key by spraying them with this stuff. It made the action a tad sloppy, but, speeded it up considerably. I wrote about this modification in Contemporary Keyboard magazine in 1979.

One of the many wonders of the Fender Rhodes was the way in which one could employ textural sound areas to enrich a composition, especially in the Jazz-Rock genre. I found that when writing, you could find yourself having your piece of music actually altered by the instrument whilst the tune was being written. In other words, the piano would subtly cause you to compose especially for it! Hooking up a few very simple outboard devices like a flanger or a Roland Space Echo (all very analogue stuff now, of course) allowed you to expand the piano's range of sounds even further.

My biggest influences were undoubtedly Chick Corea and Joe Zawinul. I always had to try hard not to derive anything from the both of them!!!! Incidentally, on a tour with Weather Report (taking in Antibes Jazz Festival, Montreux and then Hammersmith Odeon in London), I so remember a long chat with Joe Zawinul in the back of the tour bus on the way to Montreux. Joe apparently is very reticent about talking to other keyboard players. He'd seen our Brand X set at Antibes and changed seats to yap with me. I was so honored!

Amongst many pieces of advice, he suggested I learn to write with my left hand. He said doing this joins up the lazy neurons and makes your left hand enormously better… it was, he said, the secret of his dual-instrument playing. GREAT advice!!!!!!

Sadly, Brand X is not still performing… at least not in its old format. Percy and John have occasionally gone out under the name BX (or Branx D as we joking called it in the '70s / early '80s) and had a lot of fun, I gather. I'm still in close touch (mostly by e-mail) with the chaps concerned. In about 1994, I discovered a battered old cassette tape at the bottom of a cupboard, which had "BX Roxy LA 1979" scrawled on it. The tape turned out to be a monitor mix of a show at the Roxy in Los Angeles… we used to make these to assess things, like running orders of tunes or what bits needed a bit of work. These tapes used to get junked or wiped over… never saw the point of keeping them! Somehow this one survived… we had it computer-cleaned and digitalized. Although the balance and sound quality wasn't much, the performances were very good and the whole thing, including the usual Pythonic stage announcements, in my mind is a great representation of a complete gig.

Other than that, there is a silly band out here in Oz called Absolute Zero, which is soon to play at the odd jazzy club or two. *Yours Truly* is the ivories basher and some other pals of similar vintage make up the rest of the band. We called it Absolute Zero because that just about summed up the level of talent available! The repertoire comes from all members and of course there are a few old hoaries from me like "Disco Suicide" plus newer tunes in the style of the old BX.

Ray Manzarek

As one fourth of the psychedelic Sunset Strip-launched band The Doors, Ray Manzarek is a giant of Rock and Roll history. His use of jazz, Middle Eastern textures and blues is a highly influential keyboard blend in guitar dominated rock and is responsible for one of the Rhodes' most definitive and identifiable rock staples – the cool mysterioso mysticism of "Riders on the Storm." When the Doors eventually disbanded two albums after the tragic 1971 death of lead singer / poet Jim Morrison, Manzarek worked on further solo and group projects before going onto produce one of L.A.'s seminal punk outfits, X. As a solo artist, he has championed high concept works such as the rock opera Carmina Burana, a collaboration with beat poet Michael McClure

titled Love Lion, the film AND soundtrack of a noir thriller titled Love Her Madly and an album of piano and guitar duets with Roy Rogers titled Ballads Before the Rain. Of the Rhodes, Ray insists there'd have been no Soft Parade of Strange Days for he and his aspiring filmmaking mates had it not been for the revolutionary sound of its Keyboard-Bass.

The Doors are basically a 4-man band: lead singer, guitar player, keyboard player and drummer, forming a diamond. When we started out, I had the Vox Continental organ, Robbie (Krieger) played through Fender Amps, John (Densmore) had his-drums, Jim (Morrison) had a Shure microphone also singing through a couple of Fender amps – but, we had no bass player.

We auditioned two bass players. With the first bass player we auditioned, we wound up sounding like the Rolling Stones. The second bass player we sounded like Eric Burdon and the Animals. I forget what we played with the first guy, some blues and stuff. With the other guy, I guess the mistake was playing the "House of the Rising Sun" – a big hit for The Animals. The bass player got all muddy and weird. It just made it strange on the bottom. It lacked cleanliness and tightness. In the psychic realm, it broke the shape of the diamond is what it did.

So we're auditioning for gigs around L.A. We did something in the South Bay in Los Angeles – I forget what the name of the club was – hoping to get a Monday or Tuesday night. The headliner, whoever the hell they were, was some slick band. You could tell by their amps. The guy had a Vox Continental and sitting on top – Eureka – is the Fender Rhodes keyboard bass – black and shiny. I never got one in black – well, I did later on – but, the first one I had was the brown one – I call it the functional woodsman, I figured if I was playing in the forest this would be a great one to have. I saw this instrument and I thought, "Oh, my God, it's a bass!" I can play the bass with my left hand, play all the keyboard parts with my right hand, chord changes, soloing and that's going to work out just absolutely "Hunky-Door-y." Sure enough – that was the secret to The Doors.

We went to Robby Krieger's father, good ol' Stu, and said we've found the instrument we need. We went shopping for it at Wallach's Music City on the corner of Sunset & Vine in dead-ass Hollywood, man. They sold records, musical instruments and sheet music. We went in and there was one in the window. We asked, "How much is that?" The guy said, "$325." [Sighs] Three hundred and twenty five dollars?! We can't pay the rent!

The rent on the place that Dorothy and I were living in with everybody chipping in was $200 a month. We had this big front living room of a beach house, right on the beach in Venice, California – absolutely gorgeous. It was an old Craftsman-style divided up into four apartments – two on top and two on the bottom. We had the front sun room, set up all the equipment and rehearsed in there. That was $200 a month; $325?! So Robbie went to his father and said, "Dad, we need this instrument." Stu said, "All right, I'm going to buy this instrument for you kids… but, you better go to the top!" "O.K. Sir, we will! Yes Sir, Stu. Thank you so much Mr. Krieger! We'll become the #1 band. Yes sir!"

We're nothing, man. We don't even have a gig… the Whiskey A-Go-Go, the London Fog, that little dive-ass bar that we played on Sunset, nothing… absolutely nothing. We had $325 and you know what? Stu never asked to be paid back. He never said, "All right you guys, 'Light My Fire' is the #1 song in America. Where's my $325?" He was so proud of Robby and so happy that Robby's band – as he saw it, it was Robby's band – became the #1 band in America.

With that bass line, A minor to B minor, what we were doing is our homage to John Coltrane's "My Favorite Things." McCoy Tyner is doing it in 3/4 and we're doing it in 4/4. It's the same kind of pattern when it came to doing a solo and "Light My Fire" was like, "Ooo, let's do something for Coltrane," just to be hip. There I was practicing little Bach variations, except my right hand was playing "Light My Fire." Great instrument… I just absolutely loved it.

That's the "Light My Fire" bass part and the Fender Rhodes, that's the baby that did it. I carried that thing around the entire career of the Doors. Just the Fender Bass – a brown one just like this – this guy played Madison Square Garden, this guy played the Forum in Los Angeles, this guy went to Europe and played, my God, played everywhere in Europe.

The sound was totally unique. I don't think there's another band I know of that the keyboard player ever did this. Guys would play Hammond B-3 doing the bass parts with the pedals. The first guy I knew of who did that in Rock and Roll was Felix Cavalieri of The Young Rascals out of New Jersey – east coast guy, but, I could never figure out how the heck you do that – it's like tap dancing or something.

"Riders on the Storm" is certainly one of The Doors' most famous songs and OUR Fender Rhodes song. That was the one that became a big hit, unfortunately, after Jim Morrison passed on – leapt upwards into the loam… entered the ether… shed his mortal coil in Paris – and we made a truncated version of "Riders on the Storm" that was from our last album, L.A. Woman. The hit single was "Love Her Madly," and then "Riders on the Storm" was played. So, let me take the opportunity to play a little of it on this great instrument and this bass line, which was very hard for bass players to play, was like nothing… it's E minor, A major and Jerry Scheff, Elvis' bass player, was playing bass on the album.

What was Jim's comment on the Fender Rhodes bass? He loved it! He said, "It's got bottom!" I remember the first time… we did it at that beach house in this big 30 foot living room, with a wall of glass, sun…

It stepped out onto the beach. Now this is from a Chicago boy – from the south side of Chicago. My dream had come true, we hadn't even made it and my dream had come true.

I was playing music with my fellows in a beach house where you step out onto sand – the Marina was off to the left and Washington Blvd. was on the right. It was just absolutely open. There were oil derricks, a couple of houses and nothing. The next house was a hundred yards over. The oil pump was a hundred yards over. The preying-mantis, you know, those things just go up and down. It was like, there was nothing, man – nothing but The Doors, the beach, the sun, the light, the ocean, my girlfriend and my guys… a bunch of acid-heads playing music, man. It's, like, late '65 / early '66 and Jim just loved the sound the first time we played it, we did "Light My Fire."

We had been playing "Light My Fire" on a Vox Continental, but an organ should only play two notes, maybe 3 notes – that's all. You can play nice chords… maybe 4 notes, but, you have to hit staccato chords. You can't play chords and a bass line. So to play "Light My Fire," it was just mushy-mushy-mushy. Then we put the Fender Rhodes keyboard bass on top of the Vox Continental – flat. The Vox is flat so the keyboard fit right on top of it. Two manuals: there's one right here and one right here. Man, when we kicked in I said, "All right, let's try 'Light My Fire.' One, two, one-two-three bah," everyone went WOAH! There was bottom – there was, like, CAJONES – there were balls to The Doors' sound. We all looked at each other, smiled and said, "We got it now!"

I never used just a Rhodes on gigs, though. I had a set up with a Rhodes, a Hammond, a Clavinet and the Vox. We had money. We could afford to do this. I didn't have to play simply the Vox anymore. Nor was I the roadie anymore. When we first played the Whiskey A-Go-Go, what was great about the Vox is that it folded up. There were two parts and I could walk into the gig carrying them like the guitar players. Later on, you know I had to have one of these on stage. You gotta have a Fender Rhodes piano! I mean, my God, got to have that!

Nobody really calls it Fender Rhodes, you know… it's a Fender Rhodes Keyboard Bass, interestingly, but it's not a Fender Rhodes piano, it's a "Rhodes." You play a Rhodes. Fabulous instrument, unique sound and I've never seen one sitting out where people can resist. Any keyboard player cannot resist sitting down and playing a few chords on the Fender Rhodes. Invariably, it's like a jazz instrument. When you play this thing, somehow you're playing jazz. You can't help but play jazz on the Fender Rhodes! Herbie Hancock plays this thing. Chick Corea plays the hell out of it. Maybe my favorite is the late Joe Zawinul from Weather Report, who played with Cannonball, then he played with Miles, then he started Weather Report – an absolutely magnificent, Slavic, Eastern European keyboard player like Raymond Manzarek – three generations removed from Warsaw, Poland. Hearing Joe Zawinul, he had a chordal structure that was superb. He's obviously one of my favorites.

You know what else I listened to – other rock bands from "The British Invasion." That's what did it to The Doors… certainly what did it to Morrison too.

I mean, here we are at UCLA, we're studying film, making movies and into Fellini, Goddard, Truffaut, Kurosawa, Satyajit Ray from India – all those filmmakers. We wanted to be filmmakers. All of a sudden, here comes Rock and Roll from London and it's the Rolling Stones with "I Can't Get No Satisfaction." It's Eric Burdon, the Animals, the Kinks and the Beatles.

Then there was some goofy stuff like Freddie and the Dreamers… but man, it was a great Rock and Roll happening. Then they became "phenomenons" with Los Angeles Times headlines like, "The Beatles in U.S." and "The Rolling Stones Come to California!" We're watching these guys that are about our age, with long hair and the girls are going absolutely crazy. Morrison's going, "I want to do that!"

I've been playing music all my life. I'm a Rock and Roller from the first generation. I was playing Little Richard and Jerry Lee Lewis. I grew up with all of that, so I was always into Rock and Roll. When I saw the Beatles and the Stones, obviously stoners long hair, man these guys are into something and we got into ingesting certain hallucinogenic psychedelic substances… one of them was illegal – the one that you smoke – however, LSD was not illegal.

So there you have it. My name is Ray Manzarek, the keyboardist of The Doors. I've played these things for a long time, and without this instrument, there are no Doors. This is the Fender Rhodes Keyboard Bass. What a thing… this is the bass player of the Doors. There's a joke in Rock and Roll circles that goes, "Who's the bass player of the Doors?" There is no bass player of the Doors. There's the Fender Rhodes Keyboard Bass… and there's my left hand.

Les McCann

One need look no further than Les McCann's amazing Live at Montreux double album on Atlantic from 1972 to experience the utter oneness this man has with the Fender Rhodes. That and a Clavinet were all he had on the stage that night and he wore them both out, wringing every emotion and nuance of soul from the keyboards – be it on extended funk vamps ("North Carolina" and "Cochise") or the most sacred of love songs: carnal ("With These Hands") and spiritual ("Comment"). On "What's Goin' On" alone, he makes the instrument grumble and growl, then caress and bless – an unparalleled showcase for what could be brought forth from a Fender Rhodes.

It's no wonder it was McCann The Man's playing that brought Harold Rhodes himself to tears in the twilight of his years, stating between sobs that what he heard Les doing with his creation is what he'd always dreamed. The legendary Les McCann waxes wistful, philosophical and adoring of the Rhodes in the stream of consciousness jewel that follows.

We had an upright piano in our house that had 12 notes that worked. So I thought all my music in the early days was Chinese music! My mom was a fake opera singer – she listened to the opera on Saturdays and mimicked it. (Cringes) "Damn Ma, give us a break," you know!

I played a Sousaphone in the high school marching band and the drums, which was my second thing. When I was in the Navy, I played snare drum in the marching Drum and Bugle Corps.

The day I discovered the Rhodes was a magic moment in my life because I knew it instantly. I was at Atlantic Records and saw a friend of mine named Joe Zawinul who was getting to be well-known at that time. He was telling me how much he liked what I did… how funky I was, and this and that. He said, "Come over here and check this out!" I said, "What is this?" and he said, "A new piano called a Fender Rhodes." So I sat down at the thing, hit one chord and [grabs heart] Oh, my God… I knew right away when I touched it and heard that chord, it was "me" – what I'd been looking for. It became a part of me. I went out as soon as I could and bought me one. It turned my whole career around. After I started playing it, that's when I started getting young people coming to my concerts. My audience became a full range of people and it was a beautiful thing.

I just got more into it the longer I had it. CBS was the parent company then. I'd bring my Rhodes in and they'd clean it up and fix anything that broke. So my Rhodes was always pristine… just beautiful. I took my Rhodes everywhere I went. When I stayed in hotels, I needed to have a Fender in my room. I almost feel like I mastered it over a period of two or three years.

Some clubs owners didn't want me to bring in my Rhodes. "What is that on the stage? What're you doing?" I said, "My piano." "Oh, no, you're not playing that in my club. I got that spinet (piano) over there – I bought that for you to play!" I said, "That ain't no piano! I'm not playing that!"

All I had to do was announce to the people that came to see my show, "The club owner does not want me to play this," and the people would say, "Are you kidding? If you don't play that we're leaving!" They got the message real quick!

I noticed that the people telling me not to do it were older. I was looking for a younger crowd anyway because I wanted everybody to hear what I was doing. I don't know if I was that conscious of it like I'm telling you now. All I knew is that once I started playing it, young people started coming to see the shows. Kids sitting in the front row going, "Wow, I'm gonna get me one of those instruments at home to play on… " "Wow, we didn't know it could sound like that!" "Whoa, I got your records and that's why I come to see you, because of that piano – the sound you get on that is like no other."

Marvin Gaye told me, "You recorded my song, 'What's Goin On' on that piano and I like your version much better than mine." I said, "Whoa, okay, okay. I accept that." I never had a negative situation. If I tried to show someone something that I was doing, soon as I hit any note on this I had 'em. It was no losing.

One of the beautiful things about having the Fender Rhodes piano was there were many times when I felt the spirit to create a song. I'd never have to do it beforehand because once I sat at the Rhodes and got my moment of peace and quiet, BAM, it would come just instantly… the complete song… melody, bridge, everything… complete. Everything about the sound of this instrument was highly spiritual and highly inspirational to me. It just turned me on in a way that you'd think a drug would do.

It was just so beautiful to experience that. I'm not talking about write a song melody out, then come to the piano and work it out. No. Just sit down and play it. It's already in you. It's already there waiting to come out. Plus, with God in your life, you don't worry about it. You know, becoming aware of that being in my life, I could do that. It was like channeling the instrument. I realized later that I can do a whole set without ever knowing what we were gonna play, it was then, I realized I was really a jazz musician.

Sound engineers came to me saying, "Would you mind if we added some speakers and other technical things with it to see if we could expand the sound?" I did one show where we had speakers all around the room and the Rhodes was on a delay... it was so beautiful. I couldn't hold myself to play because I was so taken by the sound.

My life is filled with golden moments. My album *Invitation to Openness* (1971) was one. (Producer) Joel Dorn came up with that title. That's what it sounded like to him.

I played for 4 hours. We did, like, 16 tapes – 32 tracks. The band was so supportive. "Hey, man! We don't know what you're doing, but don't stop!" Even the tracks we've never used are truly, truly beautiful. We made an album out of that called *Layers* (1973). I remember waking up in the middle of the night in New York, "I got it. I'm gonna do this record! I can hear it!" I could name every musician I wanted on it – except one. I told Joel this idea and how I couldn't figure out who the soloist would be. He suggested Yusef Lateef, so we called him and he said he'd be more than happy to come to New York and do it. That is history right there.

It was totally spontaneous. The bass player had an exact thing he was doing, but we had FIVE DRUMMERS... and each of them came in with an attitude! Alphonse Mouzon said, "Man, what you got all these other drummers in here for?" I said, "Can they do what you do?" He said, "No." "Well, that's why I hired you. I want you to do what you do." He said, "I like to solo."

I said, "Solo through the whole record." He said, "Nobody's ever said that to me before... " Bernard Purdie is a rhythm man. I wanted him to keep the tempo. Donald Dean (Les' regular drummer) was free to do whatever... he knew what I wanted him to do. Buck Clarke and Ralph McDonald (percussionists), you know they knew what to do!

That's how it happened. It's one of those kinds of records where, when it's over, you go home and the next morning you get that phone call. "Man, you gotta come and hear this! You're not gonna believe this!" That's exactly what it was... BEYOND the dream I had when I thought of it – to sit spontaneously with these guys, just give them a little thought of what it was about and mainly just go with the flow, do whatever you feel, but make sure it relates to what we're doing.

Layers and *Invitation to Openness* are what I call my most creative albums... the ones I feel most strongly about – unrehearsed and spontaneous.

The Rhodes is why it happened. I had already been creating, but it wasn't put on tape. I was just doing all this in my hotel room or at home alone. In the middle of a dream I said, "Wait a minute. You can take this further. You can do it with a whole bunch of guys."

There are 15 musicians on the record and trust that this will work and it did. But it's all based around what I was doing here on the Rhodes. I wasn't out front on the record in any way. I was the support and the inspiration for what everybody else did.

I went through the whole track showing 'em what I was going to do – what the idea was – and they were like "Whoa, why don't you do that by yourself?" I said, "We can do it together." Some of those guys had never taken a solo before. The guitar player, David Spinozza, it was the first time he'd ever taken a solo. It just all came out. I said, "Trust in the spirit that's in me," and they all went for it.

I was playing at the San Francisco Food and Wine Festival and people were going crazy. This was during the period when I first started playing Rhodes on all my gigs. A lady I know who is a Pastor walked up to the stage and said, "You're great on that grand piano, but you're a motherfucker on that Fender Rhodes!" That's something I never forgot. I hear her voice to this day saying that to me and the crowd standing around her cheering, "Yeah, Yeah!!"

When Eddie Harris and I recorded our second record, *Second Movement* (1971), the Fender that we had was from a rental studio in New York. Right in the middle of recording the song "Carry On Brother," the piano starts going out of tune. I'm almost ready to get up and stop playing… but, Joel Dorn, the producer was standin' there saying, "Don't stop! Keep playing!" The out of tune part of the record is what made it because of the sound of this

"Prince of Peace" (a spiritual from his 1988 CD *Butterfly* that he co-penned with Jon Hendricks) is one of my favorites that I recorded on Rhodes. Several of my Samba-like songs were on it (including "Vallarta" from 1977's *Music Lets Me Be* on Impulse! / ABC).

I wrote a song on it called "Someday We'll Meet Again" for my album *Another Beginning* (1974). It just fit this instrument perfectly because I could do the groove (though he played the melody and solos on acoustic piano on this). Almost everything I did was done on this piano because I trusted the sound. I knew I could come up with something… I didn't even have to worry about it – especially slow songs and ballads. In concerts, I'd be playing something then out of nowhere I'd pull out the plug here to make the "wave" [vibrato] happen and you could see the people fainting in the room… you know, the women, underwear was coming off and up on the stage! (Laughs)

I was telling my friend Margaret tonight, "I'm sexy, you know? I don't look like nobody else, but when I'm playing this instrument I feel sexy." I feel if I played this to you, you gonna be playing back to me. I used to give massage therapy. Often when I have someone that's really uptight I'd say, "Lay on the table." I'd put the earphones on their head, plug it directly into this and I'd play for them. By the time I'd finish they were totally relaxed and ready for a nice massage. So between this and me… we some sexy motherfuckers!

I never looked at this as a piano. [motions to Rhodes] *This is me*. Once I played it and knew it was me, I instantly incorporated that in my program and in my shows. I took it everywhere. I played piano and Rhodes together at the same time, but this was the dominant. This was the bottom. This was the foundation. This is what made me want to sing. Sometimes I couldn't wait to go to work at night because I couldn't wait to hear the music come from this instrument.

I got so carried away with this instrument that I wanted to hear two and three of them on stage at once with people doing what they do and I do what I do – all on this keyboard. I knew I could do the bass on this if I wanted to and get a soloist who's very good on it, but I understood the music the way I heard it. These were young guys and just couldn't get any real discipline out of it. It was a great idea and the one time we did play was truly beautiful, but, that was it. We had four Fender Rhodes' and a drummer. Yeah.

The only player that would even come close on something like that for me now would be someone like George Duke who always told me he loved the way I played this. Bill Evans said, "Wow, on that piano… when you play those soulful ballads you bring me to tears." To hear that from him… I really loved him. He was working with Miles and whenever Miles would see me – when we'd be in the same town together – he'd say "I'm comin' to see you tonight. You gonna do my song?" I'd say, "What song is that?" He'd say, "With These Hands." He wanted to hear me sing that every time – on this piano.

I was offered a job because of that with Cannonball Adderley when he first formed his group. Miles heard me play, went back to New York and said, "You getting a new piano player? Why don't you get this guy in California, Les McCann." He called me and asked me to join his band, but I said no.

I had my own ideas. I wanted to have my own band and I did. But, again, who could be more funky than Cannonball and his brother (Nat)… AND that's how I got to know Joe Zawinul – the one that introduced me to the instrument. I took it from there.

Playing this Rhodes is like therapy… having the sound the way I like it… the stereo so even when you hear it… the right balance of sound… it's just… ahhh, like breathing… like your heartbeat. So this is therapy. In his original concept of the instrument, he was 100% right about creating something that people could recover from experiences in the war. Thank God for Harold Rhodes… the king.

I didn't meet Harold Rhodes until many years later. They were doing a documentary on him – his life, how he came up with an instrument to help people in the Air Force who had been injured in war and how this was a rehabilitation instrument. While they were filming, they had a Rhodes sitting there – the one with the legs on it. I sat down to play it so I could get used to it. I wasn't supposed to play on film at all. I was just sitting there like we're doing now. His wife was there and a whole bunch of people at the house out in the valley.

As I was playing, I looked over and saw he was cry-
ing. I leaned over to his wife and asked, "Is he okay?"
She said, "He just said to me that when he invented
the piano, the way he heard you play it was the way
he imagined it should be played." I don't think I could
have had a better compliment than that… It made
me cry, you know. He also said later that he knew
he was old and he knew he would be dying soon,
but that he was so happy that he heard me play his
Rhodes the way he liked it.

This instrument and I are one. Period! Even after I
had a stroke I knew I could play this instrument, but
I didn't have the one I wanted anymore. Every time I
tried to rent a used one, it would be the stage model,
not the suitcase model like this one. The sound was
right but I couldn't do what I wanted to do.

This is me.

"Fender McCann is my name / Musicians that know
me say the same."

John Novello

Primarily known for his blistering organ playing as a member of the power trio Niacin and as an invaluable sideman to many including Mark Isham, Cheryl Bentyne and Andy Summers, John Novello nevertheless has deep Rhodes history as a close confidante of the late, great Harold Rhodes. Below he discusses his entry into music, his special relationship with Chick Corea and the coup collaborative work he did with the man that invented the Fender Rhodes.

I started playing the accordion, like Jan Hammer did. Then I started hearing cats playing the organ and I got my first Farfisa organ… shows you how old I am. Then I got a Hammond Organ and got into the B-3 thing. Right around that time is when I heard Chick Corea and what he was doing in the first Return to Forever band with Flora Purim and Airto. Right afterwards when Bill Connors got in the band and the electric "RTF" thing started to happen, that's what flipped me out. That sound grabbed me as much as the B-3. Up until then, I wasn't even a fan of piano. I was an organ cat.

The story of Chick and me is weird. I grew up in Pennsylvania. A friend came to practice one day and said, "Hey, I got 2 new records for ya," and he gives me an Edgar Winter record – the first record, *Entrance*, this amazing jazz funky sort of R&B stuff – and the other record was Chick Corea's *ARC*, a trio record where he's playing piano. They both blew my mind and that's when I first found out about Chick Corea. On the back of the record it said management in Boston or New York and I wrote him a letter. In those days you didn't think anybody was going to write you back. A couple weeks later, I get, "Hey John, thanks for all your support of my music." I asked him a couple questions and we started to become pen pals – going back and forth. He was being the sweetest cat.

Finally, I moved to Boston to study at Berklee School of Music and I wanted to get more serious. Chick is from Boston and he was coming to town to play the Orpheum. We hadn't met yet – just pen pals. Somehow I knew somebody and got backstage for sound check in the afternoon. Chick had his place in Chelsea where he lived and he comes in with his wife, Gayle (Moran). As he walks by me I said, "Hey Chick, it's Novello!" He goes "Novello!" We shook hands and I got to hang at his sound check. We went out and had dinner. It was just natural. We became best friends and started to hang out.

Later on he moved out to California. I moved out a couple years later and I started helping him with his New England Digital Synclavier – that $250,000 toy. I was programming that for him and we got to be really good friends. So he's not only been an inspiration, but a friend.

In Boston there was a jazz club called the Jazz Workshop and Paul's Mall, two clubs right in the same building. Return to Forever had just started with Connors. That's when I saw Chick live playing the Rhodes with the little Ring Modulator on top. I remember hearing *Hymn of the Seventh Galaxy* and my world was rocked. It had the fusion of unbelievable rhythm, funk and high energy – no restrictions in that music. Those guys were having a great time.

Since we were friends, I'd say, "Dude, you gotta send me this score," and Chick would send it to me free of charge. I'd be sitting there like a kid in the candy store going, "Man… " I'd be practicing all the parts – the best way. In the Renaissance days of classical music and Baroque, there was no media to record anything. How did those guys learn? They went to concerts, memorized that stuff, went home and wrote it out by ear or eventually got the manuscript and just rewrote the manuscript – that's how they'd study. So for me, having a soundbyte and the manuscript that was, like, the best school. Even though I was going to Berklee, I probably learned more getting charts for "No Mystery," "Hymn of the Seventh Galaxy," "Duel of The Jester and The Tyrant" and of course, "Spain."

When I came to California in '78, I immediately formed a quintet of sax, bass, keys, drums and guitar – progressive, funky jazz fusion. I was writing all the material. I was playing B-3 organ, I had an OB-X synthesizer on top and I had a Fender Rhodes on a right-angle. I had processed it through equalizers and gotten more of a Dyno-kind of sound. My two favorite sounds, even over piano, were the B-3 and the Rhodes.

I could comp on the Rhodes and blow on the B-3 or vice versa. I used to put the Rhodes on top of the B-3 and the back would stick out. I had to get an extra long rod for the sustain pedal. It was just ridiculous, but it was really cool to have it up there. You had to lean over to play it and I couldn't really get any leverage, but that's how all of that started.

Eventually that music turned into Niacin. I met Billy Sheehan and, again, it's one of those stories. I meet a rock bass player and he comes up after we meet and says, "I really like your B-3 playing. I've never been in a band with a B-3 player. I'd like to do something but not with vocals." So we put a power progressive rock B-3 trio together as an experiment. We called it Niacin as a joke because Niacin is vitamin B3. In fact, it wasn't a band. We just wrote a song and we had so much fun writing the song that we needed to demo it.

I had seen (drummer) Dennis Chambers playing with the Mike Stern / Bob Berg Band out at the (Santa

We called Chick's manager who knew how to get a hold of Dennis. We called him up, sent him some demos and he said, "I love it!" We flew him out to California, did the first Niacin record and the rest is history. We've got 7 or 8 records out and that band is just kickin' butt. It's mostly B-3 but I have a Kurzweil on top where I play piano, Fender Rhodes and a couple of lead synths.

I met Harold Rhodes through Steve Grom, John Shykun and Steve Woodyard – he was the tech guy down there. I went down to the factory, started playing stuff and John and me hit it off really good. Next thing you know, I got introduced to Harold and we hit it off good. Harold and I would talk and after a while he called me up and said, "I need somebody like you to do a couple of radio spots."

He'd get college radio stations and book these things. I'd meet him down there and he had cartage send up a Rhodes. We'd go into the radio station, set up the Rhodes and "5 4 3 2 1 boom – Hi, I'm Harold

Harold talked to me about his educational concepts. He knew that I had written many books on contemporary keyboard playing. My line with Hal Leonard is called "The Contemporary Keyboardist." So he would show me some of the stuff that he wrote music education-wise.

Then one day I got a call from Harold and he says, "Hey John, guess what? We're actually going to MIDI the Rhodes." Shortly before that, I got a call from somebody at West L.A. Music and somebody said, "A new interface just came out… you gotta come down!" I went down and there were about 80 or 100 people in the store. I don't know who did the demonstration, but I can't even fathom that it was a big deal now. It was like, "There's a new interface called MIDI – Musical Instrument Digital Interface," and I'm like, "What is that?!" Up until then, when you wanted to play 2 parts, you played 2 synthesizers. I was on the road with Donna Summer. They had 5 synthesizers and I'm playing them all at the same time, doubling all these parts. Keyboard players were just expected to do that. So when I went to the show and the guy sat down, played the keyboard and told me through this little 5-pin connector it could play the sound of one synth without playing the other synth from the same keyboard, I was like, "Really?" We all walked away, like, somebody invented the wheel. That was a BIG deal.

So Harold says, "We're doing a MIDI Rhodes, a factory one, and we want you to be one of the guys to help us Beta-test it." A month or two later, this Rhodes was delivered and it was amazing!

I started playing it… I was talking to Chick and Herbie because I knew they both got one. We thought this was going to be a really big deal. We were the only ones that had it at the time. They were only going to make 500 of them. Then all of a sudden, the word came down from Corporate that they did some marketing surveys. The DX-7 came out and all those little synths with the tweedy-wheety little-sounds. I hated those sounds. I was pretty upset that they didn't do that, but, we were allowed to keep them. I just played it all the time. Eventually, other MIDI Rhodes came out. Gulbransen had a retrofit and other people came out with it, but, this one and 2 or 3 others were the original ones. There's no way I could ever sell this. It's got too much history in the making. Harold would probably "Poltergeist" me to death. [Laughs] "Right, Harold? Bless your soul."

An organ doesn't have velocity sensitivity. The moment you hit the key, it makes contact and that's it. Try to play it any harder, you're gonna break the key AND your finger. I know a lot of piano players that get on the B-3 and think they can do something with it other than hitting it. You gotta play light and use your volume pedal to do it. Just like a horn player would use the wind, use your volume pedal. On velocity-sensitive instruments like a Clavinet, a Rhodes or a piano, you've got the speed of the attack. On the Rhodes, when you really got down – when that hammer hits that tine – that spike really barked. You'd think that we wouldn't want that, but after awhile, you dug it! I used to call it a turbo-charge.

I remember meeting McCoy Tyner. I went to this jazz club on the outskirts of Boston. He was playing the McCoy stuff at break-neck speed… it was barkin', man! He had that attack on the piano. Afterwards I went up and said, "McCoy, how do you play with that speed, that velocity, that double-forte, and play that fast?" I'll never forget this – he takes his hand and goes like this [holds hand out palm down fingers out] as I'm watching his hand, he does this… he put his fingers like that [flexed vertically up] on his own. He's double-jointed and his fingers from the knuckles just go up. So when he plays, he's a bit flat-fingered. He can raise his fingers really high and come down. If you try to do that with your elbow, you can't go that fast. How fast can you vibrate such a big muscle? Now, Chick's pretty good at it because he plays drums. He can do it more than some people. I can't do it that fast. Once I get to a certain place, I gotta go over to finger and wrist power to get the speed, but then I'm gonna lose that barking sound… that attack. For some reason, the Fender Rhodes bark… it's like a drug.

Harold is to the Rhodes what Laurens Hammond is to the Hammond organ and Don Leslie is to the Leslie Speaker that went with the Hammond organ, and Les Paul is to the Guitar. How amazing to sit down and invent an instrument that allowed a bunch of creative artists to be inspired to write volumes of music then go play it. My hat's off to people that can do that. It's one thing to be an artist – to play, entertain, inspire and create work – but, for somebody to have invented the instrument that you're doing that on, that's pretty astounding. Harold was just fully an inventor that pulled a couple rabbits out of the hat. He really got into this instrument and it was his baby.

I'm happy that he invented it. Chick is out there still playing his Rhodes and writing all kinds of great music. Another good friend, Gonzalo Rubalcaba, has got records out where he's playing Rhodes and piano. He's got ridiculous chops. Hearing that Rhodes mixed in with the piano is just amazing. I hope the tradition goes on and on.

David Paich

From teenage wunderkind on the L.A. session scene to California Rock and Roll royalty as founding keyboardist of Toto, David Paich is a child prodigy – son of the master orchestrator Marty Paich. With a string of award-winning and chart topping pop credits as long as Kobe Bryant's arm, he is among the music's most valuable players. In Zelig-like fashion, he tells stories below that attach him to stellar moments with artists ranging from Steely Dan, Boz Scaggs, David Foster and Cheryl Lynn to Quincy Jones, Weather Report, Miles Davis and Michael Jackson.

It's an honor and a pleasure to be here and part of this series with the Fender Rhodes, one of my favorite instruments in the world. What the electric guitar was to Jimi Hendrix, the Rhodes is to keyboard players. Like a lot of keyboard players, after the electric guitar came and piano players had been stuck on these little ratty spinet pianos with little microphones stuck in them, there wasn't a competitive electronic keyboard. Then in 1969, I was lucky enough to see a Fender catalogue. I believe that CBS and Fender had gotten together – and there was this keyboard in it. I saw that and said to my father, "I sure would love to have one of these... I could join a band!" Luckily, my dad (legendary arranger Marty Paich) had been working with a great drummer named Louie Bellson and Louie had a Fender endorsement.

I didn't know this for years – because my dad wanted it to be a surprise to me – but, he wrote two arrangements for Louie's band and Louie got me a 73 Rhodes – chrome-top with speakers – stereo and everything. I was off to the races. I could join a band, which ended up being Toto. I met (drummer) Jeff Porcaro when I was 14 (on the "The Glen Campbell Goodtime Hour" TV show). He had the finest band in the valley there and because I had that instrument, I could work gigs.

The history of this instrument is pretty amazing… made by Harold Rhodes during World War II for wounded soldiers on up to the '60s with the keyboard bass, which Ray Manzarek of the Doors made famous when they did "Light my Fire." Everybody said, "You can play bass on this thing!" With my first Rhodes, we didn't have a bass player. We had a guitar player, a drummer and me, so I was pretty much the bass player and the keyboard player. It was great… so much fun!

Jeff Porcaro and I formed a band called RSL which later became Toto. I used to sit next to Mike Lang and there were always three instruments around: a grand piano, a Hammond organ and the new bad boy on the block, the Fender Rhodes electric piano. After I got out of high school, Quincy Jones had started the TV show "Ironside." He moved onto something else, so my Dad took over the show and I moved into what's called the Rhodes spot. There were always two keyboard books when you'd go in to do movies: piano chair and the Rhodes chair. That was my chair. So I started writing songs I believe in 1973/1974 while I'm gigging the whole time having a blast playing on this instrument.

I was lucky enough to win this little Emmy award right here. The only reason I brought this out of my closet is to celebrate this instrument that Leo Fender and Harold Rhodes put together, this Fender Rhodes here. I played on this for an "Ironside" episode titled "Light the Way." I was doing sessions at the time for Seals & Crofts and various people.

Jeff Porcaro was working with a guy named Boz Scaggs who was looking to write an album which ended up being Silk Degrees (1975). I was fortunate enough to be that chosen person. I won a Grammy for the hit single "Lowdown" from that album, which Boz and I co-wrote and recorded using a Rhodes – the main ingredient on that song.

After that I formed my band Toto. In the beginning for me, it came down to the grand piano, the Hammond organ, and the Rhodes. We used that on a lot of our records. I was lucky enough, through working with various people in L.A. to meet (famed Beatles Producer) George Martin who was doing an album with (songwriting legend) Jimmy Webb – Jim was on piano and I was playing the Rhodes. After we did those sessions in 1983, Sir George asked me to write a chapter in his book called Making Music. I was asked to write the chapter on the grand piano to instill in young players why reading music is so important. Reading music doesn't mean that you can't still play funky – that was my whole chapter! It's funny because there happens to be a picture of a Rhodes in my chapter… that's what I was playing with George. This was a book written by professionals for professionals and this is a very professional instrument. George gave me a copy with my name on it and an inscription: "To David, with thanks and admiration, George Martin." He wasn't even Sir George Martin then.

While we were recording the first *Toto* album (1978), my father and I were producing a young, new talent named Cheryl Lynn. We got in the studio with her and I came up with a groove that became (her biggest hit), "Got To Be Real" (Cheryl wrote the words, I wrote the music and David Foster contributed on the back end). On guitar was Ray Parker Jr. who lives down the street from me, James Gadson on drums, and David Shields on bass. Again, the Rhodes was there… which is why David Foster ended up co-writing that song with me. Toto was over at Sunset Sound working on our album and he came in. I was on a grand piano and there was a Rhodes. We sat down and he started singing to help me piece together one of the verses. He was producing the Average White Band, in the next studio and he was playing a Rhodes at the time.

David Foster brought a lot to this instrument when he did "St. Elmo's Fire" on which he combined the sound of his piano with the Rhodes, 50% Rhodes / 50% piano.

Another big record during that era was Elton John's "Daniel," which was done on the Fender Rhodes. They should have a discography for the Fender Rhodes… how many Gold Records, how many hits and Jazz records this little puppy's been on.

Ray Charles makes this sound like nobody else… so funky.

Who can forget Stevie Wonder?! We're always, like, "How does he get such a good sound?" Everybody used to mic the Fender Rhodes speakers. Stevie, I believe, was the first guy to start taking the direct feed from it and micing it, which made it sound a little bit different.

They would run two feeds. Plus, Stevie had this thing where when he'd do his vibrato, he would do this triplet thing. Everybody told me the key to Stevie's sound is quarter-note triplets. Of course, it's Stevie Wonder playing, so no one sounds like Stevie, but that was a thing he would set it for – his own unique setting for that.

One young guy I met that scared all of us off the planet is Greg Phillinganes. We all just wanted to stop playing and retire when we heard him. He played so good it was scary!

What was great about this is there's not a lot of knobs, no paging and not too many synthesizer buttons on it, just volume and vibrato controls, EQ, then outputs from it – so work with what you have on it. People would take it direct out – 2 stereo direct outs – then mic it as well to get that nice, warm sound.

I first started doubling the piano – which became Foster's trademark – on "We're All Alone" for Boz Scaggs. You can hear what a beautiful, almost vibraphone sound, it gets… almost sounds like it's mallets at times. They used to use it in movies a lot. Some of the motion picture keyboard players would show me some of the outer limits of weird sounds. A gentleman who I sat next to for many years is Mike Lang. He did a lot of the early Clint Eastwood movies, still does all of Clint Eastwood's piano playing and all that jazzy Lalo Schifrin soloing stuff. To this day on movies, he brings in his "cherried-out" mint condition 73 Rhodes. There's nothing quite like it when Clint needs that "Dirty Harry" sound or whatever. Mike's still a formidable, legendary keyboard player today.

"Georgy Porgy" was also a combination of Fender Rhodes and my grand piano. I got that idea from a gentleman named Leon Ware who had conceived the "I Want You" album for Marvin Gaye. We just wore those records out. I said, "Man, I gotta write a song like that." So that was a combination of Leon with a little bit of Barry White thrown in. I had been working with Steely Dan at the time and I asked Walter Becker, "What are you reading these days?" He says, "Children's nursery rhyme books." So I went out and bought the book he had and the first thing he opened it up to was "Georgy Porgy Pudding Pie." That's the first time I ever told that story.

Quincy Jones was going in with Michael Jackson to make what became *Thriller*, a milestone album in all of our careers. There was a lot of Fender Rhodes on that. When I did "Human Nature," it was a combination of synth bass and stuff, but we'd double a lot of those parts and they're very subtly laid... so smooth. You can just layer it in and put the Rhodes behind it to ghost it a bit.

There was a song after the Thriller album called "I Just Can't Stop Loving You" (from Bad) that Michael did, which is one of the first tracks we ever cut. I remember sitting down on a Fender Rhodes cutting that with Quincy (engineer) Bruce Swedien, (singer / songwriter) Siedah Garrett and Michael in the room. It's really hard to know which ones I ended up playing on. You go in and Quincy would have it like a football field – 5 keyboard players sitting out there between me, Foster and Phillinganes. We're coming into the control room, like – one guy take a break the other guy comes in and plays the part, so it's hard to tell who's playing what... except I do know Phillinganes always ended playing the bass parts.

Again, we have to go back to our history books – Greg started out playing with Stevie Wonder and the first instrument he played with Stevie was the Rhodes.

God Bless you, Michael. Thank you for having us all play on that. We miss you madly.

Synthesizers started coming around – the Yamaha people started trying to compete with the Rhodes which was very hard to do because it was such a staple. A guy named John Chowning came up with a thing called FM Synthesis which used all sine waves. My band mate Steve Porcaro, film composer James Newton Howard and I were flown to Japan to unveil this keyboard. They brought us in this big room, took the veil off and it was this teeny little keyboard... like a DX-7 but small. We played it and they had pretty much duplicated – in its own synth-y chime-y way – a beautiful simulation, but not exactly the same thing, of a Fender Rhodes. It became a later competitor.

Quincy calls me and he's doing "The Color Purple." "Quincy, where are you," I say because I can hear people shouting in the background. He goes, "I'm on a cherry picker down in the south. I'm next to Steven Spielberg and we're shooting 'The Color Purple.' I'm up on the camera crane right now." Then he asks, "What was that kalimba (African thumb piano) part you played on 'Africa?'" So I ran downstairs with the phone and played a little bit for him on a Fender Rhodes. He said, "I want to take it down right now. We need that kalimba thing." So I showed him this thing that I had done on Africa which is a combination of things to make a thumb piano sound. I said, "You got that?" He says, "Yeah, that's in 5."

Then I said, "Now write down the next one." I know he can barely hear me. I stop him and ask, "Quincy, what's it like?" He said, "You know how Oscar Peterson plays the piano… what a mofo he is? That's how Steven Spielberg directs. He's like the Oscar Peterson of directors." Then he goes, "What's that last part?" Now he took it, changed it a little bit and slowed it down, but you can hear it, when they go back to Africa in "The Color Purple," there's shades of this little part in there slowed down, done Quincy Jones style.

My father, Marty Paich, graduated from USC Magna Cum Laude, and later had a lot of students. John Williams studied with him a little bit and Dave Grusin was a pupil. So I knew all these guys as family members growing up. Dave is just so awesome with his playing and accompaniment, as a film composer, with singers and when he plays with (guitarist) Lee Ritenour. All these keyboard players loved the Rhodes. There were other companies making electronic keyboards at the time, but they didn't have the piano touch and dynamic degrees of response like a Rhodes. It gave piano players like Grusin what they were looking for. It was hard for accompanists to get good grand pianos sometimes, but they'd say, "As long as you have a Fender Rhodes we have it covered." It had all the dynamics and subtleties… a blending of all the higher harmonic tones… just a magical amalgamation of sound that only certain instruments like harps and pianos make that is just so beautiful.

Weather Report used to edit some of their records at my studio because I had Studer two-track. Joe Zawinul and those guys would always be in the back editing, but, no one would ever go in there.

The door would crack open and we'd just listen to and watch them for a second. One day when I came home off a tour and my door was locked. My door would always be open because I had a front gate. Jaco Pastorius opened my door – he had just woken up. He says "Hi, man, come on in. I don't know whose house this is, but we're in the back." I said, "Well, this is my house um, nice to meet you! It's me." Then I said, "Look at this chord Joe showed me" and I played it for him on the Rhodes 'cause I had one in my living room.

My whole house was a studio and Jaco says, "Oh, man, I'll show you a better chord than that. I showed Joe all those chords." One of the chords I got for the song that Toto recorded with Miles Davis ("Don't Stop Me Now" from *Fahrenheit* – 1985) was this beautiful chord that Jaco sat down and showed me. Jaco had immense hands.

Those are the kind of things that would go down with this keyboard in the room. I have Joe Zawinul in the back editing and Jaco on the couch showing me chords – a bass player showing me chords that he showed Joe Zawinul! Joe had just shown me the same chord, only a different permutation. Zawinul – one of the GREAT musicians and gifted spiritual people of all time.

Like Quincy says, it's a beautiful stew full of lots of ingredients and spices. That's from the master Quincy Jones – my hero, one of my father's colleagues and friends and one of my teachers who will always be. So, I love Fender Rhodes and I love everybody here for allowing me to speak on behalf of Leo Fender and Harold Rhodes.

Jerry Peters

In any discussion of all around musical excellence, Jerry Peters belongs at the top of the list. His far reaching experiences in pop, R&B, gospel and film scores, plus his vast catalog of production and compositions, live performances and executive dealings, place the formally trained Peters among the most valuable players in the music industry. When Earth Wind & Fire was suffering the sudden passing of producing / arranging genius Charles Stepney, Jerry Peters is who they called to complete his work for their monumental album, Spirit. When jazz giant Blue Note Records was taking its controversial plunge into funk-jazz fusion

with productions by Larry & Fonce Mizel of artists such as Donald Byrd, Ronnie Laws, Bobbi Humphrey and Gene Harris, Jerry Peters was a key player on all of the sessions. When the talented family group The Sylvers made their debut on Pride / MGM Records in the early '70s, it was Jerry Peters and his hand-picked crew of L.A. session peers that helped distinguish them from "bubblegum" groups of the era by giving them a sophisticated sound (since heavily sampled in hip hop). When Quiet Storm vocal divas Phyllis Hyman, Deniece Williams and Brenda Russell were all making their crucial debut solo recordings,

Jerry Peters was there as an arranger, composer and / or producer to showcase their singular voices in just the optimal light. When the gospel world needed a renaissance man to bring the richness and contemporary pulse of the finest soul music to help spread the good news to a wider audience, Jerry Peters is the man to whom that industry turned to make that dream a reality. He was also a member of the stalwart '70s jazz aggregate The Writers (with Anthony Jackson, Ralph MacDonald, Jeff Mironov, Hugh McCracken and Frank Floyd). Below he discusses just a few of the Rhodes highlights of his career.

I'll never forget my first time playing a Rhodes. I was working in L.A. with The Friends of Distinction. This was in the old RCA studios on Sunset and Ivar. I had co-written a song for them with Anita Poree called "Going in Circles." We were in the studio and they brought in this big instrument. I think I'd seen the smaller one before, but they brought in the 88 and it had this low bottom on it because it was a full keyboard. I was blown away! Not long after that, somewhere between Herbie Hancock and Joe Zawinul on Miles Davis' *Bitches Brew* project, they were using the Echoplex a lot. That led me to use the Echoplex on a song for Deniece Williams called "Free" and it worked quite nicely. Maurice White (producer of Deniece's 1977 debut Lp *This is Niecy*) wanted an intro for the song. I didn't think about it too hard, just something "open"… with the Echoplex.

There's a song that closes Earth Wind & Fire's *Spirit* album called "Burning Bush." I used it on a Syreeta & Billy Preston date, a lot of Motown stuff, Marvin Gaye's *I Want You* project, the Emotions "Blessed." Those kinda stand out in the R&B world. We also used it a bit on some of the crossover jazz projects for Blue Note like Donald Byrd and flautist Bobbi Humphrey. There was a Brazilian pianist named Manfredo Fest that I produced also, that was wonderful and a great Brazilian album. I actually did another project as a producer on the great pianist Gene Harris and we used the Rhodes a bit. I used the Rhodes on the movie soundtrack for "The Wiz" in New York with Quincy Jones. I used it when I produced a band called Brainstorm.

I literally tracked Hebie Hancock down! I had been playing another brand – starts with a "W" – and was traveling with Eddie Fisher as his music director. I had done some demos, was in New York, put some stuff down on tape of this other instrument and went over to meet Herbie Hancock. I played a little and he said, "Man, you're wired for sound!" I came back to L.A. and started doing a lot of sessions. Three years later, Herbie hired me to work on a film that he was scoring called "Death Wish." I did some orchestration for it. Herbie used the Rhodes extensively on the project. (The duo Les Nubians sampled the Rhodes from our work on that soundtrack).

Acoustic pianos and Rhodes are mechanically different because of how the mechanisms work, but they were akin enough to where there was a certain amount of affinity between the two. I liked that it was a touch sensitive instrument. I can put my weight on there, or get virtually no sound. Even though it's amplified, it's depending on me to hit it. I can't necessarily do that with a digital piano. If I wanted to make it sound loud, of course I turn it up, but you can feel the natural dynamics when you hit the Rhodes. You hear all the overtones – you hear that clicking. That's what you don't get on a digital keyboard, so you appreciate that knocking sound. It gives it sort of an acoustic property. Even though the microphone isn't necessarily picking it up – especially if it's going direct – but the player is experiencing that feedback which makes it kinda friendly.

The tone controls are another advantage because you have some form of equalization, not to mention the vibrato. That gave us that dreamy feeling… we love that! So it can be really soulful, really expressive… close to the guitar. That made it great for blues-oriented / soulful stuff. Ray Charles, obviously, used that "other instrument," but later on began to use the Rhodes. I think he completely dumped that other instrument, which I thought to be very interesting if you go back and listen to some of those recordings. So, like I said, the Rhodes has left its mark.

Ronnie Foster and I met while he was at Blue Note. He asked if I would come and produce these albums for him when he signed to Columbia. We got together on that. What I love about Ronnie, you come to his place and he's got stuff stacked up everywhere! We used the Rhodes quite a bit on *Love Satellite* (1978) and *Delight* (1979).

We just had a ball in the studio. It was always a laughing time with Ronnie. Ronnie also had a great relationship with Stevie Wonder, so we spent quite a bit of time together. It was a very respectful relationship working in the studio. I actually played on Ronnie's projects too – playing other parts, which was fun.

Funny story – Ronnie is a BMW expert, so he really took good care of his cars. I had just gotten this Mercedes so he brought this car kit for me. He went outside and had a windbreaker for the whole thing. My license plate said 2MWLEAN. After that, every time he'd see me he'd say, "2 M Willie, wassup?!"

You can't get around Donny Hathaway… "Someday We'll All Be Free," "Sack Full of Dreams" and on down the line. Of course, I loved the way Bob James used it on "Mr. Magic"… how the chords were so close. I've got to give it up for "Baby Fingers" – Patrice Rushen – and George Duke.

How can you forget the stuff that Chick Corea did? Matter of fact, he and I were playing two Rhodes pianos on a date for my friend – the late Charles Veal – a violinist, conductor and concertmaster who recorded an album for Capital Records (*Only the Best* – 1980). He wanted to do a cover on a Donny Hathaway song. I played the basic piano and Chick played the solo.

I used the Rhodes on my album, *Blueprint for Discovery* (Mercury Records – 1972) on a song called "Kuri Monga Nuie," an afro-jazz tune in 7/4 featuring Ernie Watts on soprano sax (and percussionists Harvey Mason, Bobbye Hall and Joe Porcaro).

You just could not resist the Rhodes. That sound… I love that parallel movement. 13th and 11th chords are just great for it because you're using an entire harmonic spectrum – virtually the entire overtone series! You're getting all these beatings and all these colorations that sort of amplify a natural acoustic instrument. A lot of stuff going on in an acoustic instrument you don't really hear, you know, but here you actually hear because it seems to be slicing them – breaking them down sonically.

Playing live, it's cool that you can turn it up… but, it's not really dependent upon you to feel what you're playing because you turn it up. When I practice, I can play [at no volume] because I can hear the sound of the keyboard. When I practice the acoustic piano, I put my knees under the keyboard so I can feel the wood knocking. It helps me to calibrate my touch. I don't know if that would have been by design or not, but what has happened is before I actually hear the sound, I feel it, so that's gonna effect how I play it – very much how I feel what I'm playing.

The interesting thing about the Rhodes is that it had found a rightful place. You could park it in the same garage with your other piano. Especially for jazz players – non-classical players – they found a voice or an instrument that they could play, record with and especially perform with live. With the advent of sampling – where you were able to analyze a wave form and actually replicate it digitally by another process – it obviously took that element out. The beauty of this was the fact that this was based upon a technology that was very relatively fundamental.

When you look at a piano, the reality is that you hit a key and something goes "BOING!" That's different from hitting something (on a synth) and it's in another space, so to speak. That's the relationship that we miss with the Rhodes. That's the relationship that has sustained wind instruments and other touch instruments including the guitar. Even in the advent of the electric guitar, there's still this touch experience going on.

Because of these multiple personalities that have to exist on synth keyboards, I'm not convinced that they own to the idea of, "I am an instrument. I'm a problem solver more than I'm a musical instrument. I can do all these things… " That's the struggle for those of us who had an appreciation for the Rhodes, to deal with in the absence of the prominence of the instrument… from pop recording especially. The people that haven't don't know what they might be missing. I don't think I've heard a digitally sampled keyboard that sounds like a Fender Rhodes.

We just did an album on saxophonist Kirk Whalum called *The Gospel According to Jazz* and George Duke used it extensively. So it has a few diehard supporters who will go down fighting for it! [Laughs] I had my opinions about the instrument, in terms of its rightful place in the Parthenon of musical instruments. It sits rightfully next to any other of the great instruments and other inventions that had taken place including its catalyst, the piano itself. I think it's a tribute to the greatness of the piano. That's what's allowed it to sustain.

Greg Phillinganes

Though his first big time break was playing with Stevie Wonder as a teenager and later becoming a lynchpin in the recordings and rare live performances of Quincy Jones, Greg Phillinganes truly turned the heads of many when he took one of the coolest Fender Rhodes solos on an R&B record on "Your Ways" from the Jacksons' 1980 album, Triumph. He has since worked with a stunning array of talent that includes Flora Purim, Whispers, Earl Klugh, Pointer Sisters, Patti Austin, Chaka Khan, Michael McDonald, Mighty Clouds of Joy, Lionel Richie, Chanté Moore,

Roy Ayers, Dee Dee Bridgewater, Gene Page, Joe Cocker, Djavan, Whitney Houston, The Manhattan Transfer, Eric Clapton, Vanessa Williams and, of course, Michael Jackson. He even graced the album that united L.A. session guitar rivals Larry Carlton and Lee Ritenour. He's one of a handful of people who can proudly claim that Donald Fagen wrote a song especially for him ("Lazy Nina" from his second album, Pulse – 1985). The title of his 1981 debut: Significant Gains, which also describes his reflections that follow.

The first time I heard one was probably when I was listening to Stevie Wonder – between Stevie, Herbie Hancock, Weather Report with Joe Zawinul and Chick Corea – all around that time when I was a young teenager growing up in Detroit. My primary inspiration was Stevie and Herbie was an extremely close second. A little later on, I remember listening to Donny Hathaway. That sound was like butter on his *Extension of a Man* album… one of the great albums of all time. I was just mesmerized by the sound. It totally revolutionized keyboards and the sound of records.

The year I got with Stevie Wonder was the year I graduated from high school, '74, which leads into my first time seeing a Rhodes. I was playing in this band where the flute player had a Rhodes and an Arp 2600 synthesizer. He let me use the Arp for the whole summer and I just remember losing my mind in it. Every day – all day, all night – I'd be playing with the thing… much to the alarm of the neighbors! But I also got to use his Rhodes and it was just… a really exciting time for me. I think he had a stage model, but my preference was for the suitcase because it had such a full-bodied sound. Of course, with that vibrato and the speakers, you could not beat it. The challenge was lugging that thing up and down stairs in clubs – not pretty, but I had many a beautiful memories playing around town with that.

As far as how I met Stevie and how I ended up in his band, I was still in Detroit and a friend of mine was first asked to audition on drums. The night before he left, I was happy for him, so I went to his house to congratulate him and just hang out. He insisted that I play some things on a cassette and he was going to take it to Stevie. I said, "I didn't come here for that."

He said, "No, you're gonna do this!" So, I did it, I played a few songs of Stevie's that were hits at the time. I tried to play them the way I heard them on his records – to let him know I know how he thinks… musically.

Maybe three days passed… then one morning my friend called and said, "Stevie wants to see you in New York today." Imagine my reaction. I mean, I'm bouncing off the ceiling! My mom was getting ready for work at the same time, watched me running around and asked, "What is the matter with you?" I shouted, "Mom! Stevie Wonder wants to see me in New York!" She was like, "O.K., just make sure you have clean underwear"… 'cuz that's really all moms are concerned about.

So I'm packing and getting myself together. Now, before I go to the airport, I've been instructed to pick up one of Stevie's brothers at his house. So now I get to go to Stevie's house! I'd known where he lived for a long time, but, this was my first time going in the house. So I pick up one of his brothers – Timothy, I believe it was. I go in the house, I'm sitting in the living room and I'm going, "O.K., I'm in Stevie Wonder's house… this is crazy!" Then we go to the airport, it's my first trip to New York and it's feeling to me like straight out of his "Living for the City" record – "New York, just like I pictured it… skyscrapers and everything!" I get settled in the hotel then I go to the studio, which was the original Hit Factory. I'm waiting there for what seemed like years… squirming, all nervous and everything. I'm talking to the engineers trying to stay cool… All of a sudden I look in the monitor where the elevator door opens up. Out comes his sister then there He is, ambling in like this [mimics Stevie]. I go, "Oh, my god."

So Stevie comes in and I finally meet him face to face. That was one of the greatest moments of my life, period! We talked and played around a little bit. The next day was more like a formal audition. I met the rest of the band and everything, and it was between me and this older guy. I played a bit with the band and I remember a few people coming up to me individually going, "Don't worry about a thing. You got it." They were very nice. On the way back from the rehearsal place to the studio, I was riding in the car with Steve. I'm in the back seat and he's in the front. He turns around and goes, "So how does it feel to be a member of Wonderlove?" All these things are going through my mind because I heard he was such a practical joker. I'm thinking he may be messin' with me. I said, "Are you serious?" He said, "Well, of course, I'm serious!" I said, "Would you mind telling my mom that?" I figured he wouldn't lie to mom. So we get back to the studio, I pick up the phone, call the house and hand him the phone. So the first voice my mom hears is Stevie's and he's saying, "Hi Mrs. Phillinganes, this is Stevie. I want you to know that I like the way your son plays and I want to have him in my band. I'll take good care of him," and stuff like that. He handed the phone back to me and this is what you heard for the next 10 minutes: [SCREAMS!!] My mom and I screaming! She thought it was just gonna be a weekend fling and then I was coming back home – which I did. I spent the weekend there then came home… to get the rest of my stuff!

I spent the next two months in New York which was the perfect time – springtime, April and May of '75. This was just before I turned 19 and just before he turned 25. That shows you how much of a genius he was at that point. During that time I got to participate in, arguably, the last great complete Stevie album, *Songs in the Key of Life.*

I'm playing on four songs – "Isn't She Lovely," "Contusion," "Joy Inside My Tears" and "Saturn." The Rhodes played a huge part in that album and even more so in earlier albums like *Talking Book, Innervisions* and *Fullfillingness' First Finale.*

On "Isn't She Lovely" – after the big drum intro fill – that's me doing the Rhodes part (with some synths and stuff).

On "Saturn" I'm playing the synth brass parts which were done on the big Yamaha Dream Machine – the big white thing that was like a magic castle. I remember sitting next to Stevie, we're playing the parts together… and we're both whacking our heads together! It was a beautiful moment…

On "Contusion," I play this synth lead part. The only reason I'm on that is because in the B section, there's this ridiculously fast line that Michael Sembello (the composer) came up with. He played it on guitar, Steve wanted to double it, but, couldn't play it – one of the few things that gave Stevie a bit of a challenge – so I ended up doing it.

On "Joy Inside My Tears," I'm playing the string parts… heart-wrenchingly beautiful.

I didn't get to have a Rhodes, but, Stevie had about thirteen of them – and they were all pristine. When you were at Stevie's, whatever you touched, he easily had three of everything because he was "Stevie Wonder," people just gave him stuff! He had the best. He'd have the prototypes of stuff long before they came out! He had very interesting electronic keyboards and instruments. It was great! So I just got to play his stuff and that was inspiring enough.

I didn't get one until later on. You know who gave me my first and only Rhodes? Michael Jackson. I was working with him and his brothers on The Jacksons' *Destiny* album. Somehow the subject came up that I didn't have a Rhodes. So one day this truck pulls up to my house, a guy comes to my door and says, "You Greg Phillinganes?" I go, "Yeah." He says "We have something for you." He unloads the truck, this massive box comes out and it's a 73 Fender Rhodes with a note that says something like, "Well, I know you didn't have one so I hope you enjoy this." He forgot to sign it… but, I thought that was really, really sweet.

I still have the Rhodes that Michael gave me. It's deeply imbedded in storage somewhere because it needs some work, but, that's still the only one I have.

The Suitcase 88 with the three knobs. It does not get any better than this folks. Don't get it twisted with that later model that had those slides on it – oh, no-no-no – the one with the knobs, baby! That deep rich vibrato… it's butter.

The '80s was more synth-time. The advent of the Yamaha DX-7 just wiped everybody out. Nobody wanted to touch anything else after that because the DX was so new, so fresh and exciting. It supposedly had great Rhodes sounds… but, not exactly. That was the going thing at the time, so everybody jumped on that bandwagon. The Rhodes kind of got kicked to the curb for awhile. But in situations like that, it's not until years later that you realize how good of a thing you have and then you want to go back and embrace it even more.

During that time I don't remember using Rhodes too much. Later in the mid '80s, it came around again. I used it a lot on projects like Donald Fagen's *The Nightfly* album (1982). I'm on most of that album. "I.G.Y." was the first song I remember working on and it involved a Rhodes.

They started building the track with just me and a little drum machine. I fell in love with the song instantly. It was so hauntingly beautiful that I remember messing up on purpose so I could start again from the top.

My favorite sessions: all the Michael (Jackson) stuff. Also 25 years ago with Aretha Franklin on one that Arif Mardin produced (*Love All the Hurt Away* – 1981). The greatest thing about that was being able to sit next to Aretha and watch her play. Sessions with Rickie Lee Jones (*Flying Cowboys* – 1989) were great fun, also involved the Rhodes.

I had the great pleasure of working with Herbie Hancock and producing a couple of songs with him for his *Possibilities* album. First of all, I never even imagined that I would get to know Herbie Hancock, much less be producing him. His contribution on Rhodes is staggering. There was this tune he did called "Actual Proof" (from his 1974 fusion classic Lp, *Thrust*, featuring the mind-warping drums of Mike Clark). Ever since I first heard it, I was confused about where it fell on the beat meter-wise… actually conflicted with it! I mentioned it to Herbie once at his house. "Bro, what is up with 'Actual Proof'? Why doesn't it work for me?" He said, "Well you know it's all in 4." I go, "No, it's not! It's this weird… ," but, he insists it's all in straight 4/4 time.

I'm scratching my head like, "How is that scientifically possible?!" Herbie was nice enough to sit me down, played the track and counted the entire song for me. He just sat there and proved to me that it's really all in 4. I was hearing it wrong all these years. I was stunned.

I am extremely blessed to be part of George Benson's project, *Songs and Stories* (2009). It's simply the most fun I could possibly have with my clothes on. The fact is "sessions" as I used to know them are kind of dead. The whole process of recording has changed. They're still doing a lot of recording, but for various reasons I don't get nearly as many calls for Rhodes anymore.

The place of technology in music – samples, new gadgets and things – comes and goes. They're wonderful for enhancing and they're also convenient.

But nothing will ever replace an acoustic piano and nothing will ever replace a real Fender Rhodes. It's just that simple. Just like people are realizing the mystical qualities of analog sound vs. digital – how hiss was actually a major component of the sound and how the scratching of vinyl relates to the needle, played an integral part of the sound – it's the same.

Just like an acoustic guitar or a Stradivarius violin, it's not going to be replaced with anything electronic. As close as they may come and as diligently as they may work at it, there is an intrinsic beauty to the sound of a Rhodes. It's not only man-made, but it's the love that's put into each instrument that you can't really describe. There's a joy that comes from playing it because you realize you're not just playing that instrument, you're playing all of the history that's associated with it.

Stuff comes and goes… but, a Rhodes is a Rhodes.

Left: Michael Jackson and Greg Phillinganes

Right: Michael Jackson, Paul McCartney, Quincy Jones and Greg Phillinganes

James Poyser

Philadelphia soul brother James Poyser – a member of the Soulquarians clique – is among the top writer / producers in contemporary soul music. After entering the business doing gospel projects and the criminally underrated vocal quintet B.B.O.T.I., James chiseled a sterling reputation working with the cream of the crop of soul artists including D'Angelo, Erykah Badu, The Roots, Larry Gold, Eric Benet, Nikka Costa, Jill Scott, Common, Roy Hargrove's RH Factor, Chante' Moore & Kenny Lattimore, Lauryn Hill, Anthony Hamilton, Eric Roberson, Vikter Duplaix, Ronny Jordan, Leela James, Jaguar Wright, Mariah Carey and Joss Stone, to name just some.

Through remixing, his work has also enhanced vintage recordings by Nat "King" Cole, Marvin Gaye, Phyllis Hyman and Al Jarreau. The man not only knows soul, he's intimate with the soul of the Rhodes.

I first heard the Fender Rhodes on records and on the radio growing up. My father was a pastor so I grew up surrounded by Gospel music. My family listened to a lot of old Andraé Crouch records and that sound is very prevalent in those records. He had some of the same session players playing on these records that were playing on everything else like, Greg Phillinganes and Joe Sample. As I delved into other types of music more, playing and learning, it just grew from there.

Listening to Stevie Wonder, Donny Hathaway, Roy Ayers… Herbie, Chick and Miles… all that early electric stuff.

There's this music store in Philly run by an old Italian guy. He has a bunch of gear in the basement, but you can't just go in there and buy something. I had to vibe with him – listen to his bad jokes – so I was there a few hours! Then he's like, "You know, my friend, I got a Rhodes for you!" He pulled a Rhodes out of the basement for $100 – a 73 Rhodes stage piano. I gave him the money and ran out with that piano!

Then I got an 88 suitcase. This was in the mid-'90s, so I was late in acquiring one, but I've always loved the sound and I've always played one. Even a lot of the keyboard sounds when I wasn't playing a Rhodes, were Rhodes-emulated sounds, like a Voce module and the D70… back in the day. Those were great sounding, but, you know… it's not "The Real Mc-Coy." The sound of this thing, the warmness of it, was the attraction. When I finally got one… I was in Heaven.

The first major record I worked on that used the Fender Rhodes was Erykah Badu's "Other Side of the Game," which I wrote with her on the Rhodes. Erykah's voice marries well with the sonics of the Rhodes. She has a certain tone to her voice. The warmth of this thing sort of brings it to life.

On a lot of records, I come up with concepts, like a bass idea on my left hand while playing harmonic things on top, so I definitely used it as a writing tool. I did a song called "Sometimes" with (singer) Bilal. Pino Palladino played the bass on the record, but if you listen, my left hand thing is in there also.

I also have a few of those Sparkle-Top Fender Rhodes Bass things, yeah… loved them. I might have used it on the Anthony Hamilton "Cornbread Fish and Collard Greens."

Hip Hop stuff from the Native Tongues Posse and the stuff that Q-Tip was sampling helped bring the Rhodes back. They were sampling soul records from the '60s and '70s. Not only were the drum-breaks funky, but, the Rhodes thing was very prevalent in them. That definitely led to what came after with D'Angelo, Erykah and The Roots. Let's throw Tony Toni Toné in there and The Family Stand. They definitely ushered in that era of the soulful stuff.

Also influential was Roy Ayers – even the stuff he did with Ramp – great very "black" sounding music, if I can say that. It just sounds like black pride and black power really warm and strong.

Growing up in Philly, pretty much every musician that came out of Philly has been inspired by and learned from Gamble & Huff (Kenneth Gamble and Leon Huff). Mr. Gamble had a studio in the Philadelphia International building, so being around him made me listen to their records a lot closer. Hearing Leon Huff's piano playing, also his Rhodes playing. Being able to walk into that studio where a lot of those classic records were made and being able to play the Rhodes that was used on a lot of those records definitely inspired me long before I started working with the Roots and so forth. There's a lot of great local players in Philly, seeing them play it, inspired me growing up.

When I wrote "Chicken Grease" with D'Angelo, we were in the studio one night at like 4am. We were working on Common's *Like Water For Chocolate* album at Electric Lady.

I was playing, D' was playing and Ahmir (Thompson, a.k.a. "Questlove" – drummer of The Roots) was playing. We were stumped for ideas then stuff started coming like, whoa! D' listened to the track in his car because he dropped us at the hotel. He must have sat outside the hotel for like 45 minutes playing it over and over. By now it's 5 in the morning and I'm like, "I gotta go to sleep!" and D' was like, "I need this for my album!" So we took it from Common and we did it. D' did "Geto Heaven, Pt. 2" for Common and kept that song for himself – kept the track and wrote that song.

One of my favorite Rhodes songs is "4 AM" by Herbie Hancock (from his 1980 Lp, *Mr. Hands*). The interplay that Herbie, (drummer) Harvey Mason and (fretless bassist) Jaco Pastorius got into is ridiculous on that! Anything Stevie Wonder has done – the intro on "As" alone... I also love the way Donald Fagen writes – his fake-me-out progressions where it seems like it's going one place and then, ugh... like Reggie Bush running through the line – Boom.

Frank McComb and I are really good friends. He used to live in Philly for awhile. We'd get together and play. Frank's a great player and a great singer! He makes me sick!! It's pretty nuts how he knows this instrument. He actually tuned my Rhodes up a few times in Philly – borrowed it for a gig... on the CONDITION that he tune it.

When the sound of this instrument in the music became popular again, it just felt right. It wasn't a conscious decision to do certain things. I'd end up playing it. I guess my style and this instrument married well together and worked in that time period for some of those records I did with those artists – art-

ists that liked that sound. It was a perfect storm of all those things that came together. The Rhodes has cool textures percussively and melodically. In forming a song and producing – in terms of thinking – you can go from one thing to another seamlessly.

Effects-wise, I use everything – distortion, wah wah pedals, delays... things I come up with through the board... a Mutron phaser, bi-phase... all kind of things. I have quite a few old analog synths set up in my home studio. I'm using a lot of plug-ins, a weighted key controller and a lot of things out the computer. But my Rhodes is in the room. Even though I may write with some of the plug-in things, there's times when I need this thing... like, "Let me plug this in and record this."

I used a real Rhodes and a synthetic Rhodes together on a Gospel record by Tye Tribbet. There's a few songs with the combination of a Rhodes and a particular sound in the Motif that was a Rhodes, but had a different effect on it that was cool.

Playing on TV shows (formerly Dave Chappelle's "The Chappelle Show" and currently "Late Night with Jimmy Fallon"), a lot of guest bands come in and in their set up you'll see this instrument – including keyboard basses – and it's not necessarily soul music... it's used in rock and alternative bands. They may be using it in different ways than in the past, but it's still around.

The Rhodes has definitely been part of my sound on a lot of the records that I've worked on. It's pretty much my main axe... that says it all.

Patrice Rushen

Lovingly dubbed "Baby Fingers," Patrice Rushen represents a level of all around musical excellence and cool that is an inspiration to male and female players alike. A singer, songwriter, composer, producer, arranger and educator, she is still first thought of as the fiery keyboard sorceress that began her recording career in 1974 playing straight-ahead jazz, but quickly became a superstar of funky, feel-good groove. She flourished as a side woman on the records of others — from Jean-Luc Ponty, Harvey Mason and Lenny White to Lalo Schifrin, Teena Marie and Vanessa Williams — was a member of the all star group The Meeting (with Ernie Watts, Ndugu and Alphonso Johnson), and was the sole instrumental contributor to Kenneth "Babyface" Edmonds' landmark all R&B female film score for "Waiting to Exhale." Patrice also produced R&B-pop hits so indelible the first time around ("Look Up," "Haven't You Heard" and "Forget Me Nots") that they have been sampled and covered later on major pop, gospel and hip hop hits for Will Smith ("Men in Black"), Kirk Franklin ("Looking for You") and Mary J. Blige ("Remind Me"), respectively. We found the lady still steady "kickin' back," eager to impart pearls from her chameleonic career and the major role the Rhodes has played throughout.

In high school I was in this jazz band called Msingi Workshop Orchestra – we're talking early '70s. By this time, the Rhodes had begun to really make some noise. I had heard Herbie Hancock play it, I had heard Joe Zawinul play it, I heard George Duke play it. I was familiar with the sound of it. I decided the summer of '71 – the summer before my senior year in high school – I was gonna have one. So I saved my money. Our instructor Reggie Andrews was really innovative at that time. He would bring people into the fold so the students understood their responsibilities – what it really meant to be a professional musician. To wear the moniker of a musician, let alone a jazz musician, meant that you needed to be aware of lots of things – musically and technically.

Mr. Rhodes actually helped me pick the piano that I still have. It was a suitcase model 73. I remember going over at that time they housed Rhodes pianos at Fender. Reggie Andrews (Musical Director for Locke High School and Founder of Msingi) drove me out there because I was ready. I had my money and was ready to go. Harold Rhodes had heard about me and told me "well let's see if we can find something really special for you." The pianos are just rollin' down the conveyor belt, you know, and he says, "That one." I don't know if he really knew that this was a great one or if it was just the gesture of making me feel like he hand-picked my piano, but, it turned out to be super.

The sound of the Rhodes had already gotten my ear because it had the ability to both blend and be a solo instrument. It had a unique sound – a magical sound able to homogenize with other instruments. It could fill out a small horn section or any type of ensemble and sound really good.

Then on its own, it had a distinction too. You had to adjust your playing technique to be able to play it very well. Those that did usually had a really distinctive sound with it because it was very subject to weighting and un-weighting, though I don't think it was designed with that in mind. The pressure of pushing the key created the impact to the tine and a person's touch could be identified after a while.

If the keyboard happened to be really even – meaning that it wore out evenly maybe the same player was playing the same keyboard – then you could determine, besides what they were playing, who was who… which was kind of fun.

But the sound of it was the main thing and the portability because at that time, even though it's big and was a lot to move, it was way easier than trying to move a piano. With the parts it could be repaired, so mine got a lot of use. When I got my first car, I had to make sure it was big enough at least to get the Rhodes in there. I would take it to gigs and people used to hate to see me coming because, being female, I wasn't about to lift this thing, so they would see me coming! I was kind of forced into always trying to play really well because the guys were gonna have to schlep this thing in and out of my car!

I still have that particular Rhodes. A few years later I got an 88 model, again a suitcase. I prefer the suitcase because the sound was better and I liked the idea of the sound coming back to me. I modified my bottom by putting in JBL speakers. The speakers that you got with it were sufficient, but they didn't have the dynamic range that I preferred. So, I did that, which only made the bottom even heavier… which only made me have to play even better!

Since the Rhodes was a new instrument, they started a campaign to get people to see it as a viable instrument. Mr. Rhodes picked certain people to be "Rhodes Scholars" – some of his favorite customers – and I was one of them. The picture in this ad, judging from my 'fro, was probably taken around 1972/1973. This would have represented the type of Rhodes that he picked off the line for me.

The Rhodes was a great instrument, a great discovery and it revolutionized a lot about the way we approached playing. I've never approached it like it was a replacement for the piano. We looked upon it as a sound in and of itself. Even though we have great soft-synths and wonderful virtual synths that give you the impression of a Rhodes… there's nothing like a Rhodes.

While you're always looking to get your own sound, I'm a firm believer that you can't just discover your own sound. That self-discovery comes after years and years of trying to develop and learn the language. As you learn the language, you begin to gravitate towards certain kinds of things that allow you to best express yourself. Out of that comes your style – your *signature*. Just like the way you speak, the same applies to music.

From the standpoint of piano playing, I gravitated towards Herbie Hancock. I think that was because by the time I heard him, I had developed enough vocabulary to resonate with some of the things about him that I liked. I found what it was about his playing that spoke to me and I paid attention. Ironically, listening to him – especially initially – actually sent me backwards.

I paid different kinds of attention to Bill Evans, Oscar Peterson, Wynton Kelly and people like this. These were people that I guess had inspired his playing. I wanted to know where that came from.

Then there were Herbie's contemporaries Chick Corea and Keith Jarrett – also George Duke and Joe Zawinul (both out of Cannonball Adderley's groups).

These were people that fed different aspects of my piano playing in a contemporary way. Those were my heroes in terms of listening. I still revere them as masters of the language and for teaching me a lot of things… not "sit down and let me show you something," but having to really listen… and absorb concepts. As I began to understand it, it started helping me define what my style and preferences were – so it's easier for someone to say, "I know Patrice when I hear her."

Once I had a Rhodes, it was just part of what I was gonna do – only one instrument of choice. I always loved piano and I still do. The older I get, the more drawn back to the piano I am. But I will say that the Rhodes – because of its contemporary sound, its ability to blend and to be different things all at once – was really attractive as I was learning to write and playing with different people. You could do different things that you couldn't do with a piano like hooking up stuff to it – oh, my God – then it became something else! You get your wah-wah pedal, your echoplex, or whatever you could hook up to it and you could manipulate the sound. You're dealing with electronics and you can take that electronic frequency and stream that into a lot of different places.

The Vibrato – the speed of it and all – were toys that when we're playing the traditional piano we didn't have at our disposal. Suddenly piano players had these things that they could do to start manipulating sounds. This is preceding synthesizers as we know them today. There were synthesizers that existed but there were wires, you did a lot of plugging in and it wasn't a lot of playing-playing. So this was my first opportunity to experiment with a keyboard instrument… different than what you could do with organ which is a whole other ballgame. But this was important. The Rhodes allowed the frustrated guitar player to come out with that wah-wah pedal – or to do things in terms of colors and effects that you could hear, but couldn't make happen on piano. Suddenly, on a keyboard instrument you had stuff you could do. So this was really cool.

Comparing a Rhodes to a Wurlitzer, the Wurlitzer is a great instrument, but it was so distinctive. When you played a Wurlitzer, you identified with it as a Wurlitzer. With the Rhodes, you could be a chameleon – you could accompany and shadow or be way up on top. You could kind of hide then be out front with it. It gave you the best of both worlds and for a pianist, it was a logical leap. It wasn't so different from a piano that you couldn't deal with it. Anybody that could play the piano could sit down and play a Rhodes and sound pretty good. I think that's why it became popular for a long time to use in place of piano. But, when we got past that and we really understood that it was a sound in and of itself, man, it opened some doors.

I got to the point very quickly where I saw that piano and electric piano weren't the same thing. They were as distant as a trumpet is to a clarinet. You blow through both of 'em, but they don't sound alike.

You have to use a different technique, they have different characteristics. Well, Rhodes and piano were the same. They both have keys, the keys are called the same things and they're in the same places… but, the sound is different, the touch is different, the way the sound is manufactured is different, the feel when you're playing is different.

For a while there some of us wanted it to feel like a piano. I did not want that to happen because it began to speak to me as its own instrument.

You modify your technique to accommodate the difference of really wanting to get a good tone and a good sound out of it, and develop something different. The people who really pioneered using it – Herbie, Chick and Joe Zawinul – they got that too… it wasn't a substitute.

When I sit down at the Rhodes and start messing around, there's a specific kind of stuff that comes out. The sound of the instrument inspires that. I really loved playing it – the feel of it – the approach to it.

I have to say, without fail, every big hit I ever had prominently featured the Rhodes. It became the basis of the kind of sound I wanted to have. I have a classical background, a jazz background and a funk background. The hybrid of all that is what my brand of R&B, dance music – or whatever you want to call it – was at the time. By the time I had the hit song "Forget Me Nots," I had already been playing for most of my life, so I had a lot of vocabulary to draw from. Growing up listening to Prokofiev, Stevie Wonder, Miles Davis, John Coltrane and the Rolling Stones, you can imagine the bits and pieces of information that have fed the tapestry of what ultimately became what I do and it's always there.

The Rhodes was a big part of that because it was a part of the sound I was hearing and the music I grew up on. I liked the way it sounded when I soloed on it. A lot of people identify me by my use of the Rhodes. The more I used it the more it became a part of what people identified as part of my signature.

I've been on record dates recently where people ask, "Do you have a Rhodes?" I say, "Yeah," and they say, "Well, we want that – a 'Real Rhodes.'" I think we had to go through that whole (imitation) thing to find out, "This is a legitimate instrument with a precise color that does certain things really well and is valuable." Other patches don't have that thing. They're getting better all the time. It's amazing how good some of them are sounding. But there's still this idea of air moving somewhere. The Rhodes still has the ability to move through some space which makes it sound good.

I stayed in contact with Harold Rhodes earlier on. Sometimes I would run into him, sometimes I would go over to Fender and talk to him. He developed all kinds of other things. He developed a series of lessons… he was like the little guy that was always tinkering with something. He was a really nice man – very friendly and warm – and very knowledgeable about a lot of things. I think that was a big part of the initial success of the instrument. He was fearless because he was so confident that this was a great sound. He was like a mad professor, just not "mad" – always experimenting. When he got older, he wasn't finished with the Rhodes. I didn't have a lot of contact with him before he died, but I know he was experimenting still with some pretty heavy ideas that I think his "mentees" are starting to manipulate now and put into work.

As for me, these days I get to do a mixed bag. I teach a little, do guest lectures, appearances and I still get to get out and play (most recently with the bands of drummer Babatunde Lea and bassist Buster Williams).

I'm writing, doing symphonic music as well as jazz, R&B, writing for television and movies. But at the end of the day, if somebody said I could only do one, I'd still want to play.

That has been the catalyst for a lot of the other things that I've been able to do. I'm a better composer because I'm a player and it works the other way too.

I've had some grand experiences and been surrounded by some amazingly gifted genius types in all musical spheres. Now as we continue to understand the value and the importance of all communicative media and art – visual, written and musical – the connection has to be that we're aware of one another. Artists communities are growing, and everybody learns a little bit about everybody's gig, which only makes the sum of the parts that much stronger.

Joe Sample

Houston, Texas-native Joe Sample is a master musician world renowned as a founding member of the Jazz Crusaders (later known as The Crusaders) – creators of the Gulf Coast soul-jazz sound. When the group relocated from Texas to Los Angeles, Joe also became an original member of Tom Scott & The L.A. Express where he was co-creator of the classic "Sneakin' in the Back" on the all-star ensemble's seminal self-titled Lp. Just a sample of some of the Crusaders classics that feature Mr. Sample on Rhodes are "Put it Where You Want It," "Street Life," "Chain Reaction," "It Happens Everyday" and "A Message From The Inner City." His instantly identifiable touch on the Rhodes has also graced such timeless projects as "The Art of Tea" and "Sleeping Gypsy" by Michael Franks, Minnie Riperton's "Inside My Love," Donald Byrd's "Blackbyrd," Marvin Gaye's Let's Get It On and I Want You, The Claus Ogerman Orchestra's Gate of Dreams, Ronnie Laws' "Never Be The Same," Joni Mitchell's Court and Spark, Tina Turner's Private Dancer, Albert King's Truckload of Lovin', Phil Upchurch's Darkness Darkness, Andrae Crouch's No Time to Lose, Ray Barretto's Eye of the Beholder, Tavares' "Check it Out," Herb Alpert's Rise, Seals & Crofts' Get Closer and David Axelrod's Seriously Deep. While on tour with Randy Crawford, Rainbow Seeker Sample took a minute to "sermonize" our brethren on some deep Rhodes history.

Let me begin in 1968, which was a very important year in my life. I told The Crusaders that I was not going to travel with the Crusaders, we were not going out on the road, I was putting an end to working the jazz circuit of the United States, because the pianos I had to encounter in every single jazz club in America with the exception of the Penthouse Club in Seattle – everywhere else the pianos were absolute dogs! I felt that the life of the piano player was the worst life and I still feel that today. I get very angry when I hear musicians complaining on stage when I know they have their trumpet, their saxophone, their drums, their guitar, and I just have to sit over there on that dog and not say anything. By '68, I was fed up. I felt like I was wasting my life in America as a jazz "pianist." I had devolved into a jazz "dog player" – OK?!?!

In New York in '63, I witnessed the very first free jazz. By 1968, everything had moved over to intellectualism and free jazz. All of the values that I had created in myself on February 1, 1939 – my birthday – were discarded.

So in 1968 I told the Crusaders that our career as far as working the jazz circuit of the United States had come to an end. I REFUSED to play any more dogs! It happened in Cleveland, Ohio, in a jazz bar. When I sat at this piano, I thunked 88 keys, only 3 notes played. I found an old church organ hanging in a corner with a Hammond speaker – a church speaker. You can't really play jazz on that with those kinda speakers. Besides that, the club owner told us it was time for "The Flo Show" and we had to back up the shake dancers. That was it!

The Crusaders began to record and we made the decision that we could not go into free jazz,

I don't know how we did, but the real true musicianship of being born in Southeast Texas – of having Louisiana roots, of having second-line roots, of having rhythm and blues, blues and gospel roots – began to surface. For the first time in my life, I made the decision that I was not going to be ashamed of my true African American roots. We were gonna let 'em pour out! That's when we started creating some of the very first jazz-soul.

I went to a Wurlitzer and began to play them. I had heard of the Fender Rhodes and I think I had tried playing a Fender Rhodes live once. We would have an occasional gig – maybe two gigs a year – because I just totally refused to play. I tried the first Fender Rhodes on a Crusaders gig, but because I was breaking the tines, I went back to a Wurlitzer. It had its particular problems, but at least I wasn't breaking tines. Harold Rhodes heard about the problems I was having with a Fender Rhodes and was getting the same feedback from Joe Zawinul. He refused to play it because he would destroy them. We had trained all our lives on acoustic piano, so we played with that "piano touch." When I saw them coming with those silver top Rhodes, I'd say, "Get it out of here – this is a tinker toy!" Eventually, Harold called me to Fullerton and said that they had resolved the problem… and they had.

It was around 1970 when I began to record with my first Rhodes. I was very happy to do performances with the Crusaders because I did not have to contend with them dog pianos anymore. It made it possible to do more work. I had begun to do recording sessions – building up a name as a studio musician so I didn't have to work the jazz clubs. I loved the jazz clubs… but, I honestly felt it was a waste of time to go out and play pianos that were unplayable.

There was one show in the mid-'70s in Ann Arbor, MI, and the place was jam packed. I had a Rhodes and it just shut down. From that point on, I began to travel with two. You needed that back up instrument. You didn't know what would go wrong with an electronic instrument and then you couldn't do the gig. At times I had to use both.

I met Joe Zawinul in Las Vegas in '60 or '61. He was the pianist for Dinah Washington. At that time, the Crusaders were The Hollywood Nighthawks. We were a show band in Las Vegas working as a lounge act. I was playing the Hammond Organ then. We had a male singer, Larry Green, a female singer, Mickey Lynn, and a vocal group, the Titans.

Joe and I hung out in Vegas. He was there for maybe 2 weeks. I was there for 3 or 4 months! We were only there because we had to pay bills. In 1960, I was 21 years-old. Joe was 6 or 7 years older and he sort of spoke to me like a big brother. When I heard him playing with Dinah, I was like, "Who in the hell is this white dude?" When I found out he was Austrian, I was like, "How in the hell did someone in Austria learn how to play like that?" He eventually told me the GIs were there and he learned from the GIs what jazz was, what soul music was all about. Eventually, Joe began playing with Cannonball Adderley. He wrote "Mercy, Mercy, Mercy." I would see him at the Lighthouse in the mid-'60s.

Later with Weather Report, I noticed he was very fond of the synthesizers and electric pianos. Joe was a pianist, but he was very fascinated with the synthesizer world.

I was never that fascinated with that world. I was fascinated with the world of electric piano. Joe had a touch on the Fender Rhodes. There were only a handful of pianists who became, let's say, "acquainted" with the Fender Rhodes.

There were a handful of guys who realized that the Fender Rhodes was not a piano. It was a new instrument. I began to notice that I don't have to play this like a piano. It had qualities of its own – surprising things on it that I could never do on the piano. I found that you could take two notes here and two notes there, play 'em – and whooo – there would be this big beautiful sound. If I used that same sound on the acoustic piano, in that same situation, it wasn't the same thing. So I discovered the Rhodes was an instrument you know, of its self. It had its own life, its own sound, in its own world.

The Fender Rhodes has a beautiful sound if you turn the volume down, not up. When you turn it down, it forces you to use the pressure, the weight and the strength from your arms, your wrists and your fingers… I heard a distinct sound in it. When I was playing on sessions for Motown, the Rhodes was there – also the Wurlitzer, the Clavinet, the Harpsichord, the Organ and the one that I could not stand, the Farfisa! Sometimes there would be 3 keyboard players. I noticed that whenever all the other guys went over to the Rhodes, they turned it up to level 8. I told them, "What you're doing now is amplifying softness. You can't get power out of it, it's loud, but there's no power!"

I think there were only a few guys who really understood that the Rhodes was its own instrument and you had to approach it in its own way. I realized when I first sat at it that trying to play it like a piano was absolutely ridiculous. It just sounds murky and dark… Then I started finding out that I could just play 3 or 4 notes and they have this resounding beauty. I discovered another beauty in the Rhodes.

A funny thing happened. It was a Crusaders' recording we decided to run the Rhodes through a Leslie speaker. I liked it (initally). Back then we worked with (producer) Stewart Levine and (engineer) Rik Pekkonen. We recorded quite a number of records with them and I remember sitting there thinking, "Do I have to use this Leslie again?" I'd have to tell him, "Man, pull that Leslie back in the mix. Let's just put more of the Rhodes out there." I didn't know it, but they were in there thinking, "Do we have to use this Leslie speaker again?" We had both come to this exact conclusion, but didn't know it. One day it came out and I said "I'm tired of this thing" and they looked at me and said, "You're kidding! We've hated it for the last three albums!"

I used a Rhodes on a lot of recordings at Motown (including the Jackson 5 and Marvin Gaye). It established itself as one of the most unique legendary sounds ever created in music. I remember when the DX-7 came in and then it was considered that the Rhodes was obsolete. That was with that song "Bette Davis Eyes" by Kim Carnes, produced by Val Garay. I think that was the first recording on which the DX became a hit. I've always hated that one particular sound that ushered in the drone. That drone took up 60% of the space on a record.

I remember when all of a sudden, all the jazz players – somewhere in the liner notes or booklet of their albums – you saw a stage plot… a diagram of all the keyboards they were using on the record. That was the dumbest shit I had ever seen!

I've been a rebel. When everybody went over there, the Crusaders found success by goin' over here! I'd listen to the radio for six months and get bored to death hearing the same stuff. I'd say, "What would make me smile now… some shit just like this" and I'd start writing the next Crusaders record. It never failed – it'd go to #1 immediately! Those were the greatest days of the recording industry. You couldn't wait to hear Stevie Wonder's next album, you couldn't wait to hear Steely Dan's next album. Every time you heard your favorite artists you heard something different. By '82, the corporate world entered the record business and all the independent record labels vanished and all the radio stations began falling into the corporate pattern.

Before, we had all of this independent sense going on which created the great musical quality of regionalism. You had New Orleans, you had South East Texas, and San Antonio, there was Dallas, there was music coming out of Kansas City, Memphis, Nashville, Chicago, Detroit, Pittsburgh, New York, Boston, the Philadelphia sound, all the way down to the Carolinas, Florida, on out to Los Angeles, the Bay Area – all the great bands that came out of the Bay Area – all the way up to the Canadian Border. It was regionalism and that's where all that great music was coming from. The corporate world didn't get into this business for the love of music.

They got into it to make money. Because of this corporate world, I very seldom hear things that I've never heard before. That's why it's just so boring.

The Fender Rhodes was right in there in that development of the 1970's. It could have been the greatest period of American Music.

World Music is going on now. When I go over to Europe, I get really excited. I was in a taxi in Seattle a year ago. The cab driver was from India and I could hear his music playing. He was going to turn it off, but I said, "Man, what is that? Turn it up!" It was some of the most exciting music I had ever heard – simply refreshing. You could hear the musicality, the artistry, the personal feeling and the emotion of it.

I hope one day we get back to cherishing the artistry, not the formula.

It's impossible to travel with my Fender Rhodes. The airlines want too much money. A year ago, a one-way ticket from Los Angeles to Tokyo was $8,000 for the Rhodes in freight, roundtrip was $16,000. You KNOW I can't do that and I don't want them to handle it because they are going to destroy it. Once you get it there, you can't find technicians to help if there are problems. You rent one there and you don't know what sound you're going to get from note to note. I want to know that each note requires exactly the same attack. I don't want to have to hit this one harder than I hit that one.

So I started going to Motifs… to whatever I could find. I even had some guys in L.A. take one of my Rhodes and figure how to synthesize a Rhodes sound as best they could.

What I'm finding out is that when I play these keyboard instruments, I cannot get them to respond. I know exactly how I'm playing it, but what I expect to hear isn't coming out of it. So subconsciously I start to really make it obey me… and they simply cannot obey.

I'm starting to damage my hands – my wrists start to give and I'm creating pain. Two years ago I could not open my left hand. (Drummer) Steve Gadd turned me onto a really good acupuncture doctor in Tokyo. I still can't bring my thumb down, though, and I have pain all the way up my arm. That's from playing the keyboards. Everybody says, "You don't have to hit it that hard. Why don't you just turn it up?" Well, it had nothing to do with volume. It has to do with when I hit a piano a certain way, that note is going to sound a certain way. They'll never be able to (simulate) that.

I love to write on Rhodes. I would even think about going out and doing some funk gigs, but it has to be a real piano and not keyboards. There's a Yamaha studio piano at the Musician's Union. I said, "Why don't you guys take that thing – that action – and make it a keyboard?" It's just the most beautiful thing to play. That piano must cost $30k, but they won't do that.

My pianos today are in great shape because every single time I would come off the road, I would take them out to Fullerton and they would rework them. I always thought that they were bringing them back to factory specs. I was recently told that no, my pianos have something built into them and they must have done this, or throughout the years they have been changed, but I had always, whenever… I took my pianos out to the repair shop at Fullerton, when I got them back they were absolutely beautiful. So I always assumed that they were at factory specs.

Harold called me out and wanted to present to me an 88. I sat there, I began playing it and I felt like this is useless. All I could think was, "It's really heavy… my air freight is gonna go up AND I'm gonna break my back trying to lift it!" Plus, once you get up to a certain range, the notes stop being of musical quality to me. They just become brittle – metallic – and very unmusical and when you go down low – I don't even play acoustic piano that low – only every now and then.

I thought it was absolutely ridiculous to make an 88. I play a piano within a certain range. I only go up in the high range for effect and again, the Rhodes ain't a piano. Why try to make it simulate a piano? It's a Fender Rhodes! It has this incredible beauty right there in the 73. When they added lower pickups down there, the overall piano became murky… When I get my 73 with the high and the low set at the right place, it tends to record well, it fits in with other instruments and it doesn't take up a lot of room.

I've always recorded with Steinways, there are some Yamahas, but I know the Hamburg Steinways, in a trio setting, it doesn't' take up a lot of room. I have played the Bosendorfer, but I don't need that kind of massiveness. A classical pianist might like that particular sound for a particular composer. I have played some Bosendorfers that are just simply awesome, but for electric pianos, a 73 Rhodes is the thing.

NOTHING SOUNDS LIKE A RHODES

5

ON THE OTHER SIDE
OF THE RHODES

George Benson

Respected worldwide as a superstar entertainer, the great George Benson is, at essence, the supreme guitar slinger who earned his early rep as a sideman and session player who always delivered impeccable accompaniment and unforgettable solos. In the hard grinding years before his 1976 breakthrough album Breezin', "Bad Benson" shared many a bandstand and studio with an enviable group of first call peers. It is those days as a player and a leader that he reaches back to for his personal perspective on the evolution of the Fender Rhodes, particularly as it pertains to the two keyboardists that traveled with him in the Breezin' band – Ronnie Foster and the late Jorge Dalto.

The first electric piano, the Wurlitzer, had a lot of flaws in it. It wasn't too impressive except for the songs Ray Charles recorded. His bass line on "What'd I Say" was pretty impressive! Then came a finer instrument, the Fender Rhodes. Because it was a Fender, it already had a great connotation about it because Fender was very popular (for electric basses and guitars). Now they were going to keyboards, which gave keyboard players who were switching from piano a lot of hope – 'cuz they wanted to be heard! Bands started getting louder – more dynamics, more volume – so it was a natural transition for pianists and even organ players who wanted to play with a bass, to go to keyboards. The Fender Rhodes was setting the pace for electronic instruments.

A lot of people were switching to the Rhodes. Herbie Hancock, who was relatively new when I came to New York, was setting quite a pace. His popularity grew very fast and he brought the Fender into the picture and probably brought along a lot of other players that were trying to be like him.

The Rhodes was the perfect transition from standard piano as an instrument. You could take with you. One of the biggest problems of working on the road was every week you had a different piano. Some places wouldn't even bother to tune 'em, some had the wrong name on 'em, some of them were not so nice sounding and some were just worn out! But if you brought your own Fender, you knew exactly what to expect every night. So it became like the guitar, a portable instrument. You could pack up and do 2 or 3 gigs a night when you had that kind of flexibility.

The suitcase model was unique – just flip the keyboard over, plug the keyboard into the cabinet or speaker and you're in business. Then they came out with the portable one that had the legs and a sustain pedal. They started with a 73-key model because it was designed to be portable and convenient, but the greater piano players demanded more so they got the Fender 88 – a full keyboard. That became the standard.

In the beginning, I came to New York with organist ("Brother") Jack McDuff. When I left his band, I formed my own organ trio / quartet, but the organ became kind of cumbersome. I sat in around town with people who had basses and pianos in their group. So, I got used to playing with piano and bass.

It was a little more intimate and had a lot more flexibility… allowed me to do things I couldn't do with the organ. When I started playing with a keyboard band, I had an organist who switched to Fender Rhodes just so he could get the gig! He didn't like it at first. On his first gig, the first time he played a Fender Rhodes, he got the biggest applause he ever got in his life. So from that day on, he was a Fender Rhodes player. Ronnie Foster was his name.

Then I hired a second keyboard player – a guy from Argentina named Jorge Dalto – because of Stevie Wonder's records. Stevie would play rhythm lines on Clavinet along with his lead parts and I liked that combination, so I hired a guy to play Clavinet. Problem was we had two keyboard players that both liked the Fender Rhodes. Both of them wanted a Fender Rhodes in addition to the second instrument they were playing. Ronnie Foster was playing Fender Rhodes and a Moog synthesizer, and the other keyboard player was playing the Clavinet, but he liked playing the Fender Rhodes also. After battling with that for a while, I put the other keyboard player on standard piano, which he was very comfortable with. That's how I got the argument down with the Rhodes. I still have both of their instruments, though. I had to carry two Rhodes on the road, a Clavinet and a Moog synthesizer – you know… the whole trip!

Jorge Dalto passed away (in 1987). One day I invited his son, Miles Dalto, over. We were having a get together at my house in New Jersey and he lived in New York. I saw him play the piano and realized I was looking at the same identical hands that his father had – exact same anatomy… blew my mind.

Then I remembered that I had the Rhodes I'd bought for his dad to play in a storage place down in one part of my house. So, I gave him the piano. I'm really looking forward to one day seeing him take his dad's place in the world as one of the great players. He's got the clout and he's got the same attitude his dad had. I didn't know what I was going to do with that piano, but that became the perfect solution – give it to his son so that maybe it would inspire him to excel on his instrument. That was a pleasure, man.

The thing that made my band on *Breezin'* so good with Ronnie Foster on Fender Rhodes and Moog was that Jorge Dalto brought that Latino romanticism to everything he played. He was a folk player in his hometown – known as a folk player who wanted to play jazz. He came to the U.S. to have that opportunity, but he played semi-classical. He had great technique and played everything with a romantic flair. That's why "This Masquerade" was such a big record in my opinion. Now, I'd like to see how his son has progressed.

George Benson, Paul McCartney and Gerald McCauley

Stanley Clarke

Stanley Clarke is a musical renaissance man of his generation. As an acoustic and electric bassist, he swung out of the gate working in a variety of amazing contexts – from studio musician on landmark albums by Donny Hathaway and Aretha Franklin, to jazz side-man with Gil Evans and Horace Silver to jazz-rock fusion pioneer playing on Deodato's seminal "Also Sprach Zarathustra (2001)" and, of course, his co-founding of the fusion super group Return to Forever with Chick Corea. Stanley has since scaled the R&B and pop charts as a soloist and as half of The Clarke-Duke Project with George Duke,

has produced albums by artists such as Dee Dee Bridgewater (Just Family), McCoy Tyner (Looking Out), Howard Hewett ("Heaven Sent" and "Fantasy Love"), Maynard Fergusson (Hollywood) and Rodney Franklin (Learning to Love) to name only a few. He is the senior member of the all star bass trio S.M.V. (with Marcus Miller and Victor Wooten), has composed orchestral film scores and television themes, and continues to be an arbiter for the concept of music beyond boundaries. He's had his share of run-ins with the Rhodes in those travels...

When I first saw the Rhodes, the first thought I had was, "Sun Ra would love this!" His stuff was always extra-terrestrial. He would take a nasty looking keyboard and put some stuff on it to make it look like it was, "WHOOSH!!"

That was the standard ax. If you were a jazz pianist and you were going to play electrical music, you went to the Rhodes. I think the reasons were the touch was the closest thing to an acoustic piano and the clarity with which you could play chords. There was another instrument when I played with Horace Silver called a RMI. It was terrible. Every time Horace played that thing I used to think, "Such a waste," but, the Fender Rhodes has a beautiful sound. The first time I heard a stereo Rhodes was '71 or '72. I was in Pori Finland. When I met George Duke for the first time, everyone was rushing to the stage because George had this Fender Rhodes with stereo speakers (Satellite model) so the sound was going across like that [motions vibrato effect]. That was really something. It was great technology for the time and still is. It's got a very unique sound. I really haven't heard a sample yet to match it. It's not just the sound… it's something in the actual mechanics of the instrument.

When I first started playing with Chick Corea, I always thought the Fender Rhodes was bigger. Since that time, I hadn't played it or been around it for a long time. On the last Return to Forever tour – the reunion tour (2009) – he brought out one of his original Fender Rhodes. I couldn't believe that he got all that music out of such a small instrument. I'm wondering are the keys actually smaller than a regular piano…

In Deodato's case, there was one tune that was a hit, "Theme from 2001: A Space Odyssey (Also Sprach Zarathustra)" (from the album *Prelude* – CTI – 1972). I was playing electric bass – there were two bassists on that session: Ron Carter and myself. Deodato wanted to play electric and the Fender Rhodes really popped out on that record. The instrument has subtleties to it. When you played it, it was real distinctive.

You could really tell the difference between Herbie, Chick, George Duke, Deodato and others.

On *Extension of a Man* (1973) with Donny Hathaway, my memory is that I showed up at the record date late with a bunch of other guys. We were the young lions then so we had our egos goin'… We just showed up 5 or 10 minutes late and Donny got really pissed off. He must have thought that we thought he was a lesser musician – because he was an R&B musician and we were jazz musicians. So he immediately sat down and started playing "Giant Steps" on the keyboards… then, he went into another key! I'll never forget that he played that. I just stood there and said, "O.K." He was a genius, that guy… Donny Hathaway. Great musician, amazing singer, had a big heart and really knew how to put that heart into his music.

For Aretha Franklin's *Let Me in Your Life* (1974) session, I remember everything was done at one time. The strings were there, the brass were there, the background vocals were over here and the rhythm section was over here. They had a carpet for her, so Aretha walked down that carpet to where the background singers were isolated and sang. I think Jerry Wexler was the producer. Back in those days, if you played bass, drums, guitar or keyboards, you could go in the control room.

"String players, you go over there and smoke a cigarette or something!" So I got to go into the control room... and what was cool was that I heard the record. That was it... that was the record! A month or two later, it was on the radio – just like that. There was a simplicity about that.

George Duke is like a big brother to me. He's a tremendous musician. It's funny... he's had a lot of praise and a lot of accolades in his life, but, still he's underrated to me. He's one of these guys that does so many really distinctive things really well. If I was a big pop singer, I would want him to be my musical director, I'd also want him to play keyboards and I'd want him to write the song. He's a great musician and arranger. He has a long list of artists that he's produced and he's not a bad film composer too.

Ronnie Foster had a really soulful way of playing the Fender Rhodes – a great sound. I remember seeing him with George Benson. Again, the thing about the Fender Rhodes is it really took someone's uniqueness and enhanced it as opposed to some other instruments like the RMI... not that it was a bad instrument: it looked space-age, but when you played it, it was just stiff. The Fender Rhodes is loose, you know... really cool.

The first electric Return to Forever album was *Hymn of the Seventh Galaxy* (1973). The majority of the compositions were Chick's and they stemmed from him writing on the Fender Rhodes. It would have never happened if it was just acoustic piano. I believe that it empowered keyboard players to reach further out to people.

Every time I look at a Fender Rhodes, I remember all the times I used to have to help Chick carry these things down to the Village Vanguard. When we first started out, we played the Village Vanguard in New York on Seventh Avenue South – with its narrow little stairways. We didn't have roadies or people to help us, so I used to help him carry this thing. So when Chick gets a little testy with me, I look at him like [stares hard], like, hopefully he'll remember... "I used to carry your stuff, man!"

Jay Graydon

Though Jay Graydon started his musical life at age 2 singing on his father's "The Joe Graydon Show" music / talk TV program in Los Angeles followed by a short stint as a drummer, it was as a guitarist that he ultimately shined beginning in the late '60s as a member of the Don Ellis Big Band. In the '70s, he graduated into an A-list ace playing unforgettable licks filled with his sonic bag of tricks, perhaps most famously as the guy who nailed the solo on Steely Dan's Peg (from their breakthrough Aja album in 1977) after 8 other players failed to satisfy the notoriously meticulous duo.

He also crushed all of that seriously crunchin' guitar you hear up under revving engines and tire screeches in Tom Scott's mid-run theme for the TV detective series "Starsky & Hutch." As a producer, he was a major contributor to the slick sophisticated Quiet Storm / Pop breakthroughs for Al Jarreau with a string of early '80s albums that includes This Time, Breakin' Away, Jarreau and High Crime, as well as vocal quartet The Manhattan Transfer with Extensions and Mecca for Moderns — all of which heavily featured the Rhodes, usually played by his longtime partner David Foster.

Nominated over the years in a plethora of Grammy Awards categories, he is a 2-time winner as a writer in the Best Rhythm & Blues Song category for Earth Wind & Fire's "After the Love is Gone" (1979 with David Foster and Bill Champlin) and George Benson's "Turn Your Love Around" (1982 with Steve Lukather and Bill Champlin).

Greg Mathieson is the one that exposed me to the Rhodes. I grew up with Greg and went to college with him. His dad was such a great cat… responsible for so much of the knowledge that Greg and myself got. He was a jazz trombone player before he took a day gig and had a family. He used to play jazz records after rehearsals at his pad and it turned us on to so many cool things. I probably had more experience with that Rhodes when Greg bought his first one because I played with Greg all the time. There was a Rhodes in the Don Ellis band, Peter Robinson was the piano player. George Duke was also in the band for a short time and it was because of that that George got me to play on his record *Save the Country* (1969). I went on tour for a while with George – great guy – "Mr. Happy" – always smiling!

The Wurlitzer was the first electric piano and was a great tool for what it was. But when the Rhodes came along, it was a totally different sound… more practical with a really nice, lush thing to it.

I bought a stage model Fender Rhodes in 1973 or 1974. I was doing record dates as a studio musician and I always had a little studio of some sort. At this point, I had an 8 track studio and I bought a stage model. That was a mistake but I didn't know it at the time.

I didn't want the suitcase model because I didn't want to have to move it around with all the extra weight. What I didn't realize until later is that with the suitcase model, the outputs are after the active EQ and the stage model is passive EQ, so you really can't get it bright enough. It just doesn't make it for records – it's too dark. Well, Paul Rivera, a really good friend of mine, "modded" my amps. I helped him get jobs at different places over the years. He was working for Fender at the time. Shortly thereafter, I told him the dilemma. He said, "No problem! I'll get you the preamp and install it for you." So we did that.

I picked that Rhodes out of about 5 different Rhodes.

By the late '70s, I was producing and still doing record dates here and there. David Foster and I worked together all the time. We were best buds. On a session somewhere, Foster said, "I played this UNBELIEVABLE rental Rhodes the other day from Leeds" (Andy Leeds rental company which had about 5-7 Rhodes'). "It's letter 'E'!" (That's how it was cataloged in the shop). A week later we ordered it for a date. David's playing it and I'm thinking, "Man, this Rhodes sounds incredible!" So I asked Andy about the history of this Rhodes. He said, "It was in the back room of Wallach's Music City for about 10 years under a pile of stuff. I don't know how the salesman found this thing." Andy was always looking to buy gear – B-3s and Rhodes especially. Well, they pulled it out, set it up, Andy knew it sounded great, so that's how it ended up in his arsenal of Rhodes.

Now things get even better. There was a guy named Eddy Reynolds that was a piano tuner of the era. One of the nicest guys you'd ever want to meet. Other than being a piano tuner, he had technical ability. I don't know what he did to the Rhodes to modify them, but after he'd do a modification it always sounded better. So I had him tweak my Rhodes, but nothing was close to the "E" Rhodes. Well, I share information – like an unselfish person should – and I told everybody. George Duke was on the album *Breakin' Away* (1981) and played that Rhodes in the session (on "Roof Garden"). Then he started renting it all the time. What happened in the long run was, when I wanted this Rhodes for a tracking date, I'd have to book it, like, TWO MONTHS IN ADVANCE… because I'd told everybody, "Hey, look!!" So I book 2 months in advance – so what! Sharing information is important and that Rhodes was used all the time. It's on so many hit records, it's unbelievable and it's on EVERY-THING I did as soon as I discovered it. That Rhodes killed me. There wasn't even a close second.

The manager of Guitar Center, a good friend of mine said, "Do you realize you were the first guy to ever use Chorus on Rhodes?" I didn't know that, but being renowned as the guitar guy with all the effects, the very first time I recorded with Rhodes and realized I have tracks to do this, I stuck my Roland Chorus on the Rhodes and thought, "This would sound great," and it did. I'm not taking credit for this. Someone else told me that, okay?

No offense to anyone that likes the vibrato. I can't stand it. It sets up the time… this wobbling motion sets up the tempo of the track.

When you're trying to play a groove, it just gets your attention. I couldn't make it mono, either. If I ran out of tracks in the 16 track or 24 track days, I'd always record the Rhodes with the chorus on one track, but as soon as I needed tracks, I'd erase the Chorus track and just use it when I mixed – drop the level down from line to a pad, mic level run the Chorus. It was noisier, but whatever… the era of tape noise; as long as it wasn't a real exposed ballad we'd be okay.

Then the DX7 comes about and everybody's using them, including me. The Rhodes' weren't renting from Leeds. Some guy named George with a Greek last name let me know.

HE'S the guy who ended up with the E Rhodes. He called Leeds when the Rhodes' weren't rent-ing – they think its "DX7 Time" from now on – and this guy talked them into selling the E Rhodes. I'm bugged that Leeds didn't call ME and ask if I wanted to buy it! He knew how much I loved it.

Plus I got him so much business for that Rhodes! It was an impulsive move I'm sure… but, I want it man. *I want it now!*

I get contacted by this George cat and said, "I hope you're treating this thing well, man!" He says, "I've got a shrine to this thing. I hardly ever take it out on gigs." The guy lives in Santa Barbara, has another Rhodes for gigs and just saves this one. I told him, "You've gotta sample this thing. In this era, if I can't have it, the next best thing is to sample it." So he did, but I think he only did like 2 or 3 layers of samples. This was back when memory was expen-sive and it wasn't practical to sample 10+ velocities.

I've been making albums lately with Randy Goodrum. We are JaR (Jay and Randy). If you like Steely Dan you'll love this stuff. It's musical, but pop. In any case, I struggle with Rhodes samples. I use the Motif. It's the best I can find. Nobody's making a sample knocking me out yet. Someone's gotta work with George and this Rhodes!! Steely Dan is my favorite band. They write like me. The first time I heard them I thought, "They're using jazz changes in a pop tune. They're keeping the melody simple with some hip changes here and there, and their lyrics are killer." (Donald) Fagen used Rhodes a lot.

Speaking of my favorites, Stevie Wonder is the best singer that ever lived. I wear out his CDs. I can't get sick of any of it; starting from *Music of My Mind* through the last album. As Bill Champlin said about his last album, "he did Stevie outdoing Stevie." The guy is just the most amazing singer AND one of the best songwriters that ever lived… just floors me! He used Rhodes a lot, but again, the only thing that bothered me was the vibrato. Here's the time of the track – and the vibrato is not in time, but negative… Stevie? That's about where it ends!! By the way, who does Stevie dig? I mean, I'm putting him in the league with Ella and Sarah – the best singers that ever lived and my other favorites.

One of my favorites of my songs using the Rhodes is "Mornin'" by Al Jarreau (from *Jarreau* – 1983). I put Foster through the mill on that one and he hated it! I said, "Look we gotta build this from the bottom up." (Drummer) Jeff Porcaro played a great feel. Jeff never thought he could play shuffles. Well, I'd call "Mornin'" a funk shuffle and Jeff played that groove great.

He basically played the same groove on "Breakin' Away" and also on an album that Foster and I did as artists in 1979 called Airplay on "Nothing You Can Do About It" (later covered by The Manhattan Transfer on *Extensions*). I put Foster through the mill overdubbing the Rhodes. We did that first, brought Abe Laboriel in on bass then I did the guitar stuff.

I also produced an album on Dionne Warwick called *Friends in Love* (1982) that opens with a song called "For You," a delicious sounding track with David on Rhodes. The very first time Foster doubled a piano part with Rhodes was on Dolly Parton's "Here You Come Again" (1977). Dean Parks was the arranger, Gary Klein the producer. Foster either played the Rhodes part first, probably to avoid leakage on acoustic piano or the other way around, but he doubled the part and that became one of his signatures.

I don't know why I didn't have Foster play on my Grammy-winner "Turn Your Love Around." I got a call from Warner Bros. asking me to produce a couple of new tunes for the compilation *The George Benson Collection*. "You've got four days to come up with a tune!" Someone else had a tune but it wasn't going to be the single. I had to come up with the single!

So for two days I get nothing… At the end of day two, I'm sittin' on the can doing what you do and the melody came to me! I went down to the cassette machine, put it down with the changes and I got a chorus. The next night, Steve Lukather and I were going out to dinner with his wife and my girlfriend.

I said "Luke, I know this is a hang night, but I'm going to leave you at home for a half hour. Come up with a verse for this." I came back and he had a cool line. After dinner – you know we got juiced at dinner, but we were still young – I said, "Let's get (Bill) Champlin to write the lyric and come up with a bridge." We get it all done and the next night we demo it up. Luke's an okay piano player, surely better than me. He played on the demo. He wanted to play the master. I said, "Luke, you play good man, but no." Foster wasn't around, so I got Jai Winding – a really great field player. David Paich played synth bass and that was one of the very first hit records with the Linn Drum Machine.

So the Rhodes has been an essential part of my career. I still use those kinds of samples on tunes when it's clear it needs to be Rhodes. It was a new sound that got away from the monotony of using acoustic piano.

Even though I was a guitarist and was a first call studio guitar player for many years, I wrote very few tunes around guitar – okay, "Mornin'" had the guitar lick. When David and I were writing for his solo album, I came up with a lick that started the tune that was for an instrumental version for his record. Then we recorded it for Jarreau. On other tunes I had guitar licks that were the feature, but I rarely ever wrote a tune, since the mid-'70s, that was a guitar based song. I always wrote on piano. I like how I can deal with the voicings.

When I'm writing on guitar, the voicings I want to use get melodic and jazzy and fall out of the slot of being able to play the bass note on the guitar - the voicing I want. That being the case, writing on Rhodes and/or real piano was a main feature to me.

The Rhodes was a great alternative to the acoustic piano. If it was a pretty song, but didn't seem like a ballad for piano, Rhodes was the logical choice - a very big part of the stuff I've done over the years.

Lalah Hathaway

Lalah Hathaway came by her rich, soul-melting vocal tone through a combination of her classically-trained singing mother, Eulaulah Hathaway and her legendary father, musical genius Donny Hathaway. The Berklee School of Music graduate ushered in a new decade with her self-titled 1990 debut CD and has been steadily growing with each subsequent project. Highlights have included a collaborative project with Joe Sample, numerous guest appearances on albums by everyone from Marcus Miller to gospel's Donald Lawrence ("Don't Forget To Remember") and her most recent releases Outrun the Sky (2004) and Self-Portrait (2008) – the latter for a revived Stax label and both prominently featuring her own song-writing. As the daughter of Donny, Lalah knows a thing or three about the mellow magic of the Fender Rhodes vibration... And on the rare occasion that she reluctantly sits behind one on a concert stage, Heaven help your heart.

I grew up with a Fender Rhodes in my house in the '70s. We had a piano and we had a Fender Rhodes. That sound, depending on which records I hear it on, will remind me of my basement... of apartments ... or the lake front in Chicago. The sound of the Fender Rhodes is part of the soundtrack of my life.

Obviously, there are all the Donny Hathaway records, Steely Dan records, Joni Mitchell records, Chaka records, Stevie records, Doobie Brothers and Michael McDonald records... The '70s was so lush with sound, of musicians making music and the Fender Rhodes is such a part of that history – particularly soul music.

The Rhodes was always, like, THE piano – always a part of the tracking. You know, there's ALWAYS going to be a Rhodes track. It was always a part of my writing. If I didn't have access to a piano, I could find a Rhodes – somebody would have one or there'd be a practice room with one at Berklee. That's the way I wrote, so I have always recorded with the Rhodes. I didn't play on my first record so I started playing them on the second record (A Moment).

Working with Joe Sample on our The Song Lives On album was amazing. To take a classic song and try to realize it in homage to what was done before, but try to create something that will go forward as a new classic... to be able to do that with Joe – another master of the Fender Rhodes... We'd be on the bus sometimes listening to records and he'd say, "Oh, yeah, me and your dad must have been listening to the same thing around a certain time..." – listening to Herbie and all these records... Joe is a dear, dear friend of mine and he's so crazy.

The sound of the Rhodes... it can make me really happy, it can make me cry, move me to tears on certain records... Just the sound of it is so... there's such a genetic memory I have of it... of listening to it as a child. If my instrument can do the same thing for somebody, that makes me very happy.

There's a Victor Feldman solo on a Steely Dan song from Aja ["Black Cow"]. I love that solo so much, I memorized it as a kid. I remember trying to make my voice do the sound of the bells.

All my dad's records have the Rhodes on them, so I have an affinity for them. "Someday We'll All Be Free" – the beginning of that song is just heavenly. In the Stevie Wonder catalogue, pre 1985, there's so much Rhodes in those records. It's also on many, many movie soundtracks – "Three Days of the Condor" by Dave Grusin is one of my favorite movies and records of all time. Bob James just killed it with "Theme from 'Taxi'." At 4 years-old, I told my mother that I wrote a song. She said, "Ooh, play it!" I said, "It goes like this" and I ran my hands over keys. I thought I wrote that! [Laughs] But you can sit down at a Rhodes and anything that comes out is going to be beautiful. The instrument just lends itself to that.

There are just so many pieces of Rhodes history out there that are the soundtrack of people's lives and they probably don't even know it. They just hear it, like, "Oh, it's an electric piano." They probably don't even think that far.

Fans of my father's music always want to know if I can play. That's a big whoop... "If I can play." I don't play like my dad – absolutely not – but, there's such an association with singers and the Rhodes... like my dad, like Stevie, like Roberta (Flack)... being able to sit down at a Rhodes and do that. So I get asked that a lot... particularly in Japan.

My father played on Aretha Franklin records. I've got some great photographs of him playing Rhodes on one of those sessions. There are some Stax records he's on by Carla Thomas. I just got a reissue of a live record that he arranged for her that's really cool. Gosh… people send me stuff all the time and I say, "Oh wow, I never knew my dad was on that."

He was really a player. He was studying Yusef Lateef, he was studying Gershwin, he was studying a lot of things… His mind was really expansive in terms of music. If you think about it, a lot of the records my father did, he did them when he was in his mid-'20s. Those records are still highly influential. I hear guys all the time singing and playing at the Rhodes like my dad. We can only imagine having that kind of impact that early…

I met Frank McComb years and years ago… just by happenstance at a session in, like '94 - '95. People had told me about him. You'd be surprised how many times a year somebody comes up to me and says "I know this guy. Sounds just like your dad." All over the world, people say that to me all the time. When I first heard him play I could hear the influence. I could hear George Benson. I could hear Stevie Wonder. I could hear my dad. I saw him with Branford Marsalis in Amsterdam one year and I thought, "This guy, he's awesome." Frank is probably one of my favorite Rhodes players, really. His playing and singing together, for me, eclipses both his playing and his singing. Because the hand-eye-mouth coordination thing that he has is unrivaled. Not a lot of people that can do that well.

I also play with a guy named Bobby Sparks whom I love to hear on the Rhodes. I play with a guy named Michael Aaberg who's really great and really sensitive on the Rhodes. We make sure we have him on it at every gig. Then there's Tim Carmon – a lot of cats, lot of cats.

Quincy Jones

For many of the musicians interviewed in this book and for many people in general around the world, when they put the needle to Quincy Jones' Walking in Space Lp in 1969 and the first thing they heard was Bob James playing a solo 2-bar intro on the opening number "Dead End," that was their first experience hearing a Fender Rhodes electric piano. As a record producer, film music composer and all around curious soul, Quincy Delight Jones was instantly on top of utilizing the unique properties of the Fender Rhodes.

It's a testament to his resourcefulness that he drafted just about every other musician in this book at one time or another to bring their singular touch on the instrument to some form of his work over the years – from Dave Grusin and Stevie Wonder to Greg Phillinganes and Larry Williams of the band Seawind. Even his album titles Walking in Space, Body Heat and Mellow Madness could double as descriptions for the hypnotic quality of the Rhodes sound. Here now is "Q" to discuss just a few of his voluminous experiences with the Rhodes… from A to Z.

We had the first Fender Bass – early '50s. Leo Fender brought it to Monk Montgomery and we took it to Europe. We didn't know what the hell it was. We did jazz records with it. The first record with the Fender Bass was *Work of Art* by Art Farmer on Prestige Records. Without that instrument, there'd be no rock n roll… no Motown.

We used the Rhodes piano first in movies. We were always looking for new colorful sounds. I remember using the first synthesizer on (the TV show) "Ironside" in 1964 and also used it for (the film) "In Cold Blood" in 1967. It was brand new then. We were still trying to figure what to do with it. We used it to (simulate) heartbeats and so forth before the hanging and all that. We'd used it for movies because we'd get all these instruments first. There were 14 of us getting things from all the synthesizer companies… everything. The factories in Japan would send them to me, Marty Paich, Dave Grusin… a bunch of guys. We were part of the guinea pigs.

Once the Rhodes hit the street, everybody was using it. Two or three years later, the song "Brand New Me" came out – first by Jerry Butler in Chicago then Dusty Springfield in London. Then there was Miles with *Bitches Brew*. Miles played different on top of *Bitches Brew*. When you've got an electric rhythm section, it's so powerful you have to play different on top.

A man named Paul Beavers was our hi-tech guru. We had an organization back then called E.A.T.: Electronic Artistics and Technology. As composers, Dave Grusin, Johnny Mandel and all of us used to go over to Paul's house to see what other innovative instruments he had and the tech guys would suggest things to musicians. It didn't matter if the ideas made sense or not.

It was about having a cross-pollination of ideas. Paul was a genius. He's the one that created the touch-sensitive Clavinet – what Stevie Wonder played on "Superstition."

I remember once Paul said, "What about the synthesizer?" I said, "We did use that once." He said, "Man, it has 40,000 applications!" I said, "The problem is the pitch doesn't bend. If it doesn't bend, it ain't gonna be funky and if it ain't gonna be funky, brothers will not be playing it!" Sure enough, he came up with a portamento and a pitch bender. Right after that, Stevie, who was working right next door to me at the Record Plant, did 4 Grammy winning albums in a row.

As an orchestrator, I look at the Rhodes, synthesizers and other instruments in the orchestra that gave you another color – like an Eb concert Bassoon, a bass flute, alto flute or a C flute. Once it got out there, everybody used it for whatever they wanted, whether it was scoring films or jazz or pop.

Take the character of the Fender Rhodes. You don't strike a string with the intensity that you do a piano. It's got that smooth, more of a sine wave kind of a feel. So when you want warmth, mellowness and so forth, Fender Rhodes is perfect for that. We used it in "The Secret Garden" and all that (sexy) stuff. It's like part of the everyday vocabulary. Like all new instruments, when you first get it, you're still figuring out how to use it… straightening out all the kinks so it has a possibility to accomplish wherever you want to go. But everybody loved what that sound was about. Nothing else could accomplish that warm, mellow sound that the Fender Rhodes created. It's addictive… very addictive.

The first keyboard player I called in to use the Rhodes was probably Dave Grusin. He was Andy Williams' accompanist in Paris when I was over there in '59. I just fell in love with him. He's one of the greatest musicians that ever walked. In every department – composer, pianist – we used the Rhodes all the time.

Same with Bob James – we did a lot of work together. I first met him – oh, my God – when he graduated from Notre Dame. They had a festival and Henry Mancini was on the panel. I was Vice President of Mercury and Phillips then, and I was on the jury. The added attraction for whoever won the contest was I would also give them record contract. That winner was Bob James and I signed him to Mercury. He was into very esoteric stuff then… marbles on oil barrels and all that stuff. Then I got him a job with Sarah Vaughan. He was very young – 19 or 20 years old – so I felt good about that. He worked on films with me like "The Anderson Tapes." He did my album, *Walking in Space*. Years later we even did Sinatra's last record, *L.A. is My Lady*.

Between records and movies, we were rollin' all the time, man! Piano players – everybody from Greg Phillinganes, Bob James, Jerry Peters and Dave Grusin, to Artie Kane and Jimmy Rowles – we used everybody! George Duke is on a lot of the *Thriller* stuff. I've always been blessed to have the best musicians on the planet.

I was a PR man for that instrument, you know. I loved it. I don't know how many people responded, but I talked about it a lot and I walked the talk because I had it on all my records.

Richard Tee really knew how to handle a Fender Rhodes… made it his own. We worked together with Roberta Flack in the early '70s with a 37-piece orchestra – played the Greek, Pine Knob and the Circle Star Theatre up north. Richard Tee, Eric Gale, Steve Gadd… Stuff… unbelievable!

Herbie Hancock is The King – my baby brother from Chicago! Herbie and I have been working since he was 20, 21 years old. Herbie's always been ahead of the curve. His degree is in electrical engineering. I used to live on a deep canyon and a dude named Sherman Fairchild lived next to me. I didn't know who the hell he was, but these girls used to always come by my house [laughs] and I had to say, "No, he lives over there!" Herbie said, "Man, you don't know who that is? He had the Fairchild, one of the first synthesizers." There's a thing on the internet now with Herbie and I talking about that – when he first turned me onto it, you know. Herbie is a monster man. It's like Nadia Boulanger used to say to me when I was studying with her. Your music can never be any more or less than you are as a human being. It's true. Herbie is a great human being… the absolute best.

We just did something recently to celebrate (film music composer) Ennio Morricone. We did "The Good, The Bad & The Ugly" and Herbie played on it. I just saw him play with (young classical piano virtuoso) Lang Lang and a symphony at the Montreux Jazz Festival. We are each other's guardians because we run into a lot of the guys that act like we used to act – like you can only play straight jazz. We were like that up until a certain age… but, our attitude now is this: you can play whatever you're capable of playing.

During the war when I was 13 years-old, in "Bumps" Blackwell's band, we played pop music with the cup mutes wearing white cardigans at the tennis clubs. Then we'd change our uniforms and play at black clubs like the Washington Educational Social Club – Ray Charles, strippers, rhythm & blues all night long! When we finished that, we'd go down to The Elk's Club on Jackson Street – the red light district – and play bebop all night for nothing – for free – 'cause that was just coming in. We wanted to know every story about what Charlie Parker, Miles and Bud Powell were doing back east because you had no way of connecting with it then. There was no television, so we were just thirsty… had to keep our ear down to the ground all the time to copy all the new licks.

You could see the difference in the mentality with the titles to the songs. Before there was "Mares Eat Oates and Does Eat Oats," "Cement Mixer, Putty Putty," "Open the Door Richard" and all that stuff. When the Be-Boppers came in it was "Anthropology," "Epistrophy" and "Round About Midnight" – much more intellectual. I read the Koran when I was 13. I don't know why, but that was the ambience then. The origin of bebop happened because it was a group of cats that did not want to dance, entertain and roll their eyes in front of an audience anymore. They wanted to be artists like Stravinsky.

The evolution of all this is just startling… it really is. You go to Europe today and there's techno, techno, techno all over the place! It's amazing to watch when you come from an era where you just had piano, drums and an upright bass. I remember when Eddie Van Halen came in to record "Beat It" with Michael Jackson. He brought 2 Gibsons with him and these big $5,000 amplifiers.

They had built in one segment of it to sound like those old distorted amps that black musicians from the South Side of Chicago used to play with back in the '40s when they hadn't been perfected. It's interesting that in a very expensive thing like that, they still wanted to get the authentic old sound, which just came from lack of proper technology, you know… but it's all good.

I remember meeting Greg Phillinganes when I was in Detroit. I'd just done an album called *You Got It Bad, Girl*. He played hooky that day and was in line to get a record signed. I asked him did he have a Fender Rhodes yet because he was just starting off. It's ironic because once he got out here, he went with Stevie's band Wonderlove… then he started working with me. He was 19 then, now he's over 50! I told him he'd make it one day. I said, "You'll be in AARP one day… if you're lucky."

I had dinner with Stevie Wonder the other night. I'm doing an album with him and Tony Bennett next month. I met Stevie when he was 12 years-old… amazing. He wanted to know how Ray Charles got all the girls. [Cracks up] Ray Charles was one of the most independent musicians that ever lived – never used a cane, dogs or any of that stuff… walked by himself with his shoes all scuffed up! The only time Ray got "blind" was when the pretty girls came around. Then he got helpless… walking into walls and stuff. I busted him one time! I was giving Ray an award and said Stevie learned every one of his tricks! I'd say, "Stevie, did you meet my girlfriend?" He'd go, "Hi," and I'd have to say, "No, Stevie, her hands are down here!" Ray was the same way.

Do I still have a Rhodes? Hey man, I've got 3! But we were on board… the first time around.

Marcus Miller

When the Fender Rhodes was at its height of popularity in the '70s, Marcus Miller was a hot young bass player on the scene working with some of everybody on the competitive New York scene. In the process of working with the best, he swiftly became one of them, with the unique ability to scale the heights of both the jazz and R&B worlds as a major bassist, songwriter, producer and artist. The big names on his resume say it all: Miles Davis, Luther Vandross, Aretha Franklin, Wayne Shorter, David Sanborn, Roberta Flack and Donald Fagen. Hark! The composer of "Tutu," "Maputo," "Snakes," "Any Love," "Chicago Song," "Summer Nights," "Oasis," "Blast... and "Da Butt" speaks.

I came up in the glory time of the Fender Rhodes. My first memory of it is Herbie Hancock playing "Chameleon" from *Headhunters*. That was an amazing Fender Rhodes sound. Then Charles Stepney and Maurice White of Earth Wind & Fire produced a song on Ramsey Lewis called "Sun Goddess" and Ramsey was playing the mess out of a Rhodes. Earth Wind & Fire had its own songs like "Reasons" where the Fender Rhodes was the main instrument. When I was a kid learning about music, every song had a Fender Rhodes. Bob James had a song that he arranged for Grover Washington Jr. called "Mr. Magic" that starts off with the Fender Rhodes. It was just everywhere.

What was beautiful is it finally gave piano players a way to join in with the electric thing. In the '60s there was the Wurlitzer, but the Rhodes had a different sound that meshed well with the electric guitars, electric bass and the different way engineers were beginning to record drums. The Rhodes fit in there perfectly. It also had a transparency that was beautiful. It allowed you to hear all the other instruments. When you use acoustic piano, the sound is so full there's not a lot of room to clearly hear the other instruments. With the Rhodes, you heard all the harmony you needed to hear, but it still had a clarity that we really love. It was a great time for the Rhodes.

When I became a professional playing in clubs in New York, my early memories are helping the piano player move his suitcase to the gig. Then we had to put the actual keyboard on top of the suitcase and figure out how to get that sustain pedal to line up. That always took a half-hour, but it was always worth it. You knew it was a real Rhodes that had some seasonin' when there was a key that was burnt up by a cigarette that somebody left on it – a little brown circle in it, that's how you knew it was "seasoned."

Herbie Hancock plays great Rhodes. There was a guy named Jorge Dalto, who was George Benson's piano player in the '70s when George started getting really famous with his vocal hits – he was a great Rhodes player. If you were a piano player, you had to have a big car that was big enough to put your Rhodes in the back. That's how you chose a car. "Can I fit my Rhodes in there?"

When I started producing music on my own, the Rhodes was an integral part of what I was doing. It was my first choice before I even thought about an acoustic piano.

I used it on a lot of stuff I did with David Sanborn, Miles Davis and Luther Vandross. Eventually the samples started coming. The DX-7 is one of the first digital keyboards that had a Rhodes sound.

We thought it was really cool because you didn't have to carry that whole suitcase! It was very bright and had a little "ting" at the beginning of the sound that became very popular in the '80s. Now I can't stand it because it got overused. These days we're looking to hear more of the real Rhodes sound. The samples are so incredible that sometimes it's become the generic term for that sound. It's not even a Rhodes anymore… it's a "Rhodes Sound," but it's all over the place still. You know it hasn't lost any of its appeal or popularity.

The samples come close to capturing the Rhodes, but a Rhodes is a real instrument. The thing that's always great about a real instrument is that every note is not uniform. Some notes are duller, some notes are so bright that they ring; other notes are a little flat… all of that is what gives the instrument character. On a synthesizer, every note is basically the same thing, so it doesn't have the same character.

When you're sitting at a Rhodes, first of all, each keyboard sounds different. Every Rhodes has its own character. There are guys who insist on carting their own Rhodes to the session or to the gig because it has a sound that they like. So there's nothing like the real thing, but in a pinch when you just want the Rhodes for the color and you don't need that much personality, we'll use a sample. When the Rhodes is the main thing, we pull out the real thing.

In the '80s there was this big movement called "Dyno-My-Piano / Dyno-My-Rhodes!" Dyno-My-Piano (started in 1974 by Chuck Monte) was a company that would retrofit your Rhodes – (fine tune, enhance and eventually customize it). That was a big thing for a while. "Is your Rhodes a Dyno-My-Rhodes?" Then, the DX-7 came in.

The Rhodes wasn't a very reliable instrument, but if it went out of tune you could pull the top off, get in there and fix it yourself – like an old Ford Mustang! It's not a bunch of computers. It's a great instrument, man. It's never gonna go out of style because it's just too valuable and there's nothing else like it.

It's exciting that people are re-energized and are excited about the real instrument again.

Lenny White

Lenny White is a ferocious drummer… and so much more. He played with Miles Davis, Freddie Hubbard and Joe Henderson among others before joining the electric edition of Chick Corea's Return to Forever super group and played a crucial role in the mixing of the band's biggest album, Romantic Warrior (1976). He was the leader on a series of genre-defying albums in the '70s culminating with the band Twennynine that scored a funk novelty with a song shoutin' the praises of "Peanut Butter" (an earlier album was produced by Earth Wind & Fire keyboardist Larry Dunn).

An ardent supporter of talented female musicians, he was at the helm of the Echoes of an Era project that reintroduced Chaka Khan as a budding jazz singer, produced the profoundly sexy spoken word piece "Perfect Match" for Spike Lee's "School Daze" (featuring English poetess Tina Harris), and co-produced two fine CDs with singer-songwriter-multi-instrumentalist Nicki Richards. His last solo album, Edge (1999), was an astounding amalgam of all that had come before it and featured five keyboardists: Patrice Rushen, Donald Blackman, Vince Evans, Kelvin Sholar and Peter Levin.

With longtime friend, Stanley Clarke, he also co-founded the short-lived fusion super group Vertú which featured keyboardist Rachel Z, violinist Karen Briggs and guitarist Richie Kotzen. Currently completing an opera and about to drop his first album in over a decade, Anomaly, the man with the planet's flyest collection of hats and head gear talks Rhodes and Rock-Jazz history.

In Jamaica, Queens where I'm from, there was a club called the Afrodisiac and I played this gig with two drummers – Rashid Ali and myself. During the break, the trumpet player (Dion) came over and said, "Man, has Miles ever heard you play?" I said, "No." He said, "I'm gonna tell him about you." I thought, "Yeah, right, sure." Next thing I know, I get a call to come over to his house and rehearse. He said to just bring a snare drum and a cymbal. The band was Chick Corea, Dave Holland, Jack DeJohnette, Wayne Shorter and Miles. I don't think John McLaughlin was there. All we rehearsed was the beginning of "Bitches Brew" – that's all. He said, "O.K., come to Columbia Studios at 10 o'clock tomorrow." It was the actual same week of Woodstock, 1969.

We recorded for three days from 10am to 1pm – three days, that's it. The first day, it was Chick and Joe Zawinul, Jack and myself; Jumma Santos, John McLaughlin, Bennie Maupin, Wayne Shorter and Harvey Brooks played electric bass. On the second day, Larry Young also played. Chick, Larry and Joe all played Rhodes together on "Spanish Key." It was great how they all integrated what they did. I met Joe on that session.

I was scared stiff. I was 19 years-old and these were all my heroes. Miles said to be there at 10 o'clock. I got there at 9:30. The cleaning woman let me in. So I set up my stuff, playing and practicing. When Miles came in, I was still foolin' around playing. He went over the loud speaker and said, "Hey Jack, tell that young drummer to shut up!" Right away I was, like, traumatized, but he was really great. After the session, he said, "You know you're cool, come on back the next day." It was just fantastic.

With the reunion of Return to Forever in 2008, we've come full circle. I played with Stanley Clarke in Joe Henderson's band. I did *Bitches Brew* with Chick in '69. Then around 1970, I did *Red Clay* with Freddie Hubbard and Joe Henderson, then I went and played with Joe Henderson's band and Stanley came and played with Joe Henderson's band. Then I left and played with Freddie Hubbard's band, Stanley stayed and Chick Corea joined Joe's band. Then Chick and Stanley went and played with Stan Getz. Then they formed *Return to Forever* with Airto, Flora, and Joe Farrell. I was in San Francisco working with a pop band called Azteca, with bassist Paul Jackson, trumpeter Tom Harrell and guitarist Neal Schon. It was like a Santana clone with horns.

Chick gave me a call from Japan, said they were coming to the Keystone Korner in San Francisco and asked if I could play with them for a week. I said, "Sure, that'll be great." So we played for a week and it was really fantastic. Chick played Rhodes, Stanley played upright bass and I played drums.

On the last day, my friend Mingo Lewis, who played percussion with Santana, sat in and we had two guitar players sit in as well: Billy Connors and Barry Finnerty (another guitar player from the Bay Area). After that gig, Chick asked me, "Would you like to be in the band? We're gonna have an electric Return to Forever." I said, "Well, you know, Chick, I'm out here playing with Azteca and I think I want to do that." So they went back to New York and Stevie Gadd played while I stayed in San Francisco with Azteca. While I was there, I got asked to do some rehearsals with another band. I rehearsed a couple of times with them and the leader said, "The guys in the band would love for you to do this band." Chick had called me a second time, so I said, "No-no, I'm gonna go back and play with Return to Forever." That other band was Journey. Aynsley Dunbar wound up doing it.

Chick playing the Rhodes was unlike anybody else. Joe had his style and Herbie had his style, but Chick was very rhythmic because he's a drummer and also into experimentation with the Rhodes – with the Ring Modulators and everything. His Rhodes sounded like an animal! He played this Silvertop one. The Rhodes already had such a unique sound, but he took that sound and raised it up a notch. On our first album, *Hymn of the Seventh Galaxy*, he played organ on one little piece, but the whole album is just Rhodes. He wrote this music… when he came and brought in "Hymn of the Seventh Galaxy," it gave me a totally different way of thinking about playing. It was this music, the like of which I had never before played with an instrument, that fit the music… it was, like… "POW" kind of music. Quote that: "POW!" That's what it was.

I have bad hearing in this ear right now… the first couple of years with *Return to Forever* were very, very physical. They'd do like this and turn the piano up, then it got to the point where that wasn't enough so they'd plug it into an amplifier the size of a cigarette machine. You had to play to match that volume. It was crazy. At the end of the night, your hands would bleed. The music was being written to expand out of the clubs. This music was matching the volume and mass of rock and roll, but still had the sophistication of jazz, harmonically and rhythmically. As drummers, we didn't just go *boom* *smack*, *boom* *smack*. We were playing all these intricate rhythms but with a bigger sound. We were trying to match the electricity of these electric instruments. There was this whole big thing that you would judge your performance on a decibel level. You know, like the critics would, they'd say that "these guys played at 120dB. 120dB is a 747 jetliner… It was ridiculous that they played at this volume!" It was instrumental and it was turned up.

There were a lot of notes but it was much more. The emphasis was on presentation – virtuosos playing things that made people remark, "Man, that's very hard to do," as opposed to just doing notes. Today, it's sometimes just about notes… It was Rock and Roll / Jazz, which was Jazz-Rock or Rock-Jazz. It was different than what they deemed to be Fusion. That's my personal opinion.

I really liked our Lp *Where Have I Known You Before*. That was the first record that had a theme. We did these pieces of music then Chick went back in and joined them together by playing piano solos and intros between the tunes. Progressive Rock bands like Yes and King Crimson had theme-oriented records. For us it was different.

Romantic Warrior was totally our theme album. "This is what the theme is going to be, so everybody do something that adds to that theme." That's the one that put us over the edge. We no longer played clubs. We went into arenas, the crowds got bigger and it was great… People were saying that we were one of the best bands in the world. I never aspired to be the best drummer in the world, but I always wanted to be in the best band. Because if you're in the best band in the world, they'll say you're the best drummer.

It's an era of music that I've started to reinvestigate. It's not just about the people that make the music, but who was affected by the music. For some reason, that period of time has been taken out of the jazz cannon. I think Ken Burns had a great deal to do with that because he totally left it out of his "Jazz" documentary series. They stopped at, like, 1962 or whatever. There's a whole lot of stuff that happened… That music introduced a lot of younger people to the jazz art form. I believe a lot of that has been negated.

It was a great time because you could not play on the bandstand and have the band before you sound better than you. That was not gonna happen. So you had this competition between these famous bands and it was a healthy competition because it raised the music to a higher level. That was very special. We need that back. That spirit has to come back.

Maurice White

To those of us who know and love him, "Reece"... a metaphysical magician, drew upon the elements and shaped a perennial imprint in music -- Earth, Wind & Fire. Complex arrangements with poly-rhythms rooted in Africa and South America and Phenix Horns defying the middle ground, soaring high with unmatched precision. One of the most influential mainstream bands of all time greatly utilized the Fender Rhodes in their sound.

I came up in Memphis where I started out being inspired by all kinds of music available to me. That music took me for a ride into many different places... Along the way I learned that a big part of artistry is self-discovery. I didn't know I could write a song, but I soon found out I was a songwriter. I found out I was a singer, a drummer, then a producer and you know, a bottle washer, too (laughs). It's been an interesting career.

I got into producing by accident. I was in the studio one day... someone said, "Cut that tape machine off," so I hit the stop button. All of a sudden it dawned on me, "I can do this." So I became a music producer. Early on I realized how important electronic keyboards would be in the music I produced. The Fender Rhodes became a big part of that.

I can't think of albums like *Head to The Sky, Open Our Eyes, That's the Way of the World, Gratitude, Spirit, All 'N All, I Am* or *Raise!* without it. When we did the Beatles' "Got to Get You Into My Life," that sound is what gave the groove its character. I really liked that the Rhodes could also be very subtle. On "September," it sits in the pocket.

The song dictates what it needs. When you write a song and listen very carefully to the vibration of the song... the song will let you know where to take it. You need a full sound on certain things and on other things a very small sound. So, some songs need strings, other songs need horns in order to create this "wall of sound."

When I produced "Free" on Deniece Williams' debut album *This is Niecy* (1976), it was clear that the Rhodes was going to be a centerpiece on that track.

On those tracks I did with Ramsey Lewis on *Sun Goddess* (1974), I loved his approach to the electric piano and wanted to produce something really big for him that showcased those gifts. We did a couple, but, "Sun Goddess" really benefited from the Rhodes sound. I like both the studio version with Ramsey and the live arrangement we did on *Gratitude* (1975) that featured our group keyboardist, Larry Dunn. (Note: There is also a third version – a live take that features Ramsey Lewis as a special guest on the Earth Wind & Fire CD, *Alive in '75*).

I've been very fortunate to work with many great keyboard players on EWF records over the years. Larry Dunn, Charles Stepney (a huge influence on our sound)... great arranger! Eddie Del Barrio he's bad too. David Foster, Skip Scarborough, Jerry Peters, Michael Boddicker and Wayne Vaughn... all utilized the Fender Rhodes as a tool. The textures of the Rhodes lent itself to each musical direction we chose. Even today, that sound doesn't get old.

Verdine White (bass), Maurice White and Larry Dunn (On Rhodes)

Vince Wilburn Jr.

Vincent Wilburn Jr. is a drummer, an entrepreneur and the nephew of Miles Davis. He performed and recorded in Uncle Miles' band – most notably on Decoy (1983) and You're Under Arrest (1985), contributed to fellow Miles band keyboardist Robert Irving III's CD Midnight Dream (1990) and sat in with Chicago guitar legend Phil Upchurch on his CD Tell the Truth (2001). Today he stays busy tending to plenty business as co-executor of his legendary uncle's mighty estate. Top priority: bringing Miles' story to the big Hollywood screen with Don Cheadle in the lead.

Representing the man who raised the bar of the Rhodes' commercial possibilities, Vince shares a few thoughts about music, Miles and the instrument at hand.

Miles Davis was always evolving… always looking for and hearing changes in his music.

The piano is like the voice of everything, so he had a Rhodes. He signed a deal with Yamaha organ, but Rhodes was his main instrument in terms of what I always saw around the house. I used to like him to play chords because he knew voicings that he learned from Dizzy and Bird. I remember Herbie saying that the band would present songs then and when Miles got finished with them, they'd really be songs, because he just heard in his head how to arrange and complete a song.

Herbie Hancock is a genius. He and (drummer) Tony Williams were the youngest in that quintet, so the pressure was on them. I remember Herbie once saying he was comping behind Miles and he played the wrong chords. Instead of Uncle Miles turning around, like, "Herbie, why you do that," he played the notes that fit the chords. I just think anybody who was around him couldn't help but get that energy to want to be the best.

Everybody who came out of Uncle Miles' band went on to become great band leaders in their own right. I think that coming from acoustic to electric opens your ear up to another way of thinking. Uncle Miles was the one that had us all think beyond the scope.

With Miles, if he saw that picture frame and said, "Man, get some sticks and hit that so I can hear it," that's the way it was. "Let's put a mic out there and I want you to hit the side of that lawn chair!" Nothing was ever preconceived. I was doing some remixes and found a track with Tony Williams playing temple blocks that no one's ever heard. If it was in his head, he wanted you to try it. This is a man that played a wah-wah on trumpet. Who thinks like that? Miles was also one of the first to have a wireless trumpet mic because it gave him the freedom to walk across the stage.

Dig this. Acoustic music – all music, really – is sacred… but, once you've experienced acoustic music as a musician or a listener then something else opens up your ears and your mind, why not try it? It started with the electric guitar, then the Rhodes. Look how far it's taken us. A lot of electric instruments came in and went out, but the Rhodes has outlasted all of them. We just had a Fender Rhodes sent to us in Paris the other night for John Beasley – It was killin'.

The Rhodes is like another voice elevating the music to another plateau. The Rhodes opened up a different way for musicians to express themselves. Thank God there was a Rhodes. If not, where would we be? How old is the Rhodes now? It and all the music recorded on it will be around long after we're gone. We have a bunch of music in the vault – outtakes of Herbie and Chick and all those guys, so the Rhodes and that music will outlive us all – as it should.

Allee Willis

Songsmith Allee Willis recorded one 1974 album for Epic Records titled Child Star, before focusing on songwriting and penning unforgettable songs for a broad cross-section of artists – from major hits such as "September" for Earth Wind & Fire, "Neutron Dance" by The Pointer Sisters and "Lead Me On" by Maxine Nightingale to cool obscurities such as Herbie Hancock's "Come Running To Me," Thomas Dolby's "Don't Turn Away" (featuring Stevie Wonder), Phyllis Hyman's "Why Did You Turn Me On," Angela Bofill's "Something About You," Webster Lewis' "The Love You Give To Me," Al Jarreau's "If I Could Only Change Your Mind," Greg Phillinganes' "Forever Now," The Brecker Brothers' "I Love Wasting Time With You," Level 42's "Micro-Kid," Lani Hall's "Double or Nothing," and The Manhattan Transfer's vocal version of Spyro Gyra's "Shaker Song." Below, she discusses her most GINORMOUS hit… and the Fender Rhodes.

I just remember hearing the Rhodes and not knowing what it was. It just had this lush, gorgeous electronic sound. Anything that had anything to do with gadgetry I always liked. Though I never, to this day, learned how to read, write or play music, I hear every single note in my head.

So as soon as I learned it was a Rhodes, I had to have one. I bought a brand new one and never played it myself, but the fact that I had it meant that I could get people to come to me and play it. Watching Larry Dunn in Earth Wind & Fire play was the first time that I'd constantly go to the studio and see it. They'd do the original tracks with a regular piano. When the Rhodes overdubs came that was just a major deal.

It was definitely a sign of status if you had one. Especially as a songwriter who couldn't play, you know. Then… I sold it in maybe 1984… just because I had no room! Synths were starting to have sounds that kind of sounded like that, so I sold it to Donna Weiss who wrote "Betty Davis Eyes" and she still has it. She still reports to me about it and I still can't believe I sold it. Now I'm obsessed with the student Rhodes because those are so gorgeous, it's incredible. I don't even care what they sound like, they just look good!

I don't have enough to say about Larry Dunn. Earth Wind & Fire changed my life – when I first heard them because they were so amazingly distinctive and the keyboard runs were incredible. My first hit was "September." I co-wrote everything on Earth Wind & Fire's *I Am* album except for two songs and was at almost every session for that. Because that piano was something I had in my house, I really watched Larry Dunn. That was the instrument I related to the most and it was just so exciting they were the first stars I ever met. There I was in the middle of everything. His playing combined so many different influences. They made these unbelievable pop records, but they had hints of jazz and African stuff. It was just so interesting to me.

He played differently than other people played on pop records. It was just thrilling to be there and see him in action.

"Boogie Wonderland" has a real story. I co-wrote it with Jon Lind. Jon had co-written "Sun Goddess" for Earth Wind & Fire and Ramsey Lewis (and later penned another absolutely gorgeous instrumental showcase for Fender Rhodes and acoustic piano titled "Nicole" for Ramsey's 1976 album, *Salongo* – the great Charles Stepney's final production). At that point, "September" had just come out and Maurice White actually said, "You should write with Jon Lind." So we got together and wrote that song. Because Disco was so huge then, we wanted to write a song that had "Boogie" in it, but we didn't want to use "Boogie" the way that every other record was using it. I had just seen "Looking for Mr. Goodbar" with Diane Keaton. In that movie, a girl with, like, NO SENSE of self, starts going into the local disco every night. Enter "Boogie Wonderland." That first verse is:

*"Midnight creeps so slowly
into hearts of men who need
more than they get,
Daylight deals a bad hand
to a woman that has
laid too many bets… "*

Basically, she goes into a Disco every night and comes home one night with a serial killer! I was so obsessed with the theme, as I am to this day. If your life isn't working, you need to make the changes to make your life work. So "Boogie Wonderland" was almost the state of mind that your life was falling into.

"The mirror stares you
in the face and says,
'Baby, uh uh, it don't work'
You say your prayers
though you don't care;
You dance and shake the hurt.

All the love in the world can't be gone,
All the need to be loved can't be wrong,
All the records are playing
And my heart keeps saying
'Boogie Wonderland'
'Wonderland' – Dance!"

This was actually a very heavy song. The way we cut the demo had a real pop song form to it. When Earth Wind & Fire cut it, it turned into a heavily orchestrated groove. They didn't originally cut it for themselves, though the group made the track. Maurice was producing a different group at that time. So between the fact that they had changed the construction of the song and the fact that it wasn't going to be their record, Jon and I were suicidal! We begged Maurice for at least a month. One night he was finally supposed to give us the answer to whether he was going to pull it back for Earth Wind & Fire.

Jon Lind and I sat at Canter's Delicatessen from about 10 o'clock at night to 6 in the morning eating Chocolate Danishes and came home so sick... but, there was a message on the answering machine that Maurice had pulled it back for Earth Wind & Fire. I just remember being incredibly proud that it was such a different Disco record. The orchestration of it – the form of it – was "High-Art Disco." I think it has held up well through the years. The playing is incredible and the keyboard lines are really great at the turnarounds. There are so many horns and strings on that record, but if you can hear through that, the keyboard stuff that's going on is wild.

People that have Rhodes really cherish them. It's just a magic sound. It always felt like fairy dust sprinkled on top of tracks to me.

GENERATIONS
Rhodes models by years released

1965 Silvertop 73

1946 Pre-Piano

1970 Mark I Stage Piano

| 1946 | | 1959 | | 1965 | | 1970 | 1971 | 1972 | 1973 | 1974 | 1975 |

1959 Piano Bass

1972 Suitcase 88

1980 | Stage Fifty Four

1984 | Mark V Stage Piano

1980 | Mark II Stage Piano

1981 | Mark III EK-10

1976　1977　1978　1979　1980　1981　1982　1983　1984

1977 | Suitcase 73, Haigler design

1984 | Mark V Stage 73 MIDI

Afterword

The Last Rhodes
by Jim Wray

It was the Malibu Fire of 1993.

Nestled about 500 feet above the blue of the Pacific and a promenade with a breathtaking 270 degree ocean view, the beautiful, sprawling Spanish architecture of an 11 bedroom, 6.5 bathroom mansion, was home to a community of about 25 – gathered 'round my partner Jackye and myself. We had provided refuge, shelter and a home for an assortment of young aspiring actors, single parents and professionals within this Malibu home – our base in the early 1990's.

Jackye's vision of "life as service" was very resonant with the writings of Mira Alfonso (Mother Mira of the Sri Aurobindo ashram in India), and I was a devotee of the yoga founded by Aurobindo. This was our bond and the basis of our expanding a life from the two of us in 1980 to a small community by 1993. There were no belief or religious requirements of residents, and no monetary requirements either. There was only a strong filter to establish permanent residence in that one had to feel comfortable with the aura of spirituality mandatory in an association with Jackye and me. Rarely did we have to ask a person to leave since those attracted came knowing that they were given this respite from some of the cares of life in order to develop their own spirituality and focus in life.

The fire storm came through one day in The Fall of 1993. On the weekend prior, we had presented a Disney theme Halloween party for over 100 children accompanied by parents. As a house, we had created costumes and sets for 6 or 7 vignettes from Disney films. I was "Roger" from the movie "101 Dalmatians" and had set my Fender Rhodes piano up in the dog pen where I played the pianist father in the film. The lady I eventually married was the cruel "Cruella," who delighted in roaming the grounds getting hisses and boos from the children between our performances.

The Santa Ana winds were strong that day with their hot, dry 50-70 mile-per-hour gusts driving up from the San Fernando Valley to the 2500 foot peaks of the Santa Monica Mountains then down the western slopes into Malibu, spilling into the Pacific. They say the fire started in Calabasas on the eastern slopes of the mountains. Ironically, it followed the very roads I had used to drive to work that morning, only in the opposite direction.

There was nothing left but the foundation and chimney structures. The Aluminum block of the BMW 2002 model had melted and was a pool of shining silver on the ground. Four pianos went up in smoke: a grand, an upright and two electrics – one of which was my Rhodes 88 key suitcase model.

Within months, we resituated the extended family, renting a place in the Point Dume section of Malibu.

It was a piano shopping day for me when I first met Harold and Margit Rhodes. I was going from piano to piano in a west Los Angeles piano store – oblivious of my surroundings, enjoying the touch and sound of the many, many keyboards – when looking up, I found an audience of two smiling and appreciating my jazz improvisations… recognizing what, to them, was a strong Bill Evans influence. The next thing I knew, a friendship with the inventor of the Rhodes piano had begun.

Like millions of my keyboard jockey contemporaries, I had been saved from the out of tune, hard to hear, hard to play bar room uprights by the Rhodes. So I was positively in awe and appreciation of this magnificent electric piano. I was stunned to be chatting and entertaining this great man and his wife. Somehow our conversation turned to the fires and the story of my Rhodes piano that vanished without a trace. This really piqued Harold's interest. Though he was then in his '80s that winter of 1993-94, Harold's childlike curiosity and candor remained intact.

"Would you take me to your burned out house," he asked? "I'd like to see if I can find anything left of the piano." Harold Rhodes had just invited himself to my house, or at least what had been my house before the fire. Still stunned at such an encounter, of course I said yes. We made plans to meet in the next day or so.

Sifting through the ashes in a place I estimated to have been the last resting place of my Rhodes, we unearthed a few of the tines – the sounding components of the Rhodes piano. Harold was truly inspired. With the breathtaking view of the Pacific and the mountains in stark contrast with the burned out hulk of a house at his back, Harold turned to me holding the recovered tines in the palm of his outstretched hand and said, "I'm going to build you another piano"… and he did.

Harold had a garage full of Rhodes components and cannibalized pianos. From these components, he produced a custom – to my specification – suitcase model Rhodes piano. It took a couple months to assemble and get it working properly. Harold had very poor eyesight at this point in his life, so Margit had to do most of the detailed handling of screwdrivers and soldering irons in the assembly. Together, they brought the *Last Rhodes* to life. It was the summer of 1994 – 6 years prior to Harold's passing.

In those last few years of Harold's life, we became close friends. I was a frequent visitor to his house; a house full of pianos. And he and Margit always insisted that I play for them. Moved by this man's gentle nature and extraordinary story, my friend Daniel Jones and I embarked on one of many attempts, I understand, to record Harold Rhodes' life story on film. Most of the footage – interviews with artists and interviews with Harold and Margit – was filmed at his house in the Valley. A soundtrack featuring the Rhodes that we created for a movie trailer was said, by his wife, to have been his constant companion while recovering from surgery.

Harold heard the *Last Rhodes* for the last time from the other side – if he was listening – at his funeral on what would have been his 90th birthday, December 28, 2000. He had passed on December 17, 2000. The service at the Little Brown Church in Studio City was mostly music. The family had invited me to bring the *Last Rhodes*, so I played a tribute concert with my trio in a sanctuary filled with family and well wishers. In my testimonial to Harold, I shared this story you are reading now. Being Capricorns (I celebrate my birthday on the 27th), Harold and I naturally bonded. His creative genius, child-like candor and delight in a simple melodic turn embellishing a time honored jazz standard ("Do that again, Jim. How did you do that phrase?"), have elevated Harold Rhodes, the man, to almost the same level as his Rhodes piano… but not quite. Harold has passed but the Rhodes sound lives – now and forever.

Harold and Margit Rhodes, and Jim Wray at Hume House – Malibu, CA (Jim's house after fire)

Jim Wray playing Rhodes at the Hume House burn site

Acknowledgments

Our deep appreciation and thanks for your part in this great accomplishment!

INTERVIEWEES

Michael Bearden, George Benson, Stanley Clarke,
Chick Corea, D'Angelo, Eumir Deodato,
George Duke, Larry Dunn, Donald Fagen,
Ronnie Foster, Rodney Franklin, Dave Grusin,
Don Grusin, Onaje Allan Gumbs, Ellis Hall,
Herbie Hancock, Lalah Hathaway, Rami Jaffee,
Bob James, Quincy Jones, Ramsey Lewis,
Jeff Lorber, Robin Lumley, Ray Manzarek,
Les McCann, Marcus Miller, Steve Molitz,
John Novello, David Paich, Jerry Peters,
Greg Phillinganes, James Poyser, Patrice Rushen,
Joe Sample, Lenny White, Maurice White,
Vince Wilburn Jr., Allee Willis

Steve Grom, John C. McLaren, John R. McLaren,
Mike Peterson, Steve Woodyard

Harold B. Rhodes

BONUS INTERVIEWS

Robert Glasper, Jay Graydon,
Brian Jackson, Clarence McDonald

Top:
Juan Esquivel 1967 recording session

Middle:
Mercer Ellington and Duke Ellington

Bottom:
Cannonball Adderly and Joe Zawinul

Miles Davis Band -1969

Philip Woo with Roy Ayers, Philladelphia

THE FILM

PRODUCED & DIRECTED BY:
Benjamin Bove & Gerald McCauley

INTERVIEWS BY:
Benjamin Bove, Gerald McCauley, A. Scott Galloway

NARRATOR:
Dorian Harewood

Harold Rhodes narration provided courtesy of
John Novello (John Novello Productions, Inc.)

FILM EDITOR:
Chris Bove

COLOR CORRECTION:
Gabriele Gomez de Ayala

**INTERVIEWS LENSED / CAPTURED
BY (CAMERA & LIGHTING):**
Bill Totolo (Director of Photography)
*(George Benson, Stanley Clarke, Chick Corea,
Ronnie Foster, Rodney Franklin, Ellis Hall,
Herbie Hancock, Jeff Lorber, Marcus Miller,
Steve Molitz, John Novello, Jerry Peters,
Greg Phillinganes, Patrice Rushen, Joe Sample,
Lenny White, Steve Grom, Mike Peterson,
Steve Woodyard)*

Dexter Browne *(Maurice White)*
Francisco Bulgarelli *(Quincy Jones)*
Rick Burton *(Ray Manzarek)*
Keith Ebow *(Larry Dunn, Allee Willis)*
Van Elder *(Michael Bearden, Benjamin Bove,
Dave Grusin, Don Grusin, Rami Jaffee,
David Paich, James Poyser)*
Eddy Emilien *(Clarence McDonald)*
Zach Love *(Ramsey Lewis)*
Richard Marcello *(Gerald McCauley)*
Alice McGown *(Bob James)*
Matthew Skala *(Lalah Hathaway)*
Aaron Sonego *(Vince Wilburn Jr.)*
Patrick Stringer *(Les McCann)*
Toshi Tagawa *(Eumir Deodato, Donald Fagen, Onaje
Allan Gumbs, Robert Glasper, Brian Jackson)*
Thomas Worth *(George Duke, John C. McLaren,
John R. McLaren)*

ADDITONAL CAMERA OPERATORS:
Brad Carper *(Chick Corea)*
Steve Senisi *(Robert Glasper, Brian Jackson)*
Aaron Sonego *(Herbie Hancock)*

**Melbourne Production Unit /
Melbourne, Victoria, Australia:**
Jeff Brownrigg *(Director)*
James Beilharz *(Camera & Lighting)*
Robin Lumley *(Interviewee)*

HAROLD RHODES FOOTAGE:
Jim Wray *(Producer)*
Mark Daniels *(Director – Camera & Lighting)*

MUSIC SCORE:
Benjamin Bove

ADD'L MUSICIANS:
Marcus Miller – bass
Boney James – tenor sax
Julio Figueroa – drums

AUDIO ENGINEER(S):
Benjamin Bove *(all interviews + music recording)*
Alan Abrahams *(Les McCann)*
Taka Honda *(Marcus Miller)*
Ben Kane *(D'Angelo)*
Matt LeJeune *(Ramsey Lewis)*
John Novello *(John Novello)*
Dave Rideau *(Boney James)*
Steve Senisi *(Robert Glasper, Brian Jackson)*

Mixed by Dave Rideau
@ Cane River Studios (Sherman Oaks, CA)

Mastering by Steve Hall
@ Future Disc Systems (McMinnville, OR)

Top:
Richard Tee

Middle:
Richard Tee with Paul Simon

Bottom:
Jerry Peters, Ronnie Foster,
Billy Preston

"DOWN THE RHODES"

JMel, Terry Dexter, Greg & Millie Hicks, George Hill, Steve Burdick, Al Machera, Brian Hardgroove, Greg Scelsa, Noel Lee, Cheryl Standard, John Burk, Patti Austin, Randy Crawford, Nathan East, JimiJames, Kendrick Scott, Freddie Washington, Wayne Vaughn, Wanda Vaughn, Michael White, Verdine White, Alonzo Wright, Kevin F. Rose, Howard Berkson, Nick O'Toole, Chris Shepard, Nir Benjaminy (Fender Rhodes LA), Chris Carroll (Vintage Vibe), James Garfield, Frederik "Freddan" Adlers, Adam Kranitz, Horst Absmann, Dan DelFiorentino, Ron Klier, Sam Sarkoob, Rich Varga, Avid Technologies, Marianna Montague, Patrick Murphy, Patricia Rhodes, Carol Rhodes-Rice, Fender Musical Instruments Corporation, Tom Trujillo, Kenneth Manning, Aaron Tee, Jason Lockett, Steve Cohen, Ken Rich Sound Services, Jazmin Hicks, DJ Hapa, Terry Carter, Ola Washington, Dave Hampton, Myron Chandler, Lory Gardner, Michael Selma, Jackie Owen, Brian Peters, Gordon Campbell, David Levine

Patrice Rushen – 1980

CONTRIBUTORS /
ASSOCIATE PRODUCERS:
Glenda Pelliccio
Gabriele Gomez de Ayala

ARTISTS RELATED

Evelyn Brechtlein *(Chick Corea)*, Lindsay Guion *(D'Angelo)*, Randy Hoffman *(Donald Fagen)*, Marc Robbins *(Steely Dan)*, Nicole Hegeman *(Robert Glasper)*, Jessica Hancock *(Herbie Hancock)*, Melinda Murphy *(Herbie Hancock)*, Marion Orr *(Bob James)*, Debra Forman *(Quincy Jones)*, Adam Fell *(Quincy Jones)*, Rebecca Sahim *(Quincy Jones)*, Shaun Lee *(Quincy Jones)*, Shelby Shariatzadeh *(Ramsey Lewis)*, Michael Bossler *(Jeff Lorber)*, Tom Vitorino *(Ray Manzarek)*, Bibi Green *(Marcus Miller)*, Michele Aristy *(Marcus Miller)*, Patrick Raines *(Joe Sample)*, Rich Salvato *(Maurice White)*, Darryl Porter (Vince Wilburn Jr.)

VENUES AND STUDIOS

Ronnie Foster, Rodney Franklin, Don Grusin, Lalah Hathaway, Jerry Peters, Patrice Rushen –
interviews @ Triads Music (Burbank, CA),
George Duke – interview @ Le Gonks West (Los Angeles, CA),
Jeff Lorber – interview @ JHL (Pacific Palisades, CA),
George Benson – interview @ Peninsula Hotel (Beverly Hills, CA),
Joe Sample – interview @ Le Park Hotel (Los Angeles, CA),
Marcus Miller, Greg Phillinganes – interviews @ Hensen Recording (Los Angeles, CA),
Ellis Hall – interview @ Brewster Place Studio (Eagle Rock, CA),
Bob James – interview @ Elevated Basement Studio (Savannah, GA),
Ray Manzarek – interview @ Studio M (Napa, CA),
Herbie Hancock – interview @ Hancock Music (Los Angeles, CA),
John Novello – interview @ Studio 2 B3 (Valley Village, CA),
Stanley Clarke, Chick Corea, Lenny White – interviews @ Anthology (San Diego, CA),
Ramsey Lewis – interview @ Chicago Recording Company (Chicago, IL),
Larry Dunn, Allee Willis – interviews @ the Allee Willis Museum (Valley Village, CA),
Les McCann – interview @ the home of Alan & Margaret Abrahams (Agura Hills, CA),
Vince Wilburn Jr. – interview @ Dot's Way Recorders (West Hills, CA),
Quincy Jones – interview @ the home of Quincy Jones (Bel Air, CA),
Benjamin Bove, Jay Graydon, Dave Grusin, Clarence McDonald, James Poyser – interviews @ Westlake Recording (Los Angeles, CA),
Michael Bearden – interview @ Open Labs Artist Relations Showroom (Los Angeles, CA),
Rami Jaffee – interview @ Fonogenic Studios (Van Nuys, CA),
Eumir Deodato, Donald Fagen, Onaje Allan Gumbs – interviews @ Manhattan Center Studios (New York, NY),
D'Angelo – interview @ Electric Lady Studios (New York, NY),
David Paich – interview @ ATS Studios (Calabasas, CA),
Gerald McCauley – interview @ The Imagitorium (Westlake Village, CA),
Robin Lumley – interview @ Penthouse (Melbourne, Victoria, AU),
Maurice White – interview @ Kalimba Productions (Santa Monica, CA),
Steve Molitz – interview @ Johnny's Room (Tarzana, CA),
Robert Glasper – interview @ World Culture Music (New York, NY),
Brian Jackson – interview @ Out of the House Studio (New York, NY),
Harold B. Rhodes – footage @ The Home of Harold Rhodes (Topanga, CA)
Boney James – sax session @ Westlake Recording (Los Angeles, CA)
Marcus Miller – bass session footage @ Hannibal Studios (Santa Monica, CA)
Dorian Harewood – narration session @ Triads Music (Burbank, CA)

EQUIPMENT ENDORSERS
Monster Products
RefTone

PHOTO CREDITS

James Beilharz
62B, 63BR, 159

Eric Barrett
255

Joachim Bertrand
78

Dexter Browne
58BG, 130, 231

Francisco Bulgarelli
60B

Alex Bugnon
157

Marvin Dickey
150

Van Elder
58, 60T, 70, 118, 122, 140

Earl Gibson III
233BG

Don Q. Hannah
113, 210, 211, 218, 253, 257

Ingrid Hertfelder
iv, 54, 203T, 224

N Jones
230

Denise Luko
216

Susan Jane McDonald
254

Howard Pitko
110

Gary Price
251

Dave Rideau
88BG

Joe Russo
258

Steve Senesi
63TL, 127

Joshua Semolik
232BG

David Speck
63BL

Shinichiro Sugama
252

Toshi Tagawa
59, 85, 102

Bruce W. Talamon
96, 232

Bill Totolo
61T, 76T, 108, 109L, 135

Max Vadukul
208

Andrew Wo
230BG

COURTESY OF

Michael Bearden (68) **Eleana Tee Cobb** (247T, 247M) **D'Angelo** (77)
Rodney Franklin (109R) **Lalah Hathaway** (219) **Brian Jackson** (251)
Gerald McCauley (82, 88, 134, 182, 194, 208BG, 247B, 248)
Clarence McDonald (255) **Marcus Miller** (226) **David Paich** (176, 178)
Greg Phillinganes (188L, 188R, 188BG, 222) **James Poyser** (190)
Harold Rhodes Jr. and Kenneth Manning (ii, viii, xiii, 1, 2, 4BG, 5, 6T,
7-11, 14, 30, 44, 50, 64, 104, 204, 244T) **Patricia Rhodes** (6B, 12)
Lenny White (76B, 228, 230BG, 230B) **Vince Wilburn, Jr.** (72, 245T)
Philip Woo (245B) **Jim Wray** (242BL, 242BR)

Triads Music, LLC (i, vi, 15, 16, 18-25, 28, 33, 34, 38, 42, 46, 52, 53, 55,
56, 61BL, 61BM, 61BR, 62T, 63TR, 66, 71, 79, 86, 87, 91, 92, 94, 97-101,
103, 107, 114, 116, 119, 123, 128, 131, 132, 136, 141, 143, 144, 146, 149,
152, 154, 158, 160, 162, 164, 166, 170, 172, 174, 175, 179, 180, 184, 186,
189, 192, 197, 198, 200, 203BG, 206, 209, 212, 214, 217, 220, 227, 233,
235, 238, 239, 243, 252, 260)

STIPPLE, PAINTING & GRAHIC IMAGES:
Derrick Standard (70, 124, 169, 234)

PHOTO RESTORATION / IMAGE ENHANCING:
Don Q. Hannah
Ingrid Hertfelder
Matthew Martin-Vegue
Glenda Pelliccio

Gil Scott-Heron & Brian Jackson

"The Rhodes is as important an instrument as an acoustic piano or a Hammond organ. It is a masterpiece!" – PHILIP WOO

"The Rhodes was an essential element in the Earth, Wind & Fire sound." – VERDINE WHITE

Clarence McDonald

Carly Simon, James Taylor, Carole King, David Crosby, Graham Nash, Clarence McDonald – 1977

Steve Molitz

Robert Glasper Experiment

Thanks to all at Hal Leonard Corporation for helping us publish the book, including Brad Smith, John Cerullo, Carol Flannery, and Clare Cerullo.